Envision It! | Visual Skills Handbook

Author's Purpose

EI•2

Cause and Effect

Cause

An effect is something that happens. A cause is why that thing happens.

As you read, ask yourself: *What happened? Why did it happen?*

Effect

EI•3

Classify and Categorize

Classifying or categorizing means putting things that are related into groups.

Forest Life | Desert Life

Compare and Contrast

Alike

Different

Draw Conclusions

Combine what you already know with new information to draw conclusions.

What I know:

Riding uphill can make you tired.

Sometimes your face scrunches up when you work hard.

Exercise can make you feel warm.

Conclusion:

The girl is becoming hot and tired.

Fact and Opinion

A statement of fact can be proven true or false.
A statement of opinion tells someone's ideas or feelings.

Generalize

Main Idea and Details

What is the selection all about? What details support the main idea?

Graphic Sources

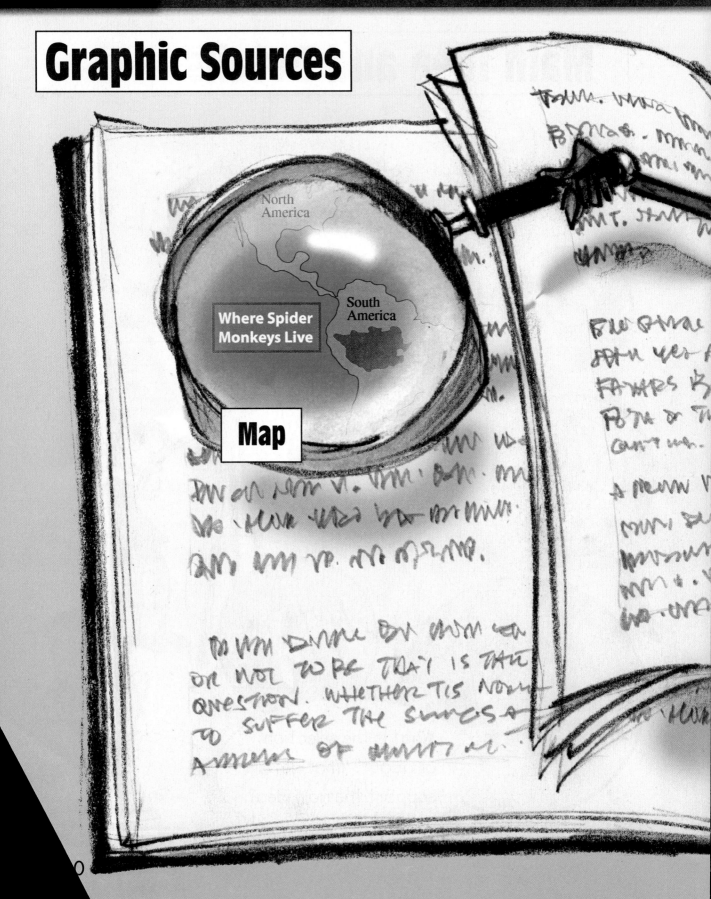

North
America

**Where Spider
Monkeys Live**

South
America

Map

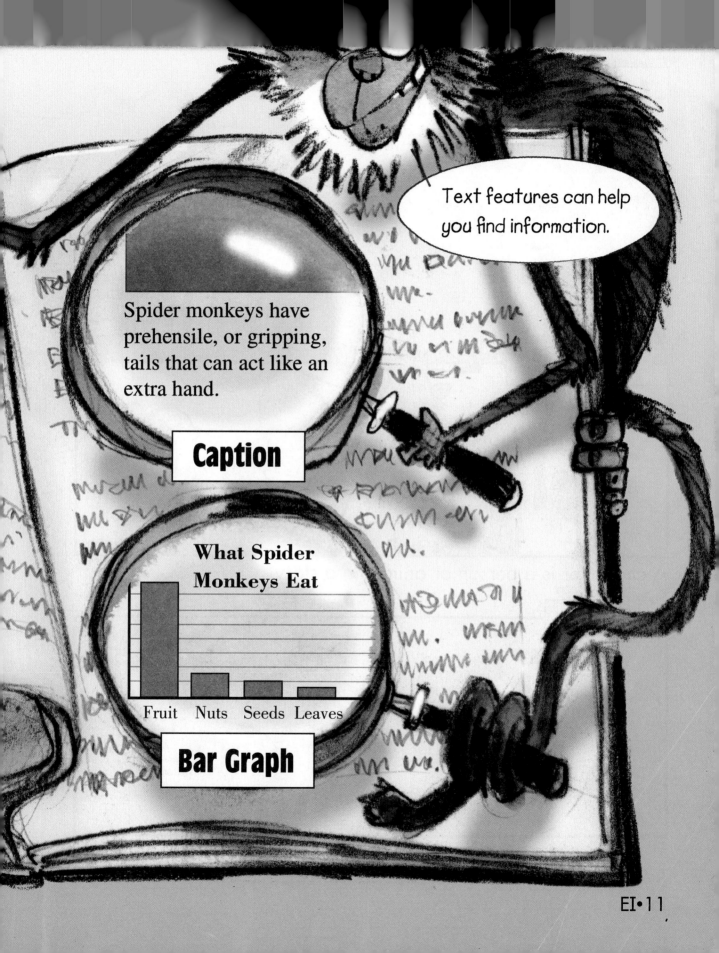

Literary Elements

Characters

A character is a person or animal in a story.

Setting

The setting is the time and place in which a story happens.

Plot

A story's plot is the important events that happen.
The plot starts with a problem and ends with a solution.

Theme

The theme is the big idea of a story.

Sequence

The sequence of a selection is the order of events.

First

Next

Last

EI•14

Steps in a Process

Envision It! | Visual Strategies Handbook

Background Knowledge

Background knowledge is what you already know about a topic based on your reading and personal experience. Make connections to people, places, and things from the real world. Use background knowledge before, during, and after reading to monitor and adjust comprehension.

To use background knowledge
- with fiction, preview the title, author's name, and illustrations
- with nonfiction, preview chapter titles, headings, graphics, captions, and other text features
- think about what you already know

This reminds me of a book I read.

Let's Think About Reading!

When I use background knowledge, I ask myself
- Does this character remind me of someone?
- How is this story or text similar to others I have read?
- What else do I know about this topic from what I've read or seen?

Important Ideas

Important ideas are essential facts in a nonfiction selection. Important ideas include details that provide clues to the author's purpose.

To identify important ideas
- read all titles, headings, and captions
- look for words in italics, bold print, or bulleted lists
- look for signal words and phrases: *for example, most important,* and others
- use photographs, illustrations, diagrams, or maps
- note how the text is organized— cause and effect, question and answer, or other ways

The caption under the photograph gives more information about wolves.

Let's Think About Reading!

When I identify important ideas, I ask myself
- What information is included in bold, italics or other special lettering?
- What details support important ideas?
- Are there signal words and phrases?
- What do illustrations, photos, diagrams, and charts show?
- How is the text organized?
- Why did the author write this?

Inferring

When we **infer** we use background knowledge with clues in the text to come up with our own ideas about what the author is trying to present.

To infer

- identify what you already know
- combine what you know with text clues to come up with your own ideas

Let's **Think** About **Reading!**

When I infer, I ask myself

- What do I already know?
- Which text clues are important?
- What is the author trying to present?

Monitor and Clarify

We **monitor comprehension** to make sure our reading makes sense. We **clarify** to find out why we haven't understood. Then we fix up problems to adjust comprehension.

To monitor and clarify

- use background knowledge as you read
- try different strategies: reread, ask questions, or use text features and illustrations

> This *doesn't* make sense! I'll slow down and reread.

ASSEMBLY INSTRUCTIONS

Let's **Think** About **Reading!**

When I monitor and clarify, I ask myself

- Do I understand what I'm reading?
- What doesn't make sense?
- What strategies can I try here?

Predict and Set Purpose

We **predict** to tell what might happen next in a story. The prediction is based on what has already happened. We **set a purpose** to guide our reading.

To predict and set a purpose
- preview the title, author's name, and illustrations or photos
- identify why you're reading
- use what you already know to make predictions
- check your predictions to confirm them

I wonder what happens next to Boone!

DANIEL BOONE

Let's Think About Reading!

When I predict and set a purpose, I ask myself
- What do I already know?
- What do I think will probably happen?
- What is my purpose for reading?

Questioning

Questioning is asking good questions about important text information. Questioning takes place before, during, and after reading.

To question
- read with a question in mind
- stop, think, and record your questions as you read
- make notes when you find information
- check your understanding and ask questions to clarify

Let's Think About Reading!

When I question, I ask myself
- Have I asked a good question with a question word?
- What questions help me make sense of my reading?
- What does the author mean?

Story Structure

Story structure is the arrangement of a story from beginning to end. You can use this information to summarize, or retell, the plot.

To identify story structure
- note what happens at the beginning, middle, and end of the story
- use this information to summarize, or retell, the story

Let's Think About Reading!

When I identify story structure, I ask myself
- What happens in the beginning, middle, and end?
- How can I use this information to summarize?
- How might this affect future events?

Summarize

We **summarize**, or retell, to check our understanding of what we've read. A summary is a brief statement. It's no more than a few sentences.

To summarize fiction
- tell what happens in the story
- include the goals of the characters
- tell how characters try to reach goals and if they are successful

To summarize nonfiction
- tell the main idea of the selection
- think about text structure
- think about how the selection is organized

...and that's how Lewis and Clark helped create new communities.

LEWIS + CLARK

Let's **Think** About **Reading!**

When I summarize, I ask myself
- What is the story or selection mainly about?
- In fiction, what are the characters' goals? Are they successful?
- In nonfiction, how is this information organized?

Text Structure

We use **text structure** to look for how the author has organized the text; for example, cause and effect, problem and solution, sequence, or compare and contrast. Analyze text structure before, during, and after reading to locate information.

To identify text structure

- before reading, preview titles, headings, and illustrations
- during reading: notice the organization
- after reading: recall the organization and summarize the text

This article uses sequence to explain how soil is formed.

Let's **Think** About **Reading!**

When I identify text structure, I ask myself

- What clues do titles, headings, and illustrations provide?
- How is information organized?
- How does the organization help my understanding?

Visualize

We **visualize** to form pictures in our minds about what is happening in a story or article. This helps us monitor our comprehension.

To visualize fiction

- combine what you already know with words and phrases from the text to form pictures in your mind
- use your senses to put yourself in the story or text

Let's Think About Reading!

When I visualize, I ask myself

- What do I already know?
- Which words and phrases help me form pictures in my mind?
- How can my senses put me in the story?

Program Authors

Peter Afflerbach

Camille Blachowicz

Candy Dawson Boyd

Elena Izquierdo

Connie Juel

Edward Kame'enui

Donald Leu

Jeanne R. Paratore

P. David Pearson

Sam Sebesta

Deborah Simmons

Alfred Tatum

Sharon Vaughn

Susan Watts Taffe

Karen Kring Wixson

PEARSON

Glenview, Illinois • Boston, Massachusetts • Chandler, Arizona • Upper Saddle River, New Jersey

We dedicate Reading Street to
Peter Jovanovich.

His wisdom, courage,
and passion for education
are an inspiration to us all.

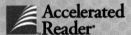

About the Cover Artist
When Leo Timmers was young he liked to putter with tape and shoeboxes to make animals, boats, and cars. Now, Leo is an illustrator and loves to draw and paint animals, boats, and cars. Some say his paintings look like they could jump off the page! Leo lives in Belgium.

Acknowledgments appear on pages 558–561, which constitute an extension of this copyright page.

ISBN-13: 978-0-328-45562-1
ISBN-10:   0-328-45562-8
3 4 5 6 7 8 9 10 V063 14 13 12 11 10
CC1

Dear Reader,

You are about to explore a special street—*Scott Foresman Reading Street*. Are you ready? We hope you'll have fun and that you'll learn new things to share with others. Along the way you will meet some interesting characters. You will read about a boy who learns to use his imagination. You will read about a lazy bear and a clever hare. You will also meet a girl who helps whales.

As you travel down *Scott Foresman Reading Street*, you may read new information that will help you in science and social studies.

While you're enjoying these exciting pieces of literature, we hope you'll find that something else is going on—you are becoming a better reader.

So, put on your walking shoes, and have a great trip!

Sincerely,
The Authors

Living and Learning

THE BIG ? **Which skills help us make our way in the world?**

Week 1

Let's **Think** About **Reading!**

narrative poem • science

by Suzanne Collins   illustrated by Mike Lester

narrative nonfiction • science

by Amy Bolt

Week 6

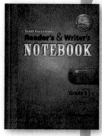

Unit 1

Envision It! A Comprehension Handbook

Smart Solutions

THE BIG **?** **What are smart ways that problems are solved?**

Week 1

Let's **Think** About **Reading!**

expository text • science

photo essay • science

Week 2

Week 3

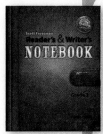
Envision It! A Comprehension Handbook

Envision It! Visual Skills Handbook EI•1–EI•16

Envision It! Visual Strategies Handbook EI•17–EI•27

***Words!* Vocabulary Handbook W•1–W•15**

People and Nature

How are people and nature connected?

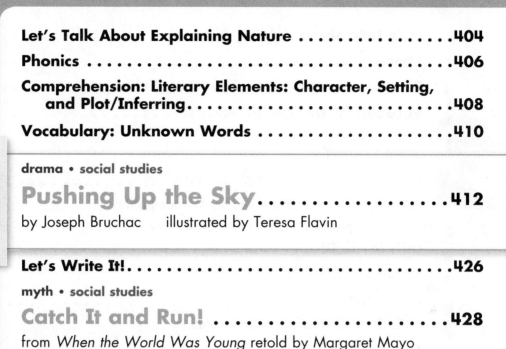
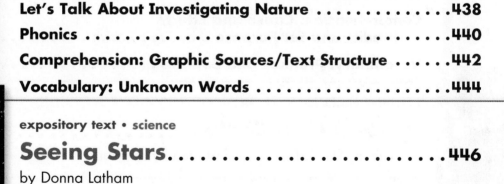

13

14

Week 6

Interactive Review

Unit 3

Envision It! A Comprehension Handbook

Envision It! Visual Skills Handbook EI•1–EI•16

Envision It! Visual Strategies Handbook EI•17–EI•27

Words! **Vocabulary Handbook W•1–W•15**

Don Leu
The Internet Guy

Right before our eyes, the nature of reading and learning is changing. The Internet and other technologies create new opportunities, new solutions, and new literacies. New reading comprehension skills are required online. They are increasingly important to our students and our society.

Those of us on the Reading Street team are here to help you on this new, and very exciting, journey.

See It!

- **Big Question Video**

- **Concept Talk Video**

- **Envision It! Animations**

- **eReaders**

- **Interactive Sound-Spelling Cards**

Hear It!

- **eSelections**

- **Grammar Jammer**

- **Vocabulary Activities**

Concept Talk Video

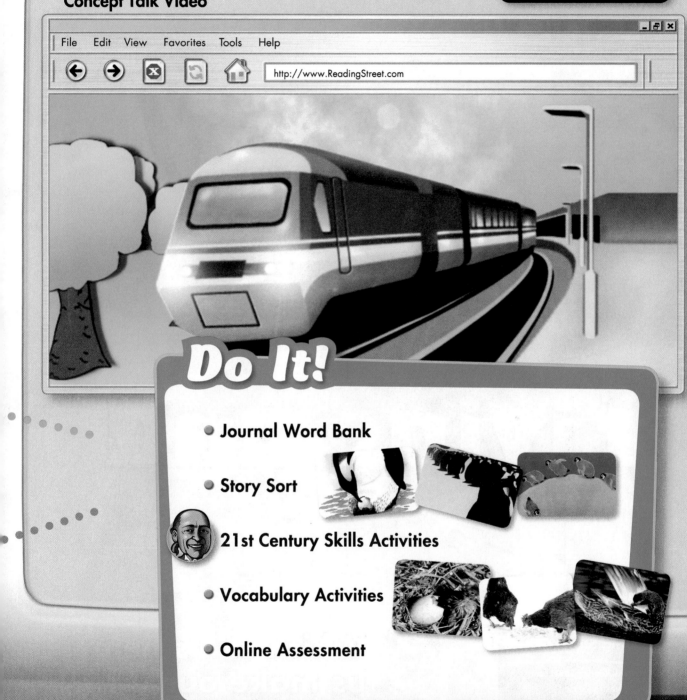

File   Edit   View   Favorites   Tools   Help

http://www.ReadingStreet.com

Do It!

- **Journal Word Bank**

- **Story Sort**

- **21st Century Skills Activities**

- **Vocabulary Activities**

- **Online Assessment**

Living and Learning

THE BIG ?

Which skills help us make our way in the world?

Objectives
- Listen closely when someone speaks, ask questions about the topic he or she is talking about, and comment about the topic. • Speak clearly and to the point while making eye contact, changing how fast, loud, and clearly you speak to communicate your ideas.

Let's Talk About

Trying New Things

- Ask what we can learn by trying new things.

- Pose and answer questions about new ways to have fun.

- Make and listen to comments about how people can encourage each other to try new things.

READING STREET ONLINE
CONCEPT TALK VIDEO
www.ReadingStreet.com

20

21

Phonics

🎯 Short Vowels: VC/CV

Words I Can Blend

invent
splendid
magnet
happen
intend

Sentences I Can Read

1. I would like to invent a splendid new computer game.

2. What will happen if you hold a magnet above paper clips?

3. Did you intend to get up early?

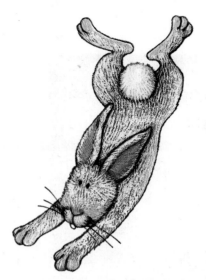

Justin missed part of the school day because of a trip to the dentist. He went to collect his lessons from Patrick. "What subjects did I miss today, Patrick?"

Patrick said, "Molly had her pet rabbit Button at school after lunch! He was hidden in a basket at first, but then she let him out. All of a sudden Button ran zigzag under desks and other objects."

"What happened next?" asked Patrick.

"Molly tried to collect him, but Button had gotten stuck in a locker. It took an hour to get him back in that basket."

You've learned

🎯 Short Vowels: VC/CV

Envision It! | Skill Strategy

Skill

Strategy

Comprehension Skill

Literary Elements: Character, Setting, and Theme

● A character is a person or animal in a story. You learn about characters, how they change, and their relationships from their actions and what they say.

● The setting is when and where a story takes place.

● The theme is what you learn from the story and can be supported with details.

● Use what you learned about character, setting, and theme as you read "Flash to Bang." Fill out a chart using details from the story.

Story Title	
Characters	**Setting**

Comprehension Strategy

Background Knowledge

Good readers connect what they are reading with what they already know. Using what you know can help you monitor and adjust your comprehension as you read.

Flash to Bang

Thomas stood in the yard and looked up at a big dark cloud. He could see lightning in the distance. It would probably rain soon. All week the weather had been sunny and warm. Now it was Saturday—no school, no karate practice, no piano lesson—and he really wanted to spend the day playing outside.

"Why can't I stay outside?" he asked his mom. "I don't mind getting wet."

"It's not the rain I'm worried about," she told him as they went inside. "Lightning is dangerous, and the storm is coming closer."

"How can you tell?" Thomas wondered.

"Lightning causes thunder," his mom replied, "but it takes time for the sound of the thunder to reach us. When you see lightning, count the seconds until you hear the thunder. For every five seconds you count, the lightning is about one mile away."

During the storm, they counted seconds from seeing the flash of lightning to hearing the bang of thunder. Thomas learned something new and had fun with his mom.

Skill What details does the first paragraph give about the setting? What details does it give about Thomas?

Strategy What do you know about storms? Why shouldn't you play outside in a storm?

Skill Describe the interaction between Thomas and his mom. How does she help Thomas change by the end? What details tell you the theme?

Your Turn!

⏸ **Need a Review?** See *Envision It! Handbook* for help with character, setting, theme, and background knowledge.

Let's Think About..

▶ **Ready to Try It?** As you read, use what you've learned about character, setting, theme and background knowledge to understand the text.

Objectives
• Use context clues to figure out words you don't know or words that have more than one meaning. • Use a dictionary or glossary to look up the meanings, syllable patterns, and ways to say words you do not know.

Envision It! | Words to Know

bat

battery

plug

blew

fuel

term

vision

Vocabulary Strategy for

🎯 Homonyms

Context Clues Sometimes when you are reading, you may come to a word you know, but it doesn't make sense in the sentence. The word might be a homograph. Homographs are words that are spelled the same but have different meanings. They may or may not be pronounced the same. When homographs are pronounced the same, they are also called homonyms. For example, *bat* can mean "a stick used to hit a ball" or "a flying animal." Look at the nearby words and sentences to help you figure out the meaning of a homonym.

1. If a word you know doesn't make sense in the sentence, it may be a homonym.

2. Look at the words around it. Can you figure out another meaning from the sentence? Does it make sense?

Read "The Inventor." As you read, look for words that might be homonyms. Look for nearby words to figure out the meaning that makes sense.

Words to Write Reread "The Inventor." Make a list of the homonyms you find. Then write both meanings of each word. Write sentences using each meaning of the words.

The Inventor

Max liked to invent things. He spent a lot of time working on projects in his lab. His neighbors admired his vision and creativity, but their children thought he was strange. They told each other that he kept a bat as a pet. They stayed out of his yard.

One hot summer day, Max had a terrific idea. He wanted to create something the children would enjoy. It would not need a battery. It would not plug into the wall or use fuel such as gasoline. Max's invention would run on a special kind of power—kid power!

Max wanted to use the invention soon, so he set a short term for the project. He worked day and night to finish. When the amazing "Summer Splasher" was ready, Max set it up in his front yard. Some children stopped to ask Max what it was. He showed them how to jump on the big pedal to pump water through the sprinkler. This also made the fan move. A cool breeze blew across the yard. Soon the children were lining up to try it out.

Your Turn!

Need a Review? For additional help with using context clues to determine the meaning of a homonym, see *Words!*

Ready to Try It? Read *When Charlie McButton Lost Power* on pp. 28–47.

When Charlie McButton Lost Power

written by
Suzanne Collins
illustrated by
Mike Lester

Genre

This **narrative poem** tells
a humorous story. The author uses
imagery to help readers experience the
way things look, sound, smell, or feel. What
details from the poem create an image for you?

Question of the Week
What can we learn by trying new things?

Let's
Think
About
Reading!

Let's **Think** About...

What are some of Charlie's electronic toys that are like your own?

⊚ **Background Knowledge**

Charlie McButton had likes and like-nots.
The things that he liked involved handsets and bots,
Computerized games where he battled bad creatures.
The things he liked-not didn't have blow up features.

30

Then one day a thunderstorm blew
into town
And brought his tech empire tumbling down.
A lightning bolt struck an electrical tower,
And Charlie McButton?
    His whole world lost power.

Let's Think About...

What has happened during a bad storm you have experienced? What might Charlie do? **Predict**

31

Let's **Think** About...

Why are the descriptions of Charlie funny? How might you react to a power outage?

Inferring

He looked left, he looked right, and his heart filled with dread.
The TV, the lights and his clock were all dead.
He jumped to his feet, his lungs gasping for air.
The room spun around and he clung to his chair.

He tried to cry "Help!" but just managed a squeak.
The blackout had blacked out his power to speak.

Thank goodness his mother had ears like a bat.
She came to his room and she gave him a pat.

Help!

32

"Oh, Charlie," she said, picking up on his fears,
"The lights will come back when the bad
weather clears.
You'll have to find something without plugs
to play.
Read a book!
Clean your room!
Sing a song!
Model clay!"

Could *anything* be any duller than clay?
Soggy gray clay on a soggy gray day?
He hated the way the clay got under his nails
And how he could only make snowmen
and snails.

Let's **Think** About...

How do you feel
when you can't
do your favorite
things? How does
the author create
this feeling in this
passage?
**Background
Knowledge**

Let's **Think** About...

You've learned a little about Charlie. Why would Charlie be excited about the old gadget?

🔘 **Background Knowledge**

He dove for a gadget he'd outgrown last spring.
It was handheld, outdated, not much of a thing.
But he clutched the old toy like a lifeline that day.
See, it ran on one battery. The size? Triple-A.

He flicked the On/Off switch to On double quick,
But no happy humming sound followed the click.
He unlatched a hatch and his blood turned to ice.
"The battery is gone from my backup device!"

World records were set in the ten-meter dash
As away down the hallway he flew like a flash,
Seeking one battery, just one triple-A
That would rescue one boy from a gray day
of clay.

But just when his search nearly drove
him insane,
He ran past the bedroom of Isabel Jane.
His three-year-old sister was happily walking
A doll back and forth, and the doll—it
was talking!

Now, dolls didn't talk on their own as a rule.
They needed a power source, some kind of fuel.
In less than a second he'd made his decision.
Call it bad judgment, a real lack of vision.

Somehow his head didn't warn of his folly,
And Charlie McButton . . .

Let's **Think** About...

When have you made a decision too quickly? What was the result?

Background Knowledge

He pounced on that dolly.
He plucked out his prize through
the baby doll's dress,
And Isabel Jane made a sound of distress.

It was just a short walk to the foot of the stair
Where resided the McButton time-out
time chair.
To add to the fun of his term in the seat,
Isabel Jane came to play at his feet.

And Isabel Jane, the Battery Queen,
Had more triple-A's than he'd ever seen.
They powered her puppies, they powered
her clocks,
They powered her talkative alphabet blocks.

Let's **Think** About...

Have you ever experienced frustration like Charlie? What happened?
 Background Knowledge

37

Let's **Think** About...

How do the words create an image of a loud sound? When do you use a loud voice?

🔄 **Background Knowledge**

Assaulted by nonstop mechanical chatter,
Charlie McButton got madder and madder.
He snapped at his sis from his time-out time zone,
"How come you can't ever

just
leave
me
alone!"

38

Her eyes filled with tears and she gave them
a rub.
She went to the bathroom and hid in the tub.
Then Charlie McButton felt totally rotten
And couldn't help thinking some things
he'd forgotten.

Let's **Think** About...

Do you understand
why Charlie feels
rotten? What might
he do? Keep read-
ing to verify your
predictions.
Predict

Mainly he thought that, for sisters that toddle,
Isabel Jane was a pretty good model.
She clearly adored him. She didn't have fleas.
At dinner she'd secretly eat up his peas.

And sometimes—although he'd most hotly deny it—
He liked to just sit there beside her in quiet.
Wrapped up in a blanket, watching TV,
Her head on his shoulder, her foot on his knee.

He sat and he thought and he stared at the rain.
When his time-out was done, he found
Isabel Jane.
From the edge of the tub she gave him a peek,
So he said, "Hey, are we playing hide-and-
go-seek?"

She was happy at once and ran into the hall,
As she loved playing hide-and-go-seek most of all.
They took turns being "it" and counting to ten.
They hid in the plants and the guinea pig pen.

And when he found Isabel Jane in her quilt,
They decided a big blanket fort should
be built.
Then the gloom made him think
about dragons and spells. . . .
So Charlie became the great wizard McSmells.
And Isabel Jane, who desired a role,
Magically changed to his faithful old troll.

Let's **Think** About...

When have you
had fun imagining
things? Can you see
why this is fun?
**Background
Knowledge**

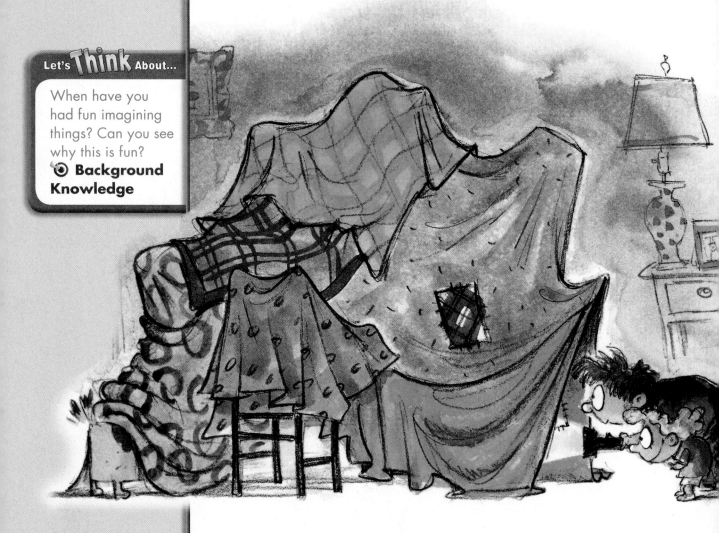

42

Between tracking down dragons and brewing
up lizards
And handling the day-to-day business
of wizards,
Like forging his faithful old troll a new sword,
Charlie McButton forgot to be bored.

Let's **Think** About...

With the power back on, what will Charlie do tomorrow?

Predict

At supper they ate under real candlelight.
The daytime had melted right into the night.
And after they'd all been asleep for an hour . . .
The world came alive with a big surge
of power.
Oh, it's finally back, Charlie thought with
a grin.
Tomorrow I'll wake up and I can plug in!

But another thought hit him he couldn't explain:
I might *also* find dragons with Isabel Jane.

Let's **Think** About...

Why do you think Charlie couldn't explain why he likes playing with Isabel Jane?
⊙ **Background Knowledge**

45

Objectives
• Describe how characters relate to each other and the changes that happen to them. • Describe different forms of poetry and how they create images in the reader's mind.

Envision It! Retell

**READING STREET ONLINE
STORY SORT**
www.ReadingStreet.com

Think Critically

1. Think about a time you experienced a power loss during a storm. Did you react like Charlie McButton? What did you do to pass the time? How long were you without power? **Text to Self**

2. Why do you think the author chose to write this story as a poem? What images did the poem help you create in your mind about Charlie McButton? **Think Like an Author**

3. How would you describe Charlie McButton? What details from the story helped you describe him?
   🎯 **Literary Elements**

4. What do you know about many of the toys and electronics that kids play with? How did it help you as you read the story? 🎯 **Background Knowledge**

5. **Look Back and Write** Look back at the question on page 29. Think about how Charlie acts when the power first goes out and what he does later in the story. Now write a paragraph explaining the changes in Charlie's behavior.

Suzanne Collins

Between writing for different Emmy-nominated television series, Suzanne Collins has written children's books. She wrote *Charlie McButton* after her own son found out he could have fun with things that didn't need power or to be plugged in by using his imagination!

Look for other books about people who use their imaginations!

Use the Reader's and Writer's Notebook to record your independent reading.

Let's Write It!

Key Features of a Narrative Poem

● tells a story

● its lines have rhythm, or a repeated accent

● often has lines that rhyme

READING STREET ONLINE
GRAMMAR JAMMER
www.ReadingStreet.com

Narrative Poem

A **narrative poem** is a poem that tells a story. The student model on the next page is an example of a narrative poem.

Writing Prompt Think about what it would be like to lose power at home. Write a narrative poem telling about it.

Writer's Checklist

Remember, you should ...

☑ create a title for your poem.

☑ tell a story with your poem.

☑ include rhyme and rhythm.

☑ include sensory details.

☑ make sure your sentences have subject-verb agreement.

Blackout

One evening last summer,

the power went out.

My brother and sister were scared.

I got out a flashlight

and turned it on bright.

"Do not be afraid!" I declared.

We made shadow puppets

and stayed up too late.

By morning the lights were repaired.

Writing Trait Careful **word choice** and sensory details make writing interesting.

Genre A **narrative poem** often has rhyming lines.

Sentences are complete.

Conventions

Sentences

Remember A **simple sentence** contains one subject and one predicate. The following is an example of a simple sentence: *The boy ran down the street.*

Objectives

● Identify the topic and find the author's purposes for writing. ● Identify the details or facts that support the main idea. ● Make connections between literary and informational texts with similar ideas and support your ideas with details from the texts.

Science in Reading

Genre
Narrative Nonfiction

● Narrative nonfiction tells about real people and real events in the form of a story.

● Narrative nonfiction can have characters, who are people living today or from history, and a beginning, middle, and end.

● Narrative nonfiction also has a topic, which is what the selection is about, a main idea about that topic, and details and facts that support the main idea.

● Now read to find out about this real person and his experiments with electricity.

How a Kite Changed the World

by Amy Bolt

Rain pours from the sky in sheets, thunder crashes all around, and the flash from lightning shines on one brave man battling the storm. Who could this brave man be? None other than our very own Benjamin Franklin.

Benjamin Franklin believed that thunderclouds carried electricity and that lightning was a large flash of electricity. He wondered if electricity could be useful and if it could, how? Benjamin Franklin also wanted to find a way to protect houses from getting hit by lightning. That is why one stormy night, Benjamin Franklin stood in the middle of a field, holding a kite.

On that famous night, Benjamin Franklin held a kite with a metal rod about a foot long placed on top of it. Benjamin Franklin believed that this rod would catch lightning. He tied a metal key to the string of the kite. If his theory was right, the electricity would travel to the key.

Benjamin Franklin took the kite to an open field. When the wind started to blow, he let the kite fly. He watched the kite and waited. Benjamin Franklin was starting to get tired and he began to think that his plan was not going to work. Then he noticed that some loose bits of kite string were standing very straight. It was working! He touched the key with the back of his hand and felt a shock. Electricity had passed from the cloud to the kite to the key.

Let's **Think** About...

What is the topic of this selection? What do you think is the main idea of that topic?
Narrative Nonfiction

51

Let's **Think** About...

Based on the facts and details you've read so far, what kind of person do you think Benjamin Franklin was? Support your answer with evidence from the text.
Narrative Nonfiction

This was not the end of Benjamin Franklin's tests of electricity. He turned his house into a laboratory by putting lightning bells in place. The bells rang when lightning was nearby.

Benjamin Franklin fixed a tall metal rod on his roof to attract the lightning. The rod would attract the electric current in the air and travel through a wire in his home. Small bells and brass balls hung from the wire. When clouds passed with electricity in them, the balls would strike the bells, the bells would ring, and a flash of electricity would travel between them.

From his experiments with the lightning bells, Benjamin Franklin hoped to show that placing a lightning rod on the roof of a building might save it from damage. If the lightning rod would attract lightning for Benjamin Franklin's experiments, then the rod could also redirect lightning away from buildings.

Let's **Think** About...

What facts and details from the page support the main idea?
Narrative Nonfiction

At first, many people were interested in Benjamin Franklin's discoveries. But they did not stay interested for a long time. To most people, watching his tests was like watching a show. The sparks, lights, and bells were fun to look at, but people didn't understand why electricity was important. With time, people began to pay more attention to ideas about electricity and how it may benefit their lives.

Before Benjamin Franklin and his kite, people knew very little about lightning and electricity. Benjamin Franklin took something found in nature, electricity, and explored everything about it. Today, every time we turn on a light, we know that Benjamin Franklin's ideas about electricity were right.

Let's **Think** About...

What happens in the beginning, middle, and end of this selection?
Narrative Nonfiction

Let's **Think** About...

Reading Across Texts What are a few of the ways that Charlie McButton used electricity? If Charlie could talk to Benjamin Franklin about electricity, what do you think he would ask? Support your answer with evidence from the story.

Writing Across Texts Pretend you are Charlie. Write a letter to Benjamin Franklin telling him what you think of his experiments with electricity.

Objectives
● Understand how information changes when moving from one type of media to another type.
● Speak clearly and to the point while making eye contact, changing how fast, loud, and clearly you speak to communicate your ideas.

Vocabulary

Homonyms

Context Clues Remember that you can use context clues to determine the meaning of homonyms. If you come to a word you know, but it doesn't make sense in the sentence, reread the words and sentences around it. They can help you find the correct meaning of the homonym.

Practice It! Select a book from your classroom library or a book you are reading from your school library. Record any homonyms you find. Then write their meanings as they were used in the book.

Fluency

Accuracy

When reading, it is important to read the words on the page as they are written. If you do not read accurately, you will not understand what is happening in the story. As you read, pay attention to each word as you read it. Think about it in the context of the story. Does it make sense? If not, go back and reread the sentence.

Practice It! With a partner, practice reading aloud *When Charlie McButton Lost Power*, page 34. Have your partner keep track of any words you read incorrectly. What were they? Reread the page, focusing on reading with increased accuracy.

Media Literacy

Get Ready For Middle School

When you give a report, speak clearly using formal language.

News Report

In a news report, a TV or radio reporter tells about important stories that are happening now. The purpose of a news report is to inform the audience about current events.

Practice It! Present a television news report to the class about the power outage in Charlie McButton's neighborhood. Include the cause of the outage and who was affected. Then discuss how your presentation would change if you were making a documentary instead.

Tips

Listening ...

- Listen attentively to speakers.
- Listen to identify mood.

Speaking ...

- Face the camera or audience.
- Use formal language.
- Use correct subject-verb agreement in complete simple sentences.

Teamwork ...

- Provide suggestions for how to turn the news report into a documentary.

Objectives
● Listen closely when someone speaks, ask questions about the topic he or she is talking about, and comment about the topic. ● Take part in discussions led by teachers and other students, ask and answer questions, and offer ideas that build on the ideas of others.

Let's Talk About

Trading with One Another

● Express opinions about the benefits of trade.

● Share ideas in teams about trading with one another.

● Pose and answer questions about trade that are based on an item's value.

READING STREET ONLINE
CONCEPT TALK VIDEO
www.ReadingStreet.com

56

You've learned
0 0 8
Amazing Words
so far this year!

57

dogs

plural -s

babies

plural -ies

peaches

plural -es

Phonics

Plurals -s, -es, -ies

Words I Can Blend

babies

smiles

nests

boxes

pennies

Sentences I Can Read

1. Babies give us lots of smiles.

2. Birds use twigs to build their nests.

3. Dad has boxes of pennies in his desk.

I Can Read!

Erin's parents are both vets, and Erin helps them out. Every day Erin spends time with puppies, cats, snakes, and even horses.

Once two girls brought in a family of foxes. They found those babies in their backyard, and the mother fox was nowhere in sight. Erin was given the job of feeding those baby foxes. She loves animals and was thrilled to do it.

When Erin is an adult, she wants to have the same job as her parents. She adores caring for kittens, dogs, birds, and any other animals that need her.

You've learned

- Plurals -s, -es, -ies

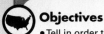

Objectives
• Tell in order the main events of a story. Explain how they will affect future events in a story. • Summarize information in a text.

Skill

Strategy

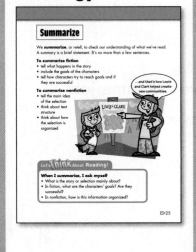

Comprehension Skill

🎯 Sequence

- Sequence is the order in which the main events in the plot happen—what occurs first, next, and last.

- Sometimes a writer uses clue words such as *first, next,* and *in the morning* or *at night.* Sometimes a writer does not. Then you can tell the order by picturing in your mind what is happening.

- Use what you've learned about sequence and the graphic organizer below as you read "Chores." Use the text and the graphic organizer to help you summarize the story events as you read.

Comprehension Strategy

🎯 Summarize

Good readers summarize what happens as they read a story. When you sum up, remember to tell the important events in the order they happen, without losing the meaning of the text. This will help you remember what you're reading.

Chores

Louisa looked at the chores list. It was her turn to fold the laundry. That was the chore she disliked most. How could she get out of it?

Louisa saw her brother J. B. in his room. "J. B., would you like to make some money?" Louisa asked.

"What's the catch?" asked J. B.

"I'll pay you 50 cents to fold the …," Louisa stopped. She remembered that she had spent her 50 cents yesterday. "Never mind."

Next Louisa saw her sister Grace pouting in the living room.

"I got the worst chore on the list today," said Grace. "I don't like dusting furniture!"

"Dusting furniture isn't bad. I have to fold the laundry! *That's* the worst!" Louisa said.

"I don't mind folding laundry," said Grace. "Anything but dusting!"

The two girls looked at each other. They both smiled. As Grace folded the laundry, Louisa hummed and dusted.

Strategy Here's a good place to stop and summarize the sequence of the plot's events so far.

Skill This paragraph begins with a time-order transition word. What happens after Louisa talks to J. B.?

Your Turn!

⏸ **Need a Review?** See the *Envision It! Handbook* for help with sequence and summarize.

▶ **Ready to Try It?** As you read *What About Me?* use what you've learned about sequence and summarize to understand the text.

61

carpenter

carpetmaker

thread

knowledge
marketplace
merchant
plenty
straying

Vocabulary Strategy for

🎯 Compound Words

Word Structure When you are reading, you may come across a long word. Look closely at the word. Do you see two small words in it? It may be a compound word. You may be able to use the two small words to help you decode the meaning of the compound word. For example, *goatseller* is a person who sells goats.

1. Divide the compound word into its two small words.

2. Think of the meaning of each small word and put the two meanings together.

3. Try the new meaning in the sentence. Does it make sense?

Read "At the Market" on page 63. Use the meanings of the small words in each compound word to help you figure out the meaning of the compound word.

Words to Write Reread "At the Market." Write a story about a special shopping trip. Tell what you see and what you do. Use compound words and words from the Words to Know list in your story.

At the Market

Imagine a small town in Europe three hundred years ago. It is market day. People come from miles around to buy and sell things. They meet in the marketplace in the center of the town. Look, there is a farmer who has come to sell his fruits and vegetables. And here is another farmer who is selling chickens and geese. He has put them in wicker cages to keep them from straying. The carpenter has made chairs and tables for people's homes. The baker has baked plenty of homemade pies, cakes, and breads. This merchant sells things for sewing–cloth, needles, and thread. And over there is a carpetmaker. He has made beautiful carpets.

People walk from stall to stall looking at the items. They know what they are willing to pay, and they use this knowledge to decide what they will buy.

Is it different from today? Not really. Just think about your last trip to a modern marketplace–the shopping mall!

Your Turn!

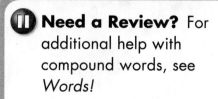 **Need a Review?** For additional help with compound words, see *Words!*

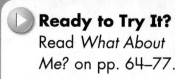 **Ready to Try It?** Read *What About Me?* on pp. 64–77.

Genre A **fable** is a story that teaches a lesson, or moral. What moral does this story teach?

64

What About Me?

by Ed Young

Question of the Week
What can we learn by trading with one another?

Once there was a boy who wanted knowledge, but he did not know how to gain it. "I shall see a Grand Master," he said. "He has plenty. Perhaps he will give me some."

When he arrived, he bowed and said, "Grand Master, you are wise. How may I gain a little bit of your knowledge?"

The Grand Master said, "You need to bring me a small carpet for my work." The boy hurried off to find a carpetmaker.

"Carpetmaker," he said, "I need a small carpet to give to the Grand Master for his work."

The carpetmaker barked, "He has needs! What about me? I need thread for weaving my carpets. Bring me some thread, and I will make you a carpet."

So the boy went off to find a spinner woman. He found her at last. "Spinner Woman," he said, "I need some thread for the carpetmaker, who will make me a carpet to give to the Grand Master for his work."

"You need thread!" she wheezed. "What about me? I need goat hair to make the thread. Get me some and you can have your thread."

So the boy went off looking for someone who kept goats.

When he came to a goatkeeper, the boy told him his needs. "Your needs! The others' needs! What about me? You need goat hair to buy knowledge—I need goats to provide the hair! Get me some goats, and I will help you."

The boy ran off again to find someone who sold goats. When he found such a man, the boy told him of his problems, and the goatseller said, "What do I know about thread or carpets or Grand Masters? I need a pen to keep my goats in—they are straying all over the place! Get me a pen, and you can have a goat or two."

The boy's head buzzed. "Everyone has a need," he mumbled to himself as he hurried off. "And what of my need for knowledge?" But he went to a carpenter who made pens, and he gave the carpenter his long story.

"Say no more," the carpenter said. "Yes, I make pens, but I need a wife, and no one will have me. Find me a wife, and we can talk about your problems."

So the boy went off, going from house to house.

Finally he met a matchmaker. "Yes, I know such a girl–she will make a good wife, but I have a need. All my life, I have wanted. . . . "

"Yes?" said the boy.

"Knowledge," said the matchmaker. "Bring me knowledge, and I will give you the young girl's name to take to the carpenter."

The boy was stunned. "But . . . but we cannot get knowledge without a carpet, no carpet without thread, no thread without hair, no hair without a goat, no goat without a pen, no pen without a wife for the carpenter."

"Stop!" said the matchmaker. "I for one don't want knowledge that bad." And she sent the boy away.

"I need a carpet," the boy chanted. "I need a carpet, I NEED A CARPET!"

And so he began to wander farther and farther from his village.

Until one day he came to a village where he saw a merchant in the marketplace, wringing his hands.

"Merchant," the young man said, "why do you wring your hands?"

The merchant looked at the young man's gentle face. "I have an only and beautiful daughter who I think is mad. I need help, but I don't know where to find it."

"**I could not** even get a piece of thread when I wanted it," said the young man. "But perhaps I can help."

And so the merchant led him to the girl. When she saw his kind face, she stopped ranting. "Oh, good young man," she said, "I have a need. My father wishes me to marry a merchant like himself, but I love a simple carpenter."

When she described the carpenter, the wanderer suddenly said, "Why, she loves the very carpenter I know!" And so he went to the other village and took the girl and her secret to him.

In thanks, the carpenter immediately gave the young man wood for a pen.

The goatseller placed the goats in the pen and gave him some goats, which he took to the goatkeeper, who gave him some of their hair, which he took to the spinner, who spun him thread.

Then he took the thread to the carpetmaker,
who made a small carpet.

This small carpet he carried back to the Grand
Master. When he arrived at the house of the wise man,
he gave the carpet to him.

"And now, Grand Master, may I have knowledge?"

"But don't you know?" said the Grand Master. "You already have it."

The Grand Master's Morals are Two:

Some of the most precious gifts that we receive are those we receive when we are giving.

and

Often, knowledge comes to us when we least expect it.

Objectives
• Tell in order the main events of a story. Explain how they will affect future events in a story. • Read by yourself for a period of time and paraphrase what you read.
• Summarize information in a text.

Envision It! | Retell

Think Critically

1. One of the morals in the story is "Often, knowledge comes to us when we least expect it." Think of a time when you learned something new when you least expected it. What did you learn? How did you learn it? **Text to Self**

2. This author makes his own pictures. Look back and find a picture that helps tell the story. Tell how it helps. What does the picture add to the story? **Think Like an Author**

3. What is important about the sequence in which this story takes place? **Sequence**

4. Summarize, or retell, what happened after the boy met the merchant. **Summarize**

5. **Look Back and Write** The merchant's daughter is important in the story. Look back at pages 73–74. Then explain how she influences the end of the story. Provide evidence from the selection to support your answer.

Ed Young

Here are other books by
Ed Young.

After working for a few years in advertising, Ed Young wanted to do something that would have more impact. Children's books gave him that challenge.

The Lost Horse

Mr. Young begins planning his illustrations as he thinks about the story. He then researches the subject so his illustrations will be accurate, even if he is illustrating a fantasy or a folk tale.

Up a Tree

Ed Young was born in Tienstin, China, and grew up in Shanghai and Hong Kong. The Chinese often pair words with their paintings. Mr. Young agrees with that idea. "There are things that words do that pictures never can, and likewise, there are images that words can never describe."

Use the Reader's and Writer's Notebook to record your independent reading.

Reading Log

79

Let's Write It!

Key Features of a Fable

- main characters are often animals

- story supports a moral or lesson

- moral or lesson is usually stated at the end of the story

READING STREET ONLINE
GRAMMAR JAMMER
www.ReadingStreet.com

Fable

A **fable** is a short story that is meant to teach a lesson or moral. The student model on the next page is an example of a fable.

Writing Prompt Write a fable that teaches a lesson.

Writer's Checklist

Remember, you should ...

✓ write a story that teaches a lesson.

✓ include animal characters.

✓ include details about the characters and setting.

✓ state the moral of the story at the end.

✓ write using complete subjects and predicates in your sentences.

The Frog in the Milk Pail

A frog was hopping around a farmyard when he decided to go inside the barn. The frog wasn't paying attention to where he was stepping, and he fell off a ledge into a pail that was half-filled with milk.

He swam around trying to reach the top of the pail. He soon realized that the sides of the pail were too steep and high for him to reach. He tried to stretch his back legs to push off from the bottom of the pail, but it was too deep.

The frog was not about to give up. He kept on trying to get out of the pail. He kicked and squirmed and kicked some more, until finally all his kicking in the milk had turned the milk into a big hunk of butter.

The butter became hard enough for him to climb onto so he could get out of the pail.

Moral: Never give up!

Writing Trait
Correct use of **conventions** such as spelling and punctuation helps make writing clear.

Complete sentences have a **subject and a predicate.**

Genre A **fable** teaches a moral.

Conventions

Subjects and Predicates

Remember A complete sentence has a **subject** and a **predicate**. The **subject** tells what or whom the sentence is about. The **predicate** tells what the subject is or does.

Objectives

● Retell themes and details in your own words. ● Explain similarities and differences between the settings of myths and folktales. ● Ask different types of questions about a text.

Pourquoi Tale

Genre
Myth: Pourquoi Tale

● *Pourquoi* [por-kwa] means "why" in French.

● Pourquoi tales are myths told to explain certain things or events in nature.

● The tales are set very long ago. They often begin with words such as "Long ago..." to show that the tale is ancient.

● The animal characters act like people. They can talk and think.

● As you read, notice how the setting compares and contrasts with other settings of myths you have read.

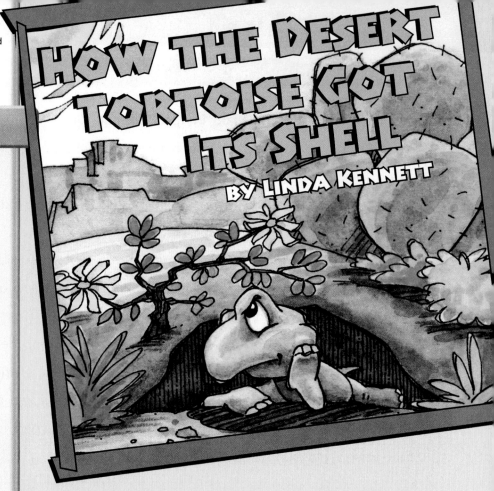

HOW THE DESERT TORTOISE GOT ITS SHELL
BY LINDA KENNETT

Long ago Desert Tortoise was a small green animal that lived in a burrow. There he hid from the heat of his enemy, Desert Sun.

From time to time, Tortoise had to leave his burrow to find food and water. One day in early spring, Desert Tortoise knew he needed go out and look for some food and water. As he crawled out, he saw that the desert was alive with beautiful wildflowers. Desert Tortoise especially liked the taste of the desert dandelion. One of the dandelions had fallen to the ground. Tortoise picked it up and carried it in his beak.

As Desert Tortoise traveled on in the sand, he got hotter and hotter. This made him angry with Desert Sun. Finally, he stopped to rest in the shade of a big rock. He put his dandelion gently on the ground. "Maybe it's time for my snack," he thought.

Suddenly, Desert Bee swooped in. "What are you doing with that flower?" he buzzed.

Let's Think About...

What characteristics of a pourquoi tale can you find?
Pourquoi Tale

"I think I will have it for lunch," replied the tortoise. "Desert Sun has been chasing me all day and I am tired and hungry."

"When someone bothers me, I just sting them with my stinger," boasted Desert Bee. If you will trade me your dandelion, I will give you my stinger. If you sting Desert Sun, he will leave you alone."

83

Desert Tortoise was excited by this news. He quickly agreed to the trade. Desert Sun began to beat down on him again as he left the shade of the rock. "You won't hurt me anymore," yelled Tortoise. He threw the stinger at Desert Sun as hard as he could. The stinger went up in the air but it didn't reach the sun and fell back to the ground only a few feet away.

Desert Tortoise picked up the stinger and continued his walk. After awhile he met Desert Cactus. She was standing with her arms stretched wide.

"What are you doing with that long, sharp thing? Is it a cactus needle?" demanded Desert Cactus when the tortoise got closer.

"Desert Bee gave me his stinger to use to fight my enemy, Desert Sun," muttered Desert Tortoise. "But it didn't work."

Let's Think About...

What things does Desert Cactus do that make it seem more like a person?
Pourquoi Tale

84

"Of course it didn't work," laughed Desert Cactus. "The best way to fight Desert Sun is with some cactus juice. If you drink my juice you will be safe. I will trade you the juice for the stinger.

This sounded like a good idea to Desert Tortoise. Desert Cactus gave him a cupful of her juice and she placed the stinger among the other spines on her arm.

Desert Tortoise took a small drink of the juice and he felt better. "Maybe Desert Cactus was right," he thought. Before he had much more to drink, Desert Tortoise came to a dry riverbed.

"What are you doing with that cactus juice?" asked Desert River.

"Desert Cactus gave it to me to fight my enemy, Desert Sun," answered the tortoise.

"I have a much better idea," Desert River said. "I am dry now, but if you pour your juice into my riverbed, it will turn into water. You will be safe from Desert Sun with me."

The thought of soaking in a river sounded very good to Desert Tortoise. He did as Desert River asked and then jumped into the water. He sunk down to the bottom and cooled himself with the wet river mud.

At last, he needed a breath of air so he came out. He was so tired from all his adventures and still so covered in mud, that he fell asleep on the banks of the river. As he slept, the mud began to dry. Soon the mud baked and cracked into a shell that covered the tortoise's body.

Finally, Desert Tortoise awoke to find himself in a place where he could always hide from the sun! To this very day, the desert tortoise can be found safe inside his shell in the American Southwest and in Mexico.

Let's Think About...

What fact of nature about Desert Tortoise does this myth explain, and is the explanation believable?
Pourquoi Tale

Let's Think About...

Reading Across Texts The boy from *What About Me?* and the tortoise from "How the Desert Tortoise Got Its Shell" both get what they want. How did they each use cooperation to help them succeed?

Writing Across Texts Rewrite the end of the myth as if no one was willing to trade with Desert Tortoise.

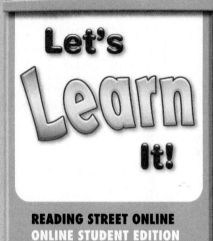

READING STREET ONLINE
ONLINE STUDENT EDITION
www.ReadingStreet.com

Vocabulary

Compound Words

Word Structure When you are reading, you may come across a long word made up of two smaller words. The word is probably a compound word. Use the two smaller words to help you understand the meaning of the compound word.

Practice It! Work with a partner to make a list of four or five compound words. Write the meaning for each compound word. Use a dictionary to check your work.

Fluency

Rate

Reading too fast or slowly can make it difficult to understand what you are reading. You might need to reread a story to practice the difficult words and phrasing so you can read at a good rate.

Practice It! Practice reading aloud *What About Me?* Listen for places where your rate slows down. What can you do to read them at a faster rate?

88

Get Ready For Middle School

When you give a description, use words that paint a picture in your listeners' minds.

Description

When you give a description, use details and images that create pictures in listeners' minds. Speak clearly, and raise your voice to make interesting details stand out.

Practice It! Describe to an audience the pictures and words found on various coins and bills. Then answer questions about what you described.

Tips

Listening ...

- Listen to determine the speaker's effectiveness.

- Ask relevant questions without interrupting.

Speaking ...

- Speak loudly enough to be heard.

- Use complete subjects and predicates in sentences.

Teamwork ...

- Ask and answer question with appropriate detail.

Objectives
● Ask questions about the topic and comment about the topic. ● Take part in discussions led by teachers and other students. Offer ideas that build on the ideas of others.

Oral Vocabulary

Let's Talk About

Achieving Goals

● Share ideas about how people work together to achieve goals.

● Discuss in teams how being prepared helps people achieve goals.

● Pose and answer questions about how specific reources help people achieve goals.

READING STREET ONLINE
CONCEPT TALK VIDEO
www.ReadingStreet.com

You've learned
0 1 7
Amazing Words
so far this year!

91

Objectives
- Read aloud words that drop the final "e" when adding an ending.
- Read aloud words that double the final consonants when adding an ending.

Envision It! | **Sounds to Know**

swimming

ending -ing

flipped

ending -ed

raced

ending -ed

taller

ending -er

smallest

ending -est

Phonics

Endings
-ed, -ing, -er, -est

Words I Can Blend

using

used

hopping

shadiest

later

dropped

Sentences I Can Read

1. The pen I was using ran out of ink so I used another one.

2. Those rabbits are hopping to the shadiest spot.

3. Dad arrived later than he'd planned because he dropped Max off at school.

I Can Read!

Hunter has always loved reading, but he got used to choosing only one kind of book. Whenever Hunter was going to the library, he always picked out adventure stories. Mom said, "Why don't you try reading a funnier title? It might make you happier."

Hunter decided he would try it on his very next visit. The first book he selected was about a talking dog. It was the silliest book he had ever read, and he walked home giggling. Now Hunter has learned that he enjoys many kinds of books, even the silly ones.

Envision It! | Skill Strategy

Skill

Strategy

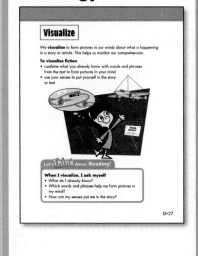

Comprehension Skill

Sequence

- Sequence is the order in which events happen in a story.

- As you read, look for clue words that tell time, or words such as *first, then, next, after that,* and *finally* to understand the sequence of events.

- A time line can help you keep track of the sequence of events.

- Use what you learned about sequence and the graphic organizer below as you read "Nalukataq, the Blanket Toss."

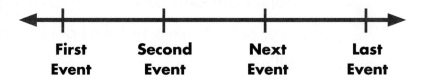

| **First Event** | **Second Event** | **Next Event** | **Last Event** |

Comprehension Strategy

Visualize

While you are reading, you can use the text to form pictures in your mind. This helps you understand and keep track of the details of what you read. Use language that appeals to your senses and other descriptions to help you create the images. If you have trouble visualizing what you are reading, reread the text until you can picture it in your mind.

NALUKATAQ, THE BLANKET TOSS

It is the end of June in Wainwright, Alaska. The whole village has come together for *Nalukataq*. This is the celebration of a good whale-hunting season. The people are glad that the whaling crew has returned.

The event begins with visiting and a big feast. Then there are games, followed by music and dancing that go late into the night. One of the games is the blanket toss. In fact, the celebration is named for this event.

The nalukataq is a large round blanket made from walrus or seal skins. It has heavy rope handles. First, about 15 people come together around the blanket. They lift it up. Then a person stands in the middle. The people holding the blanket toss and catch the person. The first jumper is always the captain of the crew that killed the whale.

The tradition comes from long ago. The blanket toss was once used in hunting. While a hunter was high in the air, he could see into the distance to find whales.

Skill What is the first thing that happens at the celebration? Add this to your time line.

Strategy What do you see in your mind as you think about the blanket toss? What should you do if you can't picture it?

Skill What clue words in this paragraph show the sequence of the blanket toss?

Your Turn!

❙❙ Need a Review? See the *Envision It! Handbook* for help with sequence and visualizing.

▶ Ready to Try It? As you read *Kumak's Fish*, use what you've learned about sequence and visualizing to help you understand the text.

Envision It! | Words to Know

gear

parka

willow

splendid

twitch

yanked

Vocabulary Strategy for

Unknown Words

Dictionary/Glossary You can use a glossary or a dictionary to find the meaning of an unknown word. A glossary appears at the back of a book. It defines important words from that book. A dictionary is a book that lists words, their meanings, and other information about the words. Glossaries and dictionaries list words in alphabetical order.

1. Look at the first letter in the word.

2. Turn to the section in the glossary or dictionary for that letter to find the entry.

3. If the word has more than one meaning, decide which meaning fits the sentence.

4. Try that meaning in the sentence to see if it makes sense.

Read "First Snow" on page 97. As you read, make a list of the highlighted words. Use a glossary or dictionary to find the meaning of each word and write it next to the word.

Words to Write Reread "First Snow." What do you think Jack and Missy missed most about Florida? Write your ideas. Use words from the Words to Know list.

First Snow

Jack and Missy had never seen snow. They lived in Florida. The weather there was too warm for snow. Then last winter they visited their cousins in Michigan.

On the second day of their visit, a snowstorm brought seven inches of the splendid white stuff. Hooray! Jack and Missy borrowed their cousin's extra boots and other outdoor gear. Then they all ran outside to play.

In the yard, the willow trees looked like they were made of snow. All the branches were covered in white. Missy went closer for a better look. Just then Jack yanked one of the branches. The snow poured down onto Missy's head. Some fell inside the neck of her parka. Brrr! The cold made her twitch and shiver, but she laughed anyway.

They took turns pulling each other in the sled. They made a snowman. Finally they were too cold and wet to stay outside. They went inside for dry clothes.

Jack and Missy had fun playing in the snow all week. By the end of the visit, though, they were glad to go back to the sunshine of Florida.

Your Turn!

Need a Review? For additional help with using a dictionary or glossary to find the meanings of unfamiliar words, see *Words!*

Ready to Try It? Read *Kumak's Fish* on pp. 98–113.

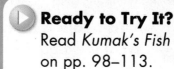

Kumak's Fish

Author and Illustrator:
Michael Bania

Genre A **Tall Tale** is a story that uses exaggeration. What is exaggerated in this story?

On a beautiful Arctic morning Kumak looked out the window of his house. Through the willows he could see the sun rising over the frozen river.

"Ahhh, spring," said Kumak to his family.

"The days are long. The nights are short, and the ice is still hard. *Good day for fish.*"

"*Good day for fish,*" said Kumak's wife, pulling on her warm parka.

"*Good day for fish,*" said his wife's mother, pulling on her warm mukluks.

"*Good day for fish,*" said his sons and daughters, pulling on their warm beaver hats and fur-lined gloves.

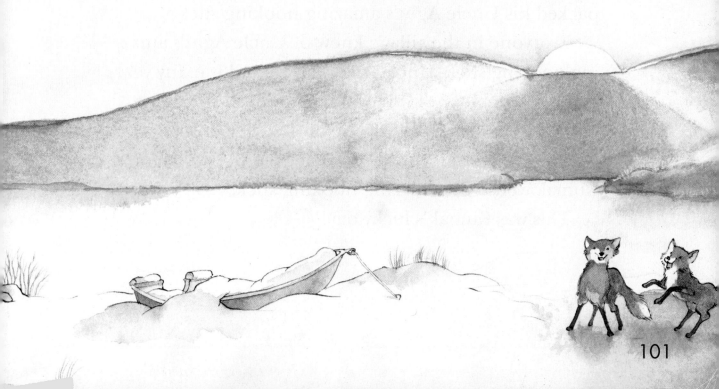

Kumak packed his fishing gear on his sled. He
packed his wife on the sled. He packed his wife's
mother on the sled. He packed his sons and daughters
on the sled. And then, in the safest place of all, Kumak
packed his Uncle Aglu's amazing hooking stick.

Everyone in the village knew of Uncle Aglu's amazing hooking stick. Uncle Aglu had carved it many years
ago out of a piece of fine willow, and each spring he
caught more fish than anyone in the village.

But this spring, Uncle Aglu's legs were stiff. He told
Kumak to use the amazing hooking stick.

This was Kumak's lucky day!

When they reached the great, frozen lake past the mouth of the river, Kumak's family dug their fishing holes and sat down to wait.

Kumak and his family sat for a long time. They were quiet. They were patient. They scooped away the ice growing around their fishing holes.

Just as the sun was starting to turn down for the day, Kumak's oldest son caught a fish. Then Kumak's two daughters each caught a fish.

Soon his wife and his wife's mother each caught a fish. *"Good day for fish!"* they said.

Kumak was quiet. He was patient. He scooped away the ice growing around his fishing hole.

Suddenly, Uncle Aglu's amazing hooking stick began to twitch. It twitched this way. It twitched that way.

It went around and around.

It gave one more twitch, then yanked Kumak toward the fishing hole. "What a big fish!" said Kumak's wife. "Biggest I can remember!" said his wife's mother. "The biggest fish ever!" said his sons and daughters.

They danced with joy, thinking about the happy
faces of the villagers when they brought the fish home.
Just then, Kumak began to twitch.

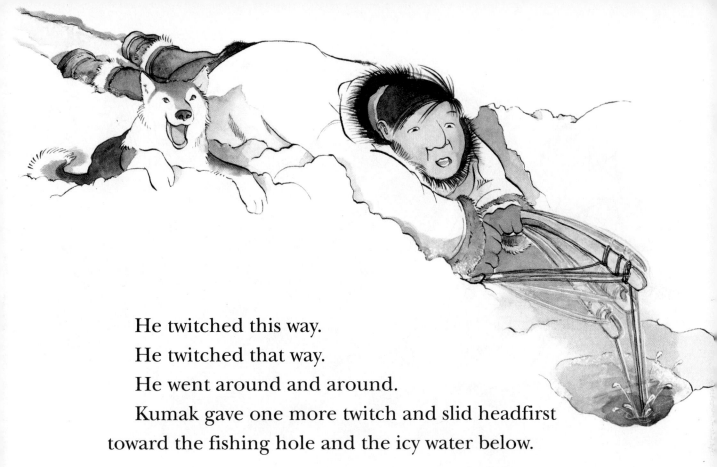

He twitched this way.

He twitched that way.

He went around and around.

Kumak gave one more twitch and slid headfirst
toward the fishing hole and the icy water below.

"Wife! Help me pull this fish!"

Kumak's wife grabbed him around the waist and
together they took two steps back.

"That fish must be as big as a seal!" yelled Kumak
happily.

"Aana! Help me pull this fish!" His wife's
mother ran to help. She took hold of Kumak's wife
and together they took three steps back. "That fish
must be as big as a walrus!" yelled Kumak happily.

"Children! Help me pull this fish!" His sons and
daughters ran to help. They lined up, one behind the
other, and never let go. Together they took six more
steps, but the stick pulled them all the way back to the
edge of the hole.

"That fish must be as big as a whale!" yelled Kumak happily. Villagers on their way home heard Kumak's shouts and ran to help. They lined up behind Kumak's family and holding on tight to the person in front of them, they pulled and pulled. But no matter how many steps they took away from the hole, they always ended up back where they started.

Soon the whole village heard about Kumak's fish and came to help. In one long line stretching across the frozen lake, they pulled and pulled and **PULLED!**

Once again, Uncle Aglu's amazing hooking stick began to twitch. It twitched this way, and all the people of the village twitched this way.

It twitched that way, and all the people of the village twitched that way.

It went around and around, and all the people of the village went around and around.

Uncle Aglu's amazing hooking stick gave one more
enormous twitch and pulled Kumak down the fishing
hole and into the icy water below!

Kumak's family and the villagers didn't give up.
Each person held on tight to the person in front of
them and never let go. All together, they gave one
more mighty pull and …

WHOOSH!

Kumak came flying back out of the fishing hole. Uncle Aglu's amazing hooking stick came flying out with him.

Stretched out in one long line, all around Kumak and the fishing hole, were hundreds of fish! Each fish held on tight to the one in front of it and never let go. Kumak had landed enough fish for the entire village to have a splendid feast.

"Hooray for Kumak!" cheered the villagers as they picked up the fish. "Hooray for Uncle Aglu's amazing hooking stick!" said Kumak as they started home.

It was a good day for fish.

Objectives
● Ask questions and clear up anything you don't understand. Support your answers with details from the text.
● Tell in order the main events of a story. ● Identify words that paint a picture in your mind.

Envision It! Retell

Think Critically

1. *Kumak's Fish* is a tall tale. Think of another tall tale you have read. How is it like *Kumak's Fish*? How is it different? **Text to Text**

2. At the beginning of the story, Kumak said it was a "good day for fish." How did the tale the author told make this phrase true at the end of the story? **Think Like an Author**

3. Create two time lines. On one, show the order in which Kumak's family caught their fish. On the other, show the order in which people lined up behind Kumak to help him pull the fish. **Sequence**

4. What do you see in your mind as everyone gives one more mighty pull on the hooking stick? **Visualize**

5. **Look Back and Write** Look back at the question on page 99. Think about the most important events that happened in the story. Now write a response to the question. Be sure to include details from the story to support your answer.

TEST PRACTICE | **Extended Response**

Meet the Author

Michael Bania

Michael Bania taught for many years in an Inuit village. Ms. Bania saw how her students loved to hear the stories the elders told. She decided to write these stories so that all children may read them. She resides in Alaska, where she continues to write. **Another book by Michael Bania is *Kumak's House*.**

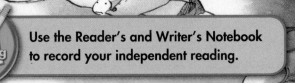

Use the Reader's and Writer's Notebook to record your independent reading.

115

Objectives
● Write essays for a certain audience and reason. ● Recognize and correctly use commas in series and dates.

Let's Write It!

Key Features of a Thank-You Note

- uses the form of a friendly letter
- has a friendly tone
- explains why the writer is grateful

READING STREET ONLINE
GRAMMAR JAMMER
www.ReadingStreet.com

Thank-You Note

A **thank-you note** is a friendly letter that expresses thanks for a thoughtful act or gift. The student model on the next page is an example of a thank-you note.

Writing Prompt Imagine you are Kumak. Write a letter to Uncle Aglu thanking him for the use of his hooking stick.

Writer's Checklist

Remember, you should . . .

☑ include a date, salutation, body, closing, and signature.

☑ use commas correctly in the date and greeting.

☑ explain how you feel about your uncle's actions.

☑ use language appropriate to your audience and purpose.

116

January 14, 20__

Dear Uncle Aglu,

Thank you for letting me use your hooking stick. **I know you usually catch more fish than anyone in the village when you use it.** Since you weren't able to fish this time, I was happy to use it for you. Just like you, I had a very lucky day of fishing!

At first, I was not sure the hooking stick would catch any fish. My kids and wife all caught fish before I did. But I was patient. **Do you know what happened?** The hooking stick began to pull this way and that way. **Everyone in the village had to get behind me and help me pull.** We were finally able to pull out enough fish for the whole village to have a feast.

Your hooking stick is amazing! Thanks again for letting me borrow it.

Sincerely,
Kumak

Conventions

Sentences

Remember A **declarative sentence** makes a statement and ends with a period. An **interrogative sentence** asks a question and ends with a question mark.

117

Objectives

● Identify the topic and find the author's purposes for writing. ● Use the features of a text to guess what will happen next.

Social Studies in Reading

Genre
Newspaper Article

● An author writes a newspaper article to inform or persuade.

● Some articles are procedural texts that use multi-step directions for the readers to follow. They can also include text features and graphic sources.

● Scan text features and graphic sources to predict what the article will be about. Then decide why you want to read it. As you read, verify your predictions.

THE MIDGEVILLE TIMES

Kids' Corner

How to Catch a Fish

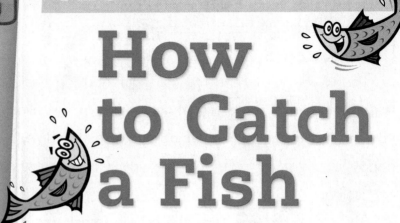

Vicki Edwards nearly broke the standing record for the largest fish caught in Lake Buchanan. Vicki follows a simple guide to catch her fish, and she wanted to share it with our readers.

Step 1. Bait the hook.
Have an adult help you bait your hook. There are different kinds of bait to choose from. Knowing what kind of fish you are trying to catch will help you decide which bait to use.

Step 2. Cast your line.
After you cast your line, watch the water. Ripples or small waves may indicate that fish are near. It is important to be quiet so you won't scare the fish away.

Step 3. Reel the fish in.

If your line tugs, that may mean you have a fish. Reel it in quickly so your fish cannot get loose.

If the fish is very heavy, you may need a net to help you get your fish into the boat.

Step 4.
See your prize.

Most lakes and rivers have rules and regulations that tell you if a fish is large enough for you to keep. Be sure to check those rules before you go fishing. Whether or not your fish is large enough to keep, be sure to take a photo of it!

Let's **Think** About...

Why did Vicki Edwards want to write about how to catch a fish? **Newspaper Article**

Let's **Think** About...

Reading Across Texts When you go fishing, will you follow the directions from this article or will you fish like Kumak did? Why? Make a Venn diagram to compare and contrast the two methods of fishing.

Writing Across Texts Write a short article for a newspaper that explains the two ways of fishing.

119

Objectives

● Read aloud and understand texts at your grade level. ● Use a dictionary or glossary to look up the meanings, syllable patterns, and ways to say words you do not know. ● Listen closely when someone speaks, ask questions about the topic he or she is talking about, and comment about the topic.

Let's Learn It!

READING STREET ONLINE
ONLINE STUDENT EDITION
www.ReadingStreet.com

Vocabulary

Unknown Words

Dictionary/Glossary If you come to a word you do not know while you are reading, you can use a dictionary or glossary to find its meaning. Words are listed in alphabetical order. Once you find the word, read the entry for the word. If there is more than one, choose the entry that fits in the sentence.

Practice It! Write the words *steady*, *stray*, and *sting* in alphabetical order. Then look up the words in a dictionary or glossary. When you find the meanings of the words in the dictionary or glossary, write them next to the word.

Fluency

Expression

As you read, change your volume, speed, and pitch to create expression. Reading with expression makes oral reading more interesting for your audience. It also allows you to give various characters different voices.

Practice It! With a partner, practice reading aloud *Kumak's Fish*, pages 100–101. Vary your volume, speed, and pitch as you read dialogue to create different voices for the characters. Ask your partner for feedback. Is there anything you can do better next time?

Listening and Speaking

Tell a Story

When telling a story, use expression and emotion to entertain your listeners. Speed up when the story gets exciting.

Practice It! With a small group, write and present a tall tale about a character who needs help achieving a goal. Then discuss your story with the audience.

Tips

Listening ...

- Determine your purpose for listening.

- Listen to identify emotional clues.

- Make relevant comments.

Speaking ...

- Speak at an appropriate pace.

- Use appropriate tone for emotional clues.

Teamwork ...

- Work productively, building on each other's ideas.

Objectives
● Ask questions about the topic and comment about the topic. ● Take part in discussions led by teachers and other students, ask and answer questions, and offer ideas that build on the ideas of others.

Let's Talk About

Wants and Needs

● Share ideas about how to grow or buy food.

● Provide suggestions for how people might manage their spending.

● Pose and answer questions about how food can be shipped.

READING STREET ONLINE
CONCEPT TALK VIDEO
www.ReadingStreet.com

You've learned
0 2 7
Amazing Words
so far this year!

123

Envision It! | Sounds to Know

bee
ee

easel
ea

snail
ai

hay
ay

soap
oa

snow
ow

READING STREET ONLINE
SOUND-SPELLING CARDS
www.ReadingStreet.com

Phonics

Long Vowel Digraphs
ee, ea; ai, ay; oa, ow

Words I Can Blend

ple**a**s**e**

free**ze**

remai**n**

know

delay

to**a**st

Sentences I Can Read

1. Please do not let the plants freeze.

2. We will remain here until we know more about the delay.

3. Would you like some toast?

I Can Read!

I received a note in the mail yesterday. Gram asked me to stay with her for a few days. She will teach me her way of making bread. I asked if I may go, and my folks said yes. They kissed my cheek, and then I was off to Gram's for an exciting week.

Baking bread is a slow process. Gram does not follow a recipe because she knows what she needs to do. She kneaded the dough in a large bowl and then we waited. After baking the bread, we made toast. Yum!

You've learned

🔊 Long Vowel Digraphs
ee, ea; ai, ay; oa, ow

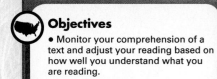
Envision It! | Skill Strategy

Skill

Strategy

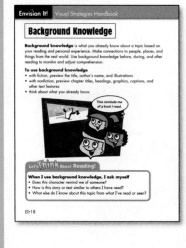

Comprehension Skill

Compare and Contrast

- When you compare, you tell how two or more things are alike.

- When you contrast, you tell only how the things are different.

- Use what you learned about compare and contrast and the graphic organizer below as you read "On the Farm."

	Farm	Subdivision
David		
Marcia		
Katie		

Comprehension Strategy

Background Knowledge

Good readers use what they already know to understand a selection. As you read, think about what you already know about the subject. Use this background knowledge to help you understand and connect with what you are reading.

126

On the Farm

The Marshall family lives on a big farm. It has eight hundred acres. An acre is about as big as a football field. There are three children in the family. David is twelve and Marcia is ten. Their little sister, Katie, is eight years old. In the spring their family plants seeds. They plant potatoes, sweet corn, and other vegetables. The children all help with the work.

Many new subdivisions have been built around the farm. David thinks all the houses look all the same. Marcia feels sorry for the families in those houses. She knows the children do not have much room to run around.

Sometimes Katie thinks about what it would be like to live in a big neighborhood. She thinks that she would like to have lots of playmates.

David and Marcia both want to be farmers someday. Katie thinks she would like to try something different.

Strategy As you read, think about your background knowledge. What do you know about life on a farm and life in a subdivision?

Skill Compare and contrast how David, Marcia, and Katie each feel about living on the farm.

Your Turn!

⏸ **Need a Review?** See the *Envision It! Handbook* for help with compare and contrast and using background knowledge.

▷ **Ready to Try It?** As you read *Supermarket*, use what you've learned about compare and contrast to understand the text.

Envision It! | Words to Know

laundry

section

shelves

spoiled

store

thousands

traded

variety

Vocabulary Strategy for

◎ Multiple-Meaning Words

Context Clues Multiple-meaning words are words that may have more than one meaning. Use context clues, or nearby words and sentences, to help you figure out the correct meaning of the word.

1. When you see a word you know but the meaning doesn't make sense, it may be a multiple-meaning word.

2. Use nearby words and sentences to figure out the correct meaning of the multiple-meaning word.

3. Try the new meaning in the sentence. Does it make sense?

Read "The Library" on page 129. Look for multiple-meaning words. Try the different meanings of the words in context. See which makes sense in the sentence.

Words to Write Reread "The Library." Write about a trip to the library. Tell how you would choose some special books. Use words from the Words to Know list.

The Library

Martita was cleaning her room. She picked up her dirty clothes and put them into the basket with the other laundry. "Let's finish our chores," her mother said. "We'll go to the library as soon as you're done."

Now Martita was eager to finish. She put her books on the shelves. Under the bed she found a variety of puzzle pieces and magazines. In the kitchen, Martita washed the dishes left from breakfast. Then she put the milk away so that it would not get spoiled. "I'm done!" she called to her mother. "Let's go!"

They stopped at the grocery store first. Martita chose the vegetables they'd cook for dinner that night.

"You've been helping so much with the chores," her mother said. "Today you can check out two books from the library instead of one."

This made Martita feel proud. At the library, she headed for the children's section. She picked a book and read the back cover. Then she traded it for another one. There were thousands of books to choose from! But she finally chose the two she wanted. "If I clean my room every day, can I check out three books next time?" she asked her mother.

Your Turn!

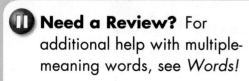 **Need a Review?** For additional help with multiple-meaning words, see *Words!*

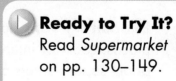 **Ready to Try It?** Read *Supermarket* on pp. 130–149.

Supermarket

Author: Kathleen Krull

Illustrator: Melanie Hope Greenberg

Question of the Week

How can we get what we want and need?

Shopping carts clang.
Magic doors whiz open and shut.
Colors glow under bright white lights.
So many breakfasts, lunches, and dinners!
It's all at a special, necessary, very real place:
the supermarket.

The supermarket is a whole world of its own.
Where does all this crunchy, munchy, sweet, sour,
fiery, frozen, fabulous food come from?

The doors don't really open by
magic. When an electric "eye"
overhead "sees" you coming, it
starts a motor to open the doors.

It all begins on farms.

Our food comes from places with lots of sunshine, rich soil, and clean water.

Certain states are famous for certain foods. Iowa for popcorn, Vermont for maple syrup, Michigan for cereal, Wisconsin for cheese, Idaho for potatoes, Massachusetts for cranberries, Florida for oranges, California for grapes, Georgia for peaches and peanuts.

Farmers make decisions every day during the long months of growing.

At harvesttime, workers pick the fruits and vegetables.

They pack everything neatly in boxes and load the boxes onto trucks.

Picking fruits and vegetables can be painful, low-paying work. César Chávez (1927-1993) became a hero for workers when he founded the National Farm Workers of America.

Small trucks, big trucks, gigantic trucks— all rev up
their engines.

Every night, drivers take off from farms or warehouses.
They zoom down the highway toward your town.

Among many other foods, American Indians introduced to the rest of the world chocolate, potatoes, tomatoes, beans, peppers, and most important, corn. Some form of corn appears in more supermarket foods today than probably anything else.

In early America, most people were farmers. American Indians taught the new arrivals what to grow.

Families grew all their own food.

Later they traded food with one another
to get other things they needed.

They started using money to buy things
at town marketplaces.

Soon there were general stores where you could buy almost anything and little, family-run grocery stores—"mom-and-pop" stores. Stores became bigger, dividing items into different departments.

Now we have an amazing place where every morning workers have a whole "super" market all ready for you.

They have unpacked thousands of boxes and arranged everything on the shelves, just so.

Bananas are the most popular fruit, followed by apples, watermelons, oranges, cantaloupes, grapes, grapefruits, strawberries, peaches, and pears.

You can find more variety in the fruit and vegetable section than anywhere else: fresh, juicy, strange, familiar.

Shoppers look, touch, sniff, compare, weigh—and watch out for automatic sprayers.

Beds of crushed ice keep the meats and fish fresh. Butchers cut or grind meat into different sizes and wrap packages in plastic.

For most of human history, food has often spoiled before it could be eaten. Not until the 1800s did people learn how to preserve food by sealing it inside metal cans. Around 1830, the English figured out a way to chill their food with machines.

According to surveys, the top reasons why shoppers pick a particular store are:
1. location
2. prices, and
3. selection

The best smells float around the bakery.
Bakers sometimes bake thousands of doughnuts a day and at least a dozen different kinds of bread.

143

Just about everyone stops in the dairy section.
Behind all the eggs, milk, yogurt, and cheese is
a refrigerated area keeping everything cold.

A stamp on many fresh foods gives
an expiration date: the day on which
the food is no longer fresh.

A sweater is handy in the frozen foods section, where the air is coldest. Zippy music makes some people hum along or dance right in the aisle.

145

The store is packed with cereal,
soups, spices, and even "nonfoods."

What is a "nonfood"? Something in
a supermarket that we don't eat—like
toilet paper, laundry soap, toothpaste,
shampoo, and magazines.

At the checkout counter, people try to pick the shortest line.

An electronic scanner "reads" the bar codes on most products and prints out the prices. A cash register adds up the cost of your food. Baggers ask "Paper or plastic?" and pack up your groceries.

Think about all the people who move food from the farms to your kitchen shelves!

The average wait in the checkout line is 8 minutes.

Americans spend more than $440 BILLION a year at our supermarkets.

Over half of shoppers, especially women, use a shopping list to make sure they don't forget anything. The average shopping list contains 22 items. Still, over half of what shoppers buy in a store is not on their list.

The supermarket is never quite the same from day to day. New items are added all the time, especially from around the world. Some markets have other stores right inside—worlds of their own.

149

Think Critically

1. The illustration on page 141 shows a variety of items that can be found in a produce section of a supermarket. What are some other unusual fruits or vegetables you might find there? Text to Self

2. The author uses notes to the reader throughout the story. Look back and find one of the notes. Why do you think that the author included these notes? Think Like an Author

3. *Supermarket* tells how people got food before there were grocery stores. Compare and contrast those methods to the way people get food now.
Compare and Contrast

4. As you read this selection, where were the places you used background knowledge? How did it help you understand the story?
Background Knowledge

5. Look Back and Write Reread pages 134–136. Think about all the different things that must happen to get food to the supermarket. Now write a list of directions explaining the process of getting fruits and vegetables from the farm to the store. Provide evidence to support your answer.

TEST PRACTICE Extended Response

Kathleen Krull

Kathleen Krull was fired from her job in the library when she was 15 years old—for reading too much! Her love of reading hasn't changed, and her love of music has greatly influenced her writing. She lives in San Diego, California, with her illustrator husband, Paul Brewer. **Ms. Krull has also written *M Is for Music* and *Lives of the Musicians*.**

Use the Reader's and Writer's Notebook to record your independent reading.

Reading Log

Key Features of a Description

○ uses sensory language

○ includes important details

○ creates a picture in the reader's mind

READING STREET ONLINE
GRAMMAR JAMMER
www.ReadingStreet.com

Description

A **description** is used to create a strong impression of a person, place, or object. The student model on the next page is an example of a description.

Writing Prompt Think about a time when you had to go to a store to get something you needed. Now write a description of a real store.

Writer's Checklist

Remember, you should . . .

☑ use your own experiences.

☑ use exact nouns and powerful verbs to appeal to the senses.

☑ use complete simple and compound sentences.

☑ use correct subject-verb agreement in each sentence.

☑ write clearly in cursive using correct spacing between words.

Peg's Gift Store

Peg's Gift Store is a really wonderful place. There are displays of bright, shiny jewelry fit for a princess. There are also shelves full of picture frames, candles, and other small gifts.

The front room has three display cases filled with necklaces, bracelets, and earrings. Some are big and some are very small. Peg stands behind a long counter and wraps each thing you buy in a pretty bag tied with a bright ribbon.

If you need a small present, you can find all kinds of choices in the back room. The walls are full of pictures and funny signs. There are pink and blue gifts for new babies and great birthday gifts just for kids.

When you leave her store, Peg always says, "Come back soon." She doesn't have to worry. I love to shop at her store!

Writing Trait Voice shows the writer's personality.

Genre A **description** creates a visual picture for the reader.

Imperative and **Exclamatory sentences** are used correctly.

Conventions

Sentences

Remember An **imperative sentence** gives a command or makes a request. An **exclamatory sentence** shows strong feeling or surprise and ends with an exclamation mark.

Objectives
● Identify the topic and find the author's purposes for writing. ● Use the features of a text to guess what will happen next. ● Ask different types of questions about a text.

Social Studies in Reading

Genre
Picture Encyclopedia

○ Picture encyclopedias provide information on a variety of topics using text and illustrations.

○ Encyclopedias often use text features such as heads, captions, and color or bold print to help the reader locate important ideas and predict the topic.

○ Entries are in alphabetical order.

○ Look at the title and the head, illustrations, and caption for each section, or entry, before you read. What do you predict this selection will be about? Verify your predictions as you read.

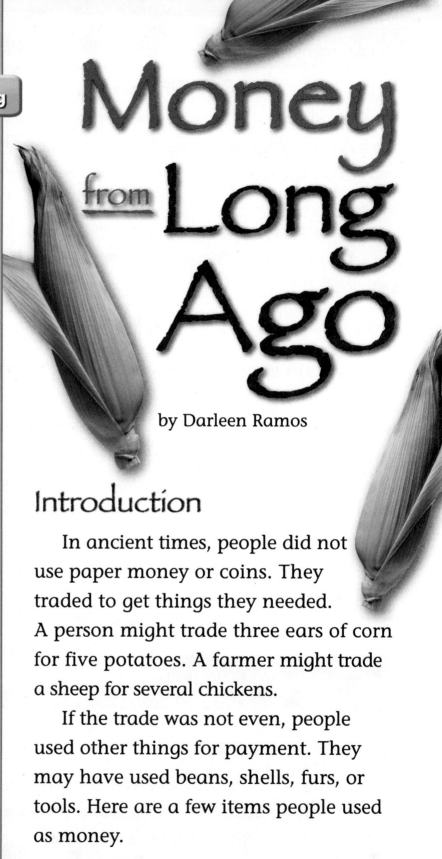

Money from Long Ago

by Darleen Ramos

Introduction

In ancient times, people did not use paper money or coins. They traded to get things they needed. A person might trade three ears of corn for five potatoes. A farmer might trade a sheep for several chickens.

If the trade was not even, people used other things for payment. They may have used beans, shells, furs, or tools. Here are a few items people used as money.

Cowrie Shells

Cowries are small snails that live in the ocean. In ancient times, their shiny shells were used as money in China,

Cowrie shells are dead snails.

India, and parts of Africa. The shells are one of the oldest forms of payment. Cowrie shells could be stored or worn. The color and size of the shell would set its price.

Feather Coils

Before there were coins and paper money, the people on the Pacific island of Santa Cruz used a feather coil for money. The coil was made from the red feathers of a honey-eating bird. The feathers were glued on the coil, which is about ten yards long. Red feather money was used in marriage contracts and to buy boats.

Red feather money coil— a wedding gift

Let's **Think** About...

What information do the caption and the photo give you? How do they help you to better understand the text? **Picture Encyclopedia**

Let's **Think** About...

Why are the words "Feather Coils" in large red letters? What does that tell you? **Picture Encyclopedia**

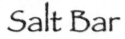
Let's Think About...

How did people in Africa and China keep food from going bad hundreds of years ago? How is this different from the ways you learned about keeping food fresh in *Supermarket*?

Picture Encyclopedia

Salt Bar

Hundreds of years ago, people from Africa and China used salt as money. Pure salt was expensive. Salt was used to keep food from going bad. The salt was cut into standard sizes and covered in reeds. This protected the salt from breaking. It also kept people from scratching off some of the salt between trades.

Reed protecting a salt bar

Stone Discs

Long ago, the people from Yap, an island in the Pacific, used large stone discs as money. The stones had holes in the middle. The giant discs were not moved when paid to a new owner. That's because the largest stones weighed more than 400 pounds! People used the stone discs to arrange marriages and to trade houses or boats.

Stone disc

Wampum

Centuries ago, Native Americans used a belt of beads for trading. This wampum was made from clam shells that were smoothed into beads. Each belt was special. The bead maker used different colors and patterns. Wampum belts were also traded during peace agreements.

Wampum belt

Let's Think About...

Reading Across Texts Which type of money from long ago would you like to use at a supermarket? Which would you not like to use? Why?

Writing Across Texts Make a chart with the heads "Good" and "Bad." List the positives and negatives of using each type of money.

Let's Learn It!

Vocabulary

Multiple-Meaning Words

Context Clues Multiple-meaning words may have different meanings. Use context clues by looking at the words surrounding a multiple-meaning word to help you figure out its meaning in the sentence.

Practice It! Make a list of four multiple-meaning words. Use each one in a sentence. Exchange papers with a partner and use context clues to figure out the meanings of your partner's words.

Fluency

Accuracy

Remember that when you read aloud it is important to pronounce words correctly. This will help everyone understand the correct meaning of the story or article you are reading.

Practice It! Read aloud *Supermarket*, pages 136–137, with a partner. Take turns listening to each other to make sure you are both reading the words correctly.

Listening and Speaking

When you give a presentation, share your ideas in an organized manner.

Panel Discussion

In a panel discussion, a group of people talk about a topic in front of an audience. The purpose is to share ideas and information.

Practice It! In a group, lead a panel discussion about different sections of a supermarket. Groups can take turns being on the panel answering the audience's questions and then being in the audience.

Tips

Listening ...

- Listen attentively.
- Ask relevant questions.

Speaking ...

- Make relevant comments.
- Make eye contact when you speak.

Teamwork ...

- Ask and answer questions with detail.
- Make suggestions that build on the ideas of others.

Oral Vocabulary

Let's Talk About

Saving and Spending

● Share ideas about how people earn and save their incomes.

● Discuss in teams the importance of saving.

● Provide suggestions for how to spend and save for the things we need.

READING STREET ONLINE
CONCEPT TALK VIDEO
www.ReadingStreet.com

160

Fresh
Lemonade 50¢

161

Envision It! | Sounds to Know

mouse

ou

owl

boy

ow

oy

oil

oi

Phonics

Vowel Diphthongs
ou, ow; oi, oy

Words I Can Blend

cookout

flowers

point

cowboy

choice

Sentences I Can Read

1. Jamie brought flowers to the cookout.
2. Point to the cowboy in the painting.
3. Which treat is your first choice?

I Can Read!

Joyce lives in a town with a lot of choice in clubs. Boys and girls can join clubs where they collect coins or old toys. Some spouses join clubs to work on their houses.

Joyce enjoys singing. She found a club called the Joyful Voices. This group allows Joyce to surround herself with beautiful voices.

Her club travels around to other nearby towns. This crowd joins with others and sings joyfully. Joyce is proud of these joyful voices!

You've learned

⊙ Vowel Diphthongs
ou, ow; oi, oy

Objectives

• Ask questions, clear up anything you don't understand, and look for facts and details. Support your answers with details from the text. • Tell in order the main events of a story. Explain how they will affect future events in a story.

Envision It! | Skill Strategy

Skill

Strategy

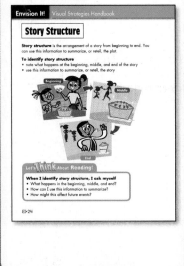

Comprehension Skill

◎ Author's Purpose

- The author's purpose is the reason an author has for writing.

- An author writes to inform, to persuade, to entertain, or to express an opinion.

- Use what you learned about author's purpose and the graphic organizer below as you read "Saturday Is Market Day." Then write a paragraph explaining how the text would change if the author's purpose were different.

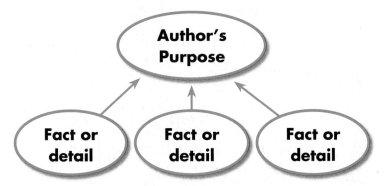

Comprehension Strategy

◎ Story Structure

As you read, think about the events that happen at the beginning, middle, and end of the story. Using the structure of a story can help you retell the story in your own words and improve your comprehension.

164

Saturday Is Market Day

My family lives in a little village in Africa. Every Saturday we go to town to sell our head scarves. Mama makes the scarves. Sometimes I help. They are the very best scarves you can buy.

Papa pulled the cart into the market as the sun came up. My sister Fusi and I laid out the scarves. It was not long before customers stopped by to look. A woman and her daughter bought two. Soon we began to sell many more.

At ten, drummers set up near us. As they played, Papa and Fusi danced. Mama and I clapped along.

Later, one customer had me turn around and around. She was looking at the scarf I was wearing that I made myself. She bought my scarf! It was a good market day. I am looking forward to next Saturday.

Skill What is the author's purpose for writing this story? What facts and details help you to know?

Strategy What happens in the beginning, middle, and end of this story?

Your Turn!

Need a Review? See the *Envision It! Handbook* for help with author's purpose and story structure.

Ready to Try It? As you read *My Rows and Piles of Coins*, use what you learned about author's purpose and story structure to help you understand the text.

Objectives

● Understand the meaning of common prefixes and common suffixes, and understand how they affect the root word.

arranged

bundles

unwrapped

dangerously

errands

excitedly

steady

wobbled

Vocabulary Strategy for

🎯 Prefixes and Suffixes

Word Structure When you read a word you don't know, see if it has a prefix or suffix. A prefix is a word part added in front of a base word to form a new word. The prefix *un-* makes a word mean "not ____ " or "the opposite of ____, " as in *unhappy:* "not happy." A suffix is a word part added to the end of a base word to form a new word. The suffix *-ly* makes a word mean "in a ____ way" as in *slowly:* "in a slow way."

1. Put your finger over the prefix or suffix.

2. Look at the base word, the part of the word without the suffix. Put the base word in the phrase "the opposite of ____" or "in a ____ way."

3. Try that meaning in the sentence. Does it make sense?

As you read "A Gift for Cletus," look for words that begin with *un-* or end with *-ly.* Use the prefix or suffix to help you figure out the meanings of the words.

Words to Write Reread "A Gift for Cletus." What do you think Cletus should save his money for now? Write your ideas. Use words from the Words to Know list.

A GIFT FOR CLETUS

Every Saturday Cletus ran errands for his neighbors to earn money. They gave him lists of things to buy in town. They gave him bundles to drop off. Sometimes Cletus had so much piled on the front of his bike that he could not keep the bike steady. He wobbled dangerously from side to side, and the bundles would almost fall into the street. Cletus had to ride very slowly, keeping one hand on the bundles.

Cletus wanted to buy a big basket for the back of his bike. He knew that with the bundles arranged behind him, it would be easier and safer to ride back and forth to town. But he had been unable to save enough money yet.

The neighbors really appreciated what Cletus did for them. They wanted a way to say thank you. So they got together and bought Cletus a basket for his bike. He unwrapped the gift and excitedly put the new basket on his bike. He thanked his neighbors, and then off he went again with their lists and bundles.

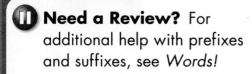
Your Turn!

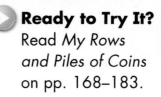
Need a Review? For additional help with prefixes and suffixes, see *Words!*

Ready to Try It? Read *My Rows and Piles of Coins* on pp. 168–183.

MY ROWS AND PILES OF COINS

by Tololwa M. Mollel

illustrated by E. B. Lewis

 **Genre**

Realistic fiction is a story that could really happen. Has anything like this ever happened to you?

Question of the Week

What do we need to know about saving and spending?

169

After a good day at the market, my mother, Yeyo, gave me five whole ten-cent coins. I gaped at the money until Yeyo nudged me. "Saruni, what are you waiting for? Go and buy yourself something."

I plunged into the market. I saw roasted peanuts, *chapati,* rice cakes, and *sambusa.* There were wooden toy trucks, kites, slingshots, and marbles. My heart beat excitedly. I wanted to buy everything, but I clutched my coins tightly in my pocket.

At the edge of the market, I stopped. In a neat sparkling row stood several big new bicycles. One of them was decorated all over with red and blue.

That's what I would buy!

For some time now, Murete, my father, had been teaching me to ride his big, heavy bicycle. If only I had a bicycle of my own!

A gruff voice startled me. "What are you looking for, little boy?"

I turned and bumped into a tall skinny man, who laughed at my confusion. Embarrassed, I hurried back to Yeyo.

That night, I dropped five ten-cent coins into my
secret money box. It held other ten-cent coins Yeyo had
given me for helping with market work on Saturdays.
By the dim light of a lantern, I feasted my eyes on the
money. I couldn't believe it was all mine.

I emptied the box, arranged all the coins in piles
and the piles in rows. Then I counted the coins and
thought about the bicycle I longed to buy.

Every day after school, when I wasn't helping Yeyo to prepare supper, I asked Murete if I could ride his bicycle. He held the bicycle steady while I rode around, my toes barely touching the pedals.

Whenever Murete let go, I wobbled, fell off, or crashed into things and among coffee trees. Other children from the neighborhood had a good laugh watching me.

Go on, laugh, I thought, sore but determined. Soon I would be like a cheetah on wheels, racing on errands with my very own bicycle!

Saturday after Saturday, we took goods to market, piled high on Yeyo's head and on my squeaky old wooden wheelbarrow. We sold dried beans and maize, pumpkins, spinach, bananas, firewood, and eggs.

My money box grew heavier.

I emptied the box, arranged the coins in piles and the piles in rows. Then I counted the coins and thought about the blue and red bicycle.

After several more lessons Murete let me ride on my own while he shouted instructions. *"Eyes up, arms straight, keep pedaling, slow down!"* I enjoyed the breeze on my face, the pedals turning smoothly under my feet, and, most of all, Yeyo's proud smile as she watched me ride. How surprised she would be to see my new bicycle! And how grateful she would be when I used it to help her on market days!

The heavy March rains came. The ground became so muddy, nobody went to market. Instead, I helped Yeyo with house chores. When it wasn't raining, I helped Murete on the coffee farm. We pruned the coffee trees and put fallen leaves and twigs around the coffee stems. Whenever I could, I practiced riding Murete's bicycle.

It stopped raining in June. Not long after, school closed. Our harvest—fresh maize and peas, sweet potatoes, vegetables, and fruits—was so big, we went to market on Saturdays *and* Wednesdays. My money box grew heavier and heavier.

I emptied the box, arranged the coins in piles and the piles in rows. Then I counted the coins and thought about the bicycle I would buy.

A few days later I grew confident enough to try to ride a loaded bicycle. With Murete's help, I strapped a giant pumpkin on the carrier behind me. When I attempted to pedal, the bicycle wobbled so dangerously that Murete, alongside me, had to grab it.

All right, Sarufi, the load is too heavy for you," he said, and I got off. Mounting the bicycle to ride back to the house, he sighed wearily. "And hard on my bones, which are getting too old for pedaling."

I practiced daily with smaller loads, and slowly I learned to ride a loaded bicycle. No more pushing the squeaky old wheelbarrow, I thought. I would ride with my load tall and proud on my bicycle—just like Murete!

On the first Saturday after school opened in July, we went to market as usual. Late in the afternoon, after selling all we had, Yeyo sat talking with another trader.

I set off into the crowd. I wore an old coat Murete had handed down to me for chilly July days like today. My precious coins were wrapped in various bundles inside the oversize pockets of the coat.

I must be the richest boy in the world, I thought, feeling like a king. *I can buy anything.*

The tall skinny man was polishing his bicycles as I came up. "I want to buy a bicycle," I said, and brought out my bundles of coins.

The man whistled in wonder as I unwrapped the money carefully on his table. "How many coins have you got there?"

Proudly, I told him. "Three hundred and five."

"Three hundred and . . . five," he muttered. "Mmh, that's . . . thirty shillings and fifty cents." He exploded with laughter. "A whole bicycle . . . for thirty shillings . . . and fifty cents?"

His laugh followed me as I walked away with my bundles of coins, deeply disappointed.

On our way home, Yeyo asked what was wrong.

I had to tell her everything.

"You saved all your money for a bicycle to help me?" she asked. I could tell she was amazed and touched. "How nice of you!" As for the tall skinny man, she scoffed, "*Oi!* What does he know? Of course you will buy a bicycle. One day you will."

Her kind words did not cheer me.

The next afternoon, the sound of a *pikipiki* filled the air, *tuk-tuk-tuk-tuk-tuk*. I came out of the house and stared in astonishment. Murete was perched on an orange motorbike.

He cut the engine and dismounted. Then, chuckling at my excited questions about the *pikipiki,* he headed into the house.

When Murete came out, Yeyo was with him, and he was wheeling his bicycle. "I want to sell this to you. For thirty shillings and fifty cents." He winked at me.

Surprised, I stared at Murete. How did he know about my secret money box? I hadn't told him anything.

Then suddenly, I realized the wonderful thing that had just happened. "My bicycle, I have my very own bicycle!" I said, and it didn't matter at all that it wasn't decorated with red and blue. Within moments, I had brought Murete my money box.

Murete gave Yeyo the box. Yeyo, in turn, gave it to me. Puzzled, I looked from Yeyo to Murete and to Yeyo again. "You're giving it . . . back to me?"

Yeyo smiled. "It's a reward for all your help to us."

"Thank you, thank you!" I cried gleefully.

The next Saturday, my load sat tall and proud on my bicycle, which I walked importantly to market. I wasn't riding it because Yeyo could never have kept up.

Looking over at Yeyo, I wished she didn't have to carry such a big load on her head.

If only I had a cart to pull behind my bicycle, I thought, *I could lighten her load!*

That night I emptied the box, arranged
all the coins in piles and the piles in rows.
Then I counted the coins and thought
about the cart I would buy. . . .

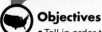

Objectives
● Tell in order the main events of a story. Explain how they will affect future events in a story. ● Support your answers with details from the text. ● Identify whether the speaker or person telling a story is a first- or third-person narrator.

Envision It! Retell

**READING STREET ONLINE
STORY SORT**
www.ReadingStreet.com

Think Critically

1. In the story, Saruni saves his money to buy a bike. Think of a time you saved your money to buy something you really wanted. What did you want? What did you do to make money? **Text to Self**

2. What point of view does the author use throughout the story? Why did the author write the story from this point of view? Be sure to include details from the story to support your answer. **Think Like an Author**

3. The author of the story could have just described what happened without using dialogue. Why do you think he showed the words spoken by the characters? **Author's Purpose**

4. What problem did Saruni have at the beginning of the story? How was his problem resolved at the end? **Story Structure**

5. **Look Back and Write** Look back at page 180. Did Yeyo's kind words make Saruni happy? Use details from the selection to tell how he felt and why. Provide evidence to support your answer.

TEST PRACTICE Extended Response

Tololwa Mollel

Tololwa Mollel grew up in a small village in Tanzania, Africa. Like the boy in *My Rows and Piles of Coins*, Mr. Mollel often went to the market with his grandmother. "It was the only time I got any money!" he says. Mr. Mollel says that it is very unusual for kids in Tanzania to have bicycles. The boy in the story doesn't want the bicycle just for himself. He wants to use it to help his mother. "Children in Tanzania help the family earn a living," he says.

E. B. Lewis

E. B. Lewis decided to follow in the footsteps of two uncles who were artists. For the illustrations in *My Rows and Piles of Coins*, he won a Coretta Scott King Honor Award.

About painting in his studio, Mr. Lewis says, "I don't know what's going to happen. The music is blasting–everything from rap to classical to jazz. Paint is everywhere. It's not a bad way to make a living."

Talkin' About Bessie: The Story of Aviator Elizabeth Coleman

Here are other books written by Tololwa Mollel or illustrated by E. B. Lewis.

Kele's Secret

Use the Reader's and Writer's Notebook to record your independent reading.

Objectives
● Write stories that are creative, build to an ending, and include details about the characters and setting. ● Show agreement between subjects and verbs in simple and compound sentences.

Let's Write It!

Key Features of a Realistic Story

● made up, but could be possible

● characters' actions are believable

● has a clear beginning, middle, and end

READING STREET ONLINE
GRAMMAR JAMMER
www.ReadingStreet.com

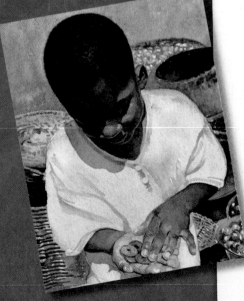

Realistic Story

A **realistic story** is a made-up story that seems as though it could really happen. The student model on the next page is an example of a realistic story.

Writing Prompt Think of something you would like to buy. Now write a realistic story about how you would save for it.

Writer's Checklist

Remember, you should . . .

☑ include events that could happen in real life.

☑ add details about the characters and setting.

☑ make sure all sentences have subject-verb agreement.

☑ reread your story to make sure it makes sense.

Earning Money

I decided to buy my little sister a tea set for her birthday. My dad says it costs $15, so I needed to figure out what to do to earn the money. My sister's birthday is only a week away!

First, I asked Mom and Dad if I could do some extra chores to earn some money. Mom loved the idea, so Dad made me a list of things I need to do: clean up the basement, pull the weeds in the garden, and wash the car.

They agreed to pay me $10 if I do everything on the list by Sunday. If I finish them in time, I'll only need $5 more!

After I talked to my parents, I went next door and offered to walk Mrs. Case's dog after school. I explained to her why I was trying to earn money. Mrs. Case said she would be happy to pay me fifty cents each time I walk Skipper, but then she had another idea. "I'll pay you $3 to help me give Skipper a bath tomorrow," she said.

Now I know that I'll be able to earn enough for my sister's gift. She'll be so excited!

Writing Trait Different kinds of **sentences** help make writing interesting.

Genre A **realistic story** seems as though it could really happen.

Compound sentences are correctly punctuated.

Conventions

Compound Sentences

Remember A **compound sentence** contains two simple sentences joined together by a comma and a word such as *and, or,* or *but.*

187

21st Century Skills

~~INTERNET GUY~~

Web sites Want to quickly find information at a Web site? Type Control and F. Then type the information you are looking for. Hit return. A great trick!

• Web sites are found on the Internet. Each Web address is also called a URL, which usually begins with http://. The home page introduces the Web site and works as a table of contents.

• Web sites can be valuable sources of information on many topics, using colors, shapes, and sometimes sounds to highlight key information.

• Read "Learning About Money" to learn about interactive communication and the conventions of Web sites. How can shapes and colors influence the message?

Learning About Money

In *My Rows and Piles of Coins,* Saruni saves his money for a new bicycle. This story may have made you wonder how young people can learn about money. After searching the Internet, you might find a Web site that helps kids learn about money.

188

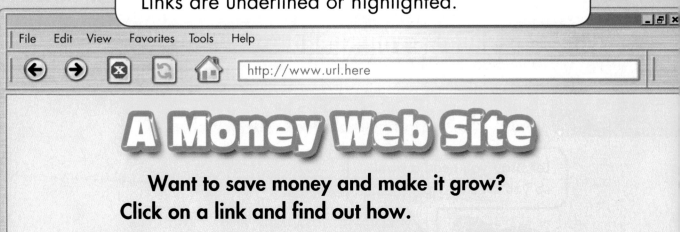

Colors and shapes make the different options stand out. Each option is a link to a new page. Links are underlined or highlighted.

A Money Web Site

**Want to save money and make it grow?
Click on a link and find out how.**

Open a Savings Account

Let's say you need a plan, so you click here.

Save as You Spend

Buy Savings Bonds

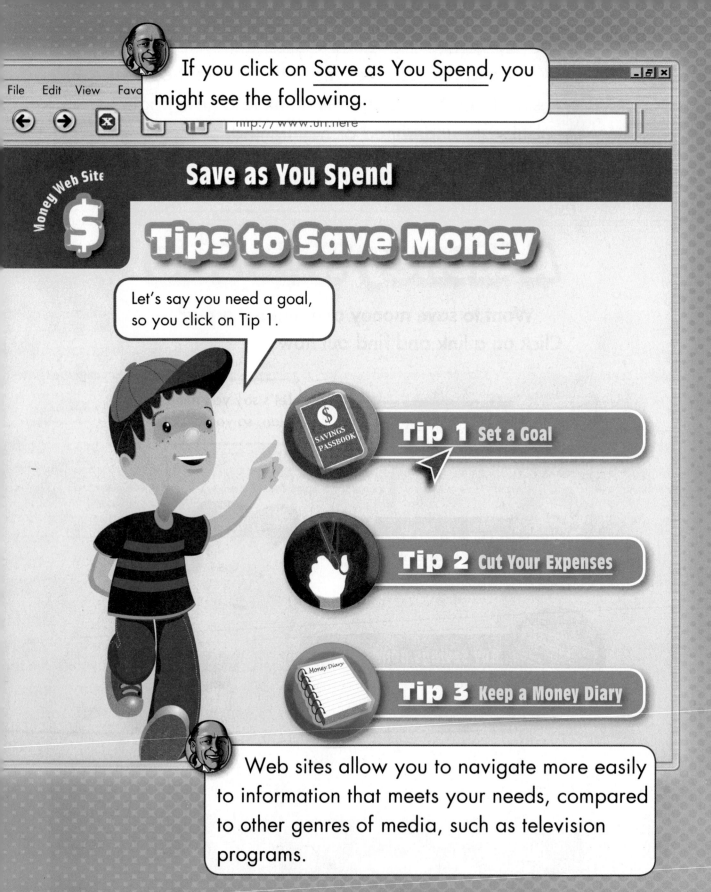

If you click on Save as You Spend, you might see the following.

Save as You Spend

Money Web Site

Tips to Save Money

Let's say you need a goal, so you click on Tip 1.

Tip 1 Set a Goal

Tip 2 Cut Your Expenses

Tip 3 Keep a Money Diary

Web sites allow you to navigate more easily to information that meets your needs, compared to other genres of media, such as television programs.

If you click on Tip 1 <u>Set a Goal</u>, you will find this information.

Money Web Site

$

Set a Goal

Suppose your goal is a new pair of sneakers that costs $48, and you earn $12 a week mowing lawns. What's your plan? How quickly do you want those sneakers?

Plan 1 If you save $6 a week, it will take you eight weeks to save enough to buy them (6 × 8 = 48). Are you patient enough to wait nearly two months?

Plan 2 If you save $12 a week, you can buy the sneakers in only four weeks (4 × 12 = 48). That's twice as fast! But then you won't have any extra spending money during those four weeks. Which goal would you set? It's up to you.

Compare the short phrases, informal language, and other conventions on this Web site to the language and conventions in an online article about saving money.

for more practice

Get Online!
www.ReadingStreet.com
Use a Web site to find out about money.

21st Century Skills Online Activity
Log on and follow the step-by-step directions about using a Web site to learn how to save money.

Objectives
- Speak clearly and to the point while making eye contact, changing how fast, loud, and clearly you speak to communicate your ideas. • Understand the meaning of common prefixes and common suffixes, and understand how they affect the root word. • Read aloud and understand texts at your grade level. • Show agreement between subjects and verbs in simple and compound sentences.

**READING STREET ONLINE
ONLINE STUDENT EDITION
www.ReadingStreet.com**

Vocabulary

Prefixes and Suffixes

Word Structure When you come to a word you don't know, look to see if the word has a prefix or suffix added to the base word. A prefix is a word part added in front of the base word. A suffix is a word part added to the end of a base word. If you know the meaning of the base word and the meaning of the prefix or suffix, you can figure out the meaning of the word.

Practice It! Choose four Words to Know from the story. Underline the base word and circle the prefix or suffix for each word. Write the meaning of the base word, the meaning of the suffix or prefix, and the meaning of the word.

Fluency

Appropriate Phrasing

As you read, use the punctuation marks in the text. Remember that you should pause at commas and stop briefly at end marks to make your reading sound smooth.

Practice It! With a partner, practice reading aloud *My Rows and Piles of Coins*, page 170. Pause at commas and stop at end marks. Did you sound like you would have if you were having a conversation?

192

Listening and Speaking

When you present a book report, follow etiquette, or rules, for conversation.

Book Report

A book report explains what a book is about, and makes inferences about the characters, events, or ideas in the book.

Practice It! Give an oral book report about *My Rows and Piles of Coins*. Tell about the characters, setting, and important events in the order in which they occurred. Would you recommend this book to a friend? Why?

Tips

Listening ...

• Ask relevant questions and make relevant comments about the literature.

Speaking ...

• Use appropriate verbal cues.

• Speak clearly, distinctly, and loudly enough to be heard.

• Use correct subject-verb agreement in compound sentences.

Teamwork ...

• Ask and answer questions with details.

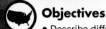

Objectives
● Describe different forms of poetry and how they create images in the reader's mind. ● Identify words that paint a picture in your mind and appeal to your senses.

Poetry

- Poetry helps us see, feel, and think about things in a different way.

- Poets carefully choose words to create **imagery**, or pictures in the mind or imagination. Imagery is used in all kinds of poems.

- **Narrative poems** tell a story. The stories they tell can be simple, dramatic, humorous, or even a little sad.

- Sometimes poets repeat ideas and words. This **repetition** can create **rhythm**.

- Poems that **rhyme** have lines with the same sounds, usually at the end. But some poems rhyme before the ends of the lines.

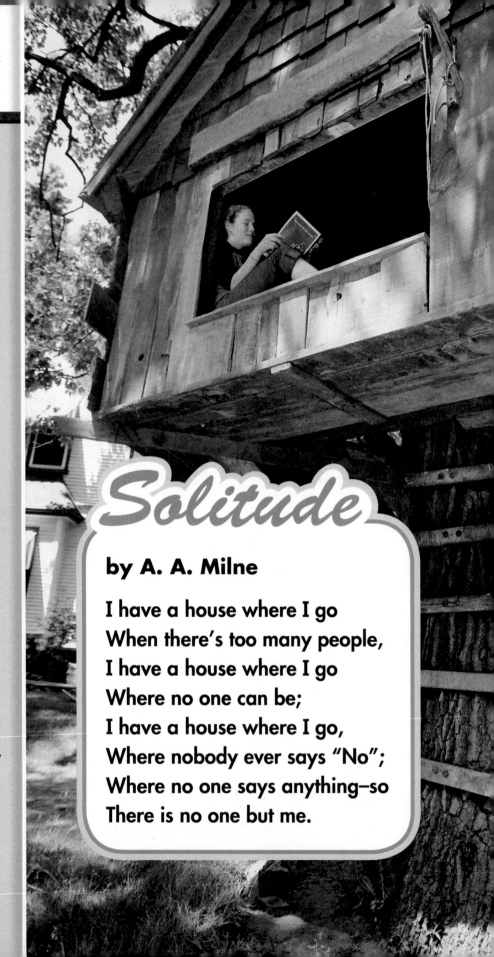

Solitude

by A. A. Milne

I have a house where I go
When there's too many people,
I have a house where I go
Where no one can be;
I have a house where I go,
Where nobody ever says "No";
Where no one says anything—so
There is no one but me.

The World's So Big

by Aileen Fisher

Think of all the people
I'll never get to know
Because the world's so big
And my wagon's so slow.

Think of all the places
I'll never get to see
Because the street's so long
And Mother's calling me!

Let's **Think** About...

How can you tell that "The World's So Big" is a **narrative poem**? Tell what is happening in the poem.

Let's **Think** About...

Can you find the **repetition** and **rhyme** in "Solitude"? Which poem has the stronger **rhythm**?

Let's **Think** About...

What specific words in the poems help create imagery?

Money

by Richard Armour

Workers earn it,
Spendthrifts burn it,
Bankers lend it,
Shoppers spend it,
Forgers fake it,
Taxes take it,
Dying leave it,
Heirs receive it,
Thrifty save it,
Misers crave it,
Robbers seize it,
Rich increase it,
Gamblers lose it . . .
I could use it.

Transportation

by Betsy Franco

Cars, trucks,
rockets, planes,
canoes, boats,
bikes, and trains.
Motorbikes, buses,
skateboards, feet,
subways, taxis,
trolleys in the street.
So many ways
to travel around:
in water, in air,
or down on the ground.
We'll fly to Mars
or rocket to the moon
in passenger spaceships
very, very soon.
We can drive or pedal
or walk or row.
Transportation takes us
wherever we go!

Smart Solutions

THE BIG

What are smart ways that problems are solved?

Objectives

● Listen closely when someone speaks, ask questions about the topic he or she is talking about, and comment about the topic. ● Speak clearly and to the point while making eye contact, changing how fast, loud, and clearly you speak to communicate your ideas.

Oral Vocabulary

Let's Talk About

Plant and Animal Structures

● Ask questions about how plants and animals adapt to their environments.

● Describe how plants and animals protect themselves in nature.

● Offer suggestions about what people can learn from the behavior of plants and animals.

READING STREET ONLINE
CONCEPT TALK VIDEO
www.ReadingStreet.com

You've learned
0 4 7
Amazing Words
so far this year!

201

Objectives
- Read aloud words that have syllables ending in consonants.
- Read aloud words that have syllables ending in vowels.

Envision It! | Sounds to Know

tiger

V/CV

lemon

VC/V

**READING STREET ONLINE
SOUND-SPELLING CARDS**
www.ReadingStreet.com

Phonics

Syllable Patterns V/CV, VC/V

Words I Can Blend

v e t o

o p e n

f i n i s h e d

t o t a l

e v e r

Sentences I Can Read

1. Mom would veto me staying out past dark.

2. We will stay open until the work is finished.

3. The total amount was more than Beth had ever spent before.

I Can Read!

Last week Kevin went on his first airplane trip ever. What an exciting day! He even got to meet the pilot of the plane.

After he entered the plane's wide body, he saw a tiny baby with her mom in the seat next to him. The baby opened her eyes and began to smile. Kevin smiled back.

The attendant finished the safety instructions, and the plane took off. The ground below seemed to vanish. After the landing, the door opened and Kevin was met by his grandpa. Kevin cannot wait to return to the airport.

Objectives

• Monitor your comprehension of a text and adjust your reading based on how well you understand what you are reading. • Identify the topic and find the author's purposes for writing. • Identify the details or facts that support the main idea.

Envision It! Skill Strategy

Skill

Strategy

Comprehension Skill

Main Idea and Details

• The topic is what a piece of writing is about. The main idea is the most important idea about the topic.

• Supporting details are small pieces of information that tell more about the main idea.

• Use what you know about main ideas and details and the graphic organizer below as you read "The Coldest Continent." Then use the organizer to help you write a one-paragraph summary.

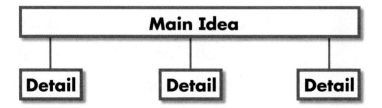

Comprehension Strategy

Monitor and Clarify

While you are reading, it's important for you to know when you understand something and when you don't. If you are confused, stop and reread the section aloud. Looking back and reading is one way to clarify or adjust your understanding.

The Coldest Continent

Antarctica is not like any other continent. It is as far south as you can go on Earth. The South Pole is found there. Ice covers the whole land. In some places the ice is almost three miles thick! Beneath the ice are mountains and valleys.

The weather in Antarctica is harsh. It is the coldest place on Earth. The temperature does not get above freezing. It is also one of the windiest places in the world.

Not many living things are found in Antarctica. People go there to study for only a short time. Very few animals can live there. Yet many animals live on nearby islands. Seals and penguins swim in the ocean waters. They build nests on the land. Some birds spend their summers in Antarctica. But most of the continent is just ice, snow, and cold air.

Skill Read the title and the first sentence. What do you think is the main idea?

Strategy Why can very few animals live in Antarctica? If you don't understand, how can you clarify or adjust your comprehension?

Your Turn!

⏸ **Need a Review?** See the *Envision It! Handbook* for help with main idea and details and monitoring and clarifying.

Let's **Think** About..

▶ **Ready to Try It?** As you read *Penguin Chick*, use what you've learned about main idea and details and monitoring and clarifying to understand the text.

Objectives
• Use context clues to figure out words you don't know or words that have more than one meaning.
• Identify words that are opposites and words that are similar.

Envision It! | **Words to Know**

hatch

pecks

preen

cuddles
flippers
frozen
snuggles

READING STREET ONLINE
VOCABULARY ACTIVITIES
www.ReadingStreet.com

Vocabulary Strategy for

🎯 Synonyms

Context Clues Sometimes when you are reading, you come across a word you don't know. The author may give you a synonym in the context of the word. A synonym is a word that has the same or almost the same meaning as another word. Look for a nearby word that might be a synonym to help you understand the meaning of the word you don't know.

1. Look at the words very near the word you don't know. The author may give a synonym in the sentence.

2. If not, look in the sentences around the sentence with the unfamiliar word for a synonym.

3. Try the synonym in place of the word in the sentence. Does it make sense?

Read "Penguins Are Birds" on page 207. Look for synonyms to help you understand the meanings of the vocabulary words.

Words to Write Look at the pictures on pages 208–221. Choose a picture to write about. Use words from the Words to Know list and synonyms in your writing.

Penguins Are Birds

All birds come from eggs. The mother bird lays the eggs, and then the mother bird or the father bird sits on the eggs until it is time for them to hatch. Each baby bird pecks, or hits the shell of its egg with its beak, until the shell breaks open. The baby bird cannot fly or get food. It needs its parents to bring it food and keep it warm. When a parent bird sits on the nest, the baby bird snuggles, or presses, into the parent's belly. The parents preen their own feathers. Then they also brush the baby bird's soft feathers. This helps keep the baby bird warm.

Penguins are birds. They have flippers instead of wings, and they swim rather than fly. But they have feathers and lay eggs just as other birds do. Baby penguins hatch from eggs, and they need their parents to give them food and warmth. Some penguins live in Antarctica, where the land and much of the water around it are frozen. Penguins don't have nests, so a penguin parent cuddles, or hugs, the egg or the chick to keep it warm.

Your Turn!

⏸ **Need a Review?** For additional help with synonyms, see *Words!*

▶ **Ready to Try It?** Read *Penguin Chick* on pp. 208–221.

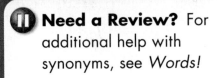

Penguin Chick

by Betty Tatham

illustrated by Helen K. Davie

Question of the Week

How do the structures of plants and animals help them solve problems?

Let's
Think
About
Reading!

A fierce wind howls. It whips snow across the ice. Here, a female emperor penguin has just laid an egg. It is the only egg she will lay this year.

Most birds build nests for their eggs. But on the ice in Antarctica, there are no twigs or leaves. There is no grass or mud. Nothing to build a nest with. Nothing but snow and ice.

The new penguin father uses his beak to scoop the egg onto his webbed feet.

Let's **Think** About...

What details are you learning about Antarctica? Why are they important?

Monitor and Clarify

He tucks it under his feather-covered skin, into a special place called a *brood patch*. The egg will be as snug and warm there as if it were in a sleeping bag.

One of the penguin parents must stay with the egg to keep it warm. But where penguins lay their eggs, there is no food for them to eat.

The penguin father is bigger and fatter than the mother. He can live longer without food. So the father penguin stays with the egg while the mother travels to the sea to find food.

Let's **Think** About...

Do you understand why the father penguin stays with the egg?

⊙ **Monitor and Clarify**

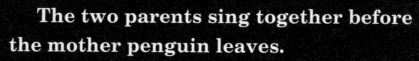

The two parents sing together before the mother penguin leaves.

Along with many other penguins, the mother penguin leaves the rookery, where she laid her egg.

The mother walks or slides on her belly. This is called *tobogganing*. She uses her flippers and webbed feet to push herself forward over ice and snow.

Because it's winter in Antarctica, water near the shore is frozen for many miles. After three days the mother penguin comes to the end of the ice. She dives into the water to hunt for fish, squid, and tiny shrimplike creatures called *krill*.

Let's **Think** About...

Do you understand why some of the words are in italic type? How can you learn their meanings?

◎ **Monitor and Clarify**

Fish

Squid

Krill

Let's Think About...

Do you understand why a huddle is important?

Monitor and Clarify

Back at the rookery, the penguin fathers form a group called a *huddle*. They stand close together for warmth. Each keeps his own egg warm.

For two months the penguin father always keeps his egg on his feet. When he walks, he shuffles his feet so the egg doesn't roll away. He sleeps standing up. He has no food to eat, but the fat on his body keeps him alive.

Finally he feels the chick move inside the egg. The chick pecks and pecks and pecks. In about three days the egg cracks open.

The chick is wet. But soon his soft feathers, called *down,* dry and become fluffy and gray. The father still keeps the chick warm in the brood patch. Sometimes the chick pokes his head out. But while he's so little, he must stay covered. And he must stay on his father's feet. Otherwise the cold would kill him.

The father talks to the chick in his trumpet voice. The chick answers with a whistle.

Let's **Think** About...

What details help you understand more about a brood patch?

⊙ Monitor and Clarify

215

The father's trumpet call echoes across the ice. The penguin mother is on her way back to the rookery, but she can't hear him. She's still too far away. If the mother doesn't come back soon with food, the chick will die.

Two days pass before the mother can hear the father penguin's call.

At last the mother arrives at the rookery. She cuddles close to the chick and trumpets to him. He whistles back. With her beak she brushes his soft gray down.

Let's Think About...

What do you picture when you think about a father penguin trumpeting?
Visualize

216

The mother swallowed many fish before she left the ocean. She brings some of this food back up from her stomach and feeds her chick. She has enough food to keep him fed for weeks. He stays on her feet and snuggles into her brood patch.

The father is very hungry, so he travels to open water. There he dives to hunt for food. Weeks later the father returns with more food for the chick.

Each day the parents preen, or brush, the chick's downy coat with their beaks. This keeps the down fluffy and keeps the chick warm.

Let's Think About...

What questions do you have about the information on this page?

Monitor and Clarify

Let's **Think** About...

What does the word *nursery* mean in your life? How is that similar here?
Background Knowledge

As the chick gets bigger, he and the other chicks no longer need to stay on their parents' feet. Instead they stay together to keep warm.

This group of chicks is called a *crèche,* or a nursery. The chick now spends most of his time here. But he still rushes to his mother or father to be fed when either one comes back from the ocean.

WINTER		SPRING
August	*September*	*October*

Sometimes the chick and the other young penguins dig their beaks into the ice to help them walk up a slippery hill. They toboggan down fast on their fluffy bellies.

The chick grows and grows. After five months, he has grown into a junior penguin. He is old enough to travel to the ocean.

SUMMER

November   *December*   *January*

Let's **Think** About...

How does the time line help you understand the text?

🔄 **Monitor and Clarify**

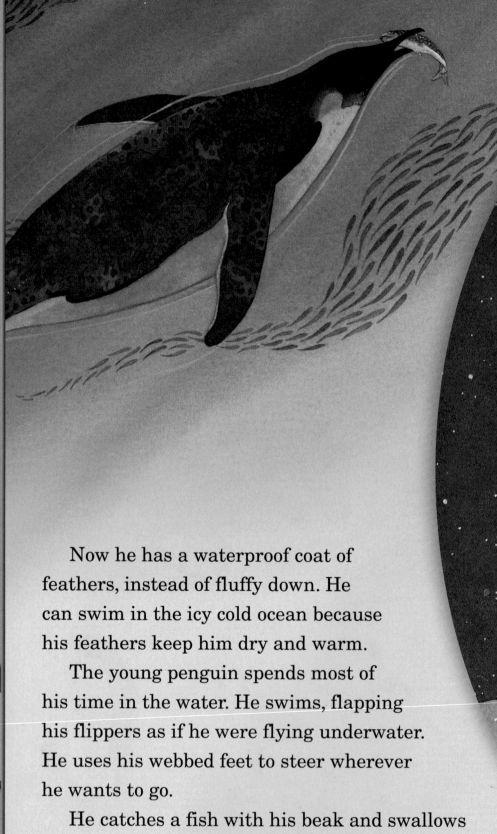

Now he has a waterproof coat of feathers, instead of fluffy down. He can swim in the icy cold ocean because his feathers keep him dry and warm.

The young penguin spends most of his time in the water. He swims, flapping his flippers as if he were flying underwater. He uses his webbed feet to steer wherever he wants to go.

He catches a fish with his beak and swallows it headfirst.

Let's **Think** About...

How do you picture the penguin using his webbed feet to steer? **Visualize**

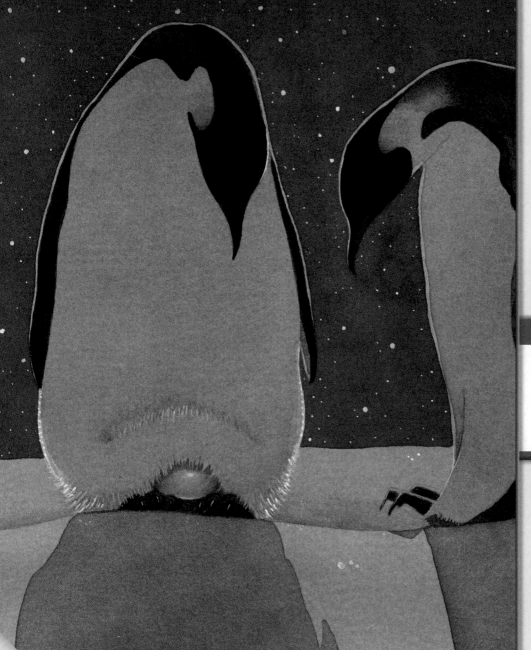

Now the young penguin can catch his own food and take care of himself. In about five years he'll find a mate. Then he'll take care of his own egg until the chick can hatch.

Let's Think About...

What will the penguin do when he has his own egg to take care of? **Summarize**

221

Envision It! Retell

READING STREET ONLINE
STORY SORT
www.ReadingStreet.com

Think Critically

1. Skim the text to identify information from the article. How do penguin chicks survive in Antarctica? **Text to World**

2. The author italicized many words in the story, like *brood patch* on page 211. Skim the text to find them. Why do you think she did that? How do the italicized words help readers? **Think Like an Author**

3. Look back at pages 214–216. What details support the idea that the penguin father and mother take care of the chick? **Main Idea and Details**

4. Did you use any reference sources to help you understand what you were reading? Which ones? If not, what sources could you have used for this selection? **Monitor and Clarify**

5. **Look Back and Write** Look back at the question on page 208. Find information in the text about how penguins protect their chicks against the extreme cold weather. Write a response to the question.

TEST PRACTICE Extended Response

222

Betty Tatham

Betty Tatham says that penguins are her favorite animals. "I write mostly about things I like, and I love animals." When she researched penguins, she read about all seventeen species of penguins. She then chose to write about the emperor penguins because they were the most interesting. "I liked the fact that the dad takes care of the egg and that the mother penguin finds her mate by listening for his voice. I liked the loving relationship both parents have with their chick."

Ms. Tatham has never seen real emperor penguins, but she would love to go to Antarctica to see them. She has been able to see blue penguins in Australia and king penguins in New Zealand. Threatened and endangered animals are a major concern for Ms. Tatham. She supports several organizations that help make sure animals survive.

Here are other books by Betty Tatham.

How Animals Communicate

How Animals Shed Their Skin

Use the Reader's and Writer's Notebook to record your independent reading.

Objectives
● Write poems that appeal to the five senses and use rhyme, meter, and patterns of verse. ● Use and understand how nouns work.

Let's Write It!

Key Features of Poetry

● sometimes written in meter

● usually includes some rhyming lines

● often uses figurative language

READING STREET ONLINE
GRAMMAR JAMMER
www.ReadingStreet.com

Poem

A **poem** is a piece of writing that expresses the writer's imagination. In a poem, the patterns made by the sounds of the words have special importance. There are many forms of poetry, such as cinquain and diamante. The student model on the next page is an example of a cinquain poem.

Writing Prompt Write a poem about penguins.

Writer's Checklist

Remember, you should . . .

✓ use the correct pattern for the form of poetry you are writing.

✓ include sensory details.

✓ give your poem a title.

✓ use common and proper nouns correctly.

Student Model

The Penguin

penguin

black, white

waddling, swimming, leaping

a **tuxedo** in **Antarctica**

emperor

Genre
A cinquain **poem** is made up of five lines and uses rhythm.

Writing Trait Word Choice
Figurative language helps paint a picture.

Common and proper nouns are used correctly.

Conventions

Common and Proper Nouns

Remember A **common noun** names any person, place, or thing. A **proper noun** names a particular person, place, or thing. The word *boy* is a common noun. The name *Jack* is a proper noun.

Objectives
● Identify the cause-and-effect relationships among ideas in the text.
● Use the features of a text to guess what will happen next.

Science in Reading

Genre
Photo Essay

● A photo essay is expository nonfiction usually written to inform the reader about a topic.

● Photo essays use photographs and text to give facts and details. They use text features to help the reader predict, locate, and verify information.

● Photo essays can have cause-and-effect relationships. Look for clue words that signal cause-and-effect relationships.

● Read the title, the blue and red heads, and the bold and italicized words to predict what this selection will be about. Verify your predictions as you read.

Plants
Fitting into Their World

from *Seeds, Stems, and Stamens*
by Susan E. Goodman

photographs by Michael J. Doolittle

226

Getting Sun

Almost all plants need sun to live. They use a process called *photosynthesis* to turn sunlight into food or energy. But sometimes getting enough light can be a problem. Tall plants and trees get it by growing higher than those around them. To do so, they use a lot of energy growing a strong stem or trunk. Other plants have different ways to grab their share of sunshine.

Hitching a Ride

This **morning glory** spends its energy climbing instead. This vine uses its flexible stem to wind around strong objects and get to the light.

This **bromeliad** is a different kind of hitchhiker. It is an air plant. It grows high on a tree and uses its roots to anchor itself to the tree's trunk or upper branches.

Leaf Placement

Many plants arrange their leaves so they can get as much sun as possible. **Mint** leaves grow in crossed pairs. That way, the leaves cast less shadow upon their neighbors.

Let's **Think** About...

What does it mean if a word is italicized? What does it mean if a word is in bold?
Photo Essay

Let's **Think** About...

Can you find and explain the cause-and-effect relationships that the author uses on this page?
Photo Essay

Let's **Think** About...

Why are some heads in red and some in blue?
Photo Essay

Let's **Think** About...

Locate the names of two plants that eat meat. How are the plants alike and different?
Photo Essay

Getting Nutrients

Most plants get their nutrients from the soil. Some plants have evolved a different way to get their "vitamins."

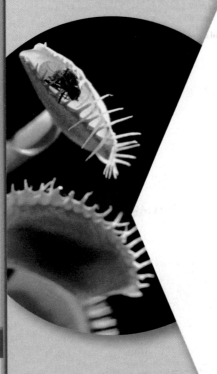

Meat-Eaters

The leaf tips of a **Venus's-flytrap** look very tempting to an insect. They are an easy place to land. They shine with what looks to be food. Mistake! Less than a second after a bug crawls in, the trap springs shut. The bristles on the leaves point outward to keep the insect from escaping as the trap closes. The plant then uses chemicals to digest its meal. In this picture, one leaf tip has just captured a fly, while a bigger leaf tip below is in the middle of digesting another.

The inventor of sticky flypaper might have gotten the idea from a **sundew plant.** A sundew's leaves are covered with hairs. And these hairs are covered with "sundew glue." The insect that lands on a sundew is there for good. It sticks to the hairs, which fold over and trap it.

Staying Safe

Plants can't run away from hungry insects and animals. They have developed other ways to protect themselves.

Physical Defenses

Freeloaders like bromeliads and vines don't directly harm their host tree, but they can do damage. They soak up water and sun that the tree could have used. If too many of them pile onto a tree, they can break off its branches. This **terminalia tree** has a great defense. Every so often, it sheds its bark—and with it, most of its unwanted company.

This **floss-silk tree** has what scientists call bark prickles all over its trunk. No matter what you call them, you wouldn't want to run into these things. And that's the point—a lot of painful ones.

Let's **Think** About...

Where can you find facts and details about how plants defend themselves? **Photo Essay**

Let's **Think** About...

Reading Across Texts Which do you think has a harder time surviving—penguin chicks or the plants in this selection?

Writing Across Texts Create a chart to explain why you think as you do.

Objectives

● Use context clues to figure out words you don't know or words that have more than one meaning.
● Identify words that are opposites, words that are similar, words that have more than one meaning, and words that sound the same even though they mean different things.
● Listen closely when someone speaks, ask questions about the topic he or she is talking about, and comment about the topic.

Let's Learn It!

READING STREET ONLINE
ONLINE STUDENT EDITION
www.ReadingStreet.com

Vocabulary

Synonyms

Context Clues As you are reading, you may come to a word you do not know. Reread the words and sentences nearby. The author may give you a synonym—a word that has the same or almost the same meaning—for the word. If you can identify the synonym, you can use it to help you figure out the meaning of the unknown word.

Practice It! Choose four Words to Know and find them in the story. Use context clues to try to find a synonym for each word, or come up with your own. Write each synonym in a sentence.

Fluency

Accuracy

It is important to read with accuracy so you can understand the text. Read each word as it is written on the page. Make sure what you are reading makes sense, or you may have to slow down or reread.

Practice It! With a partner, practice reading aloud *Penguin Chick*, page 212. Have your partner make a list of each word you read incorrectly. Look back at each word. Reread the page again. Did your accuracy improve?

Listening and Speaking

When you research and present a speech with a group, be sure to make contributions.

Speech

In an informational speech, a speaker tells an audience about people, things, ideas, or events. The purpose is to inform.

Practice It! With a small group, research penguins. Write an informational speech using the facts you gathered. Include your opinions about the facts you found. Give your speech to your class.

Tips

Listening ...

- Face the speaker to listen attentively.
- Take notes on what the speaker says.

Speaking ...

- Have good posture and eye contact.
- Speak at an appropriate pace.
- Determine your purpose for speaking.

Teamwork ...

- Ask and answer questions with detail.
- Build on each other's ideas.

231

Objectives
● Ask questions about the topic and comment about the topic. ● Take part in discussions led by teachers and other students, and offer ideas that build on the ideas of others.

Oral Vocabulary

Let's Talk About

Good Solutions

● Pose and answer questions about how you can tell if a solution is a good solution.

● Work together to make pertinent comments on how you might reach a good solution.

● Express opinions in teams about how good solutions help others.

READING STREET ONLINE
CONCEPT TALK VIDEO
www.ReadingStreet.com

Objectives

• Read aloud words that have final stable syllables.

Envision It! | Sounds to Know

candle

-le

READING STREET ONLINE
SOUND-SPELLING CARDS
www.ReadingStreet.com

Phonics

🎯 Final Syllable *-le*

Words I Can Blend

puzzle

table

kettle

tremble

needle

Sentences I Can Read

1. We put together the puzzle at the table.

2. Caleb took stew from the kettle.

3. I began to tremble when I saw the doctor's needle.

I Can Read!

A fable can be interesting to read. Most fables have a gentle lesson to teach people. A fable may feature an animal, such as an eagle or a turtle. These animals may be fickle and try to trick each other.

A fable may make you chuckle or giggle at the way the animals handle each other. Sometimes the animals battle. In the middle of the battle, a lesson becomes clear. Try reading a fable and you may learn a simple lesson.

You've learned

🔘 Final Syllable -le

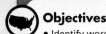

Objectives
• Identify words that paint a picture in your mind and appeal to your senses. • Monitor your comprehension of a text and adjust your reading based on how well you understand what you are reading.

Envision It! | Skill Strategy

Skill

Compare and Contrast

As you read, think about what is alike and what is different.

Alike | Different

EI·5

Strategy

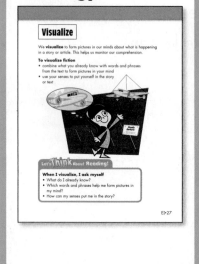

Visualize

We **visualize** to form pictures in our minds about what is happening in a story or article. This helps us monitor our comprehension.

To visualize fiction
• combine what you already know with words and phrases from the text to form pictures in your mind
• use your senses to put yourself in the story or text

Let's Think About Reading!

When I visualize, I ask myself
• What do I already know?
• Which words and phrases help me form pictures in my mind?
• How can my senses put me in the story?

EI·27

Comprehension Skill

🎯 Compare and Contrast

• Compare by telling how two or more things are alike or different.

• Contrast by telling only how two or more things are different.

• Use what you learned about compare and contrast and the graphic organizer below as you read "Snuggles and Tippy." Use the text and the graphic organizer to write a short paragraph that compares and contrasts Snuggles and Tippy.

Snuggles	Tippy

Comprehension Strategy

🎯 Visualize

As you read, picture in your mind the characters, the setting, and the events of the story. Use the details that tell you how something looks, sounds, tastes, feels, or smells to help form images. If you are unable to visualize what you are reading, stop and reread until you can picture it.

Snuggles and Tippy

Rita had a small black cat named Snuggles. The cat had bright green eyes. Her neighbor Joe had a big black dog he called Tippy. Tippy had a white spot on the tip of his tail.

Joe was busy playing catch with his dog when Rita walked out into the backyard. "Where is your cat?" asked Joe. "Does she play outside? Tippy loves to be with people."

"Cats are much more particular," replied Rita. "They will not play with just anyone."

Just then Snuggles walked out of the house. Tippy barked and Snuggles ran. She was so frightened that she climbed right up into the branches of the nearest tree.

"Well," said Joe, "that is another difference between cats and dogs. My dog would never run up a tree."

Snuggles hissed at Tippy from the safety of her branch. Rita was upset. "Well, my cat would never scare your dog!"

"I am not sure about that," laughed Joe, as he rescued the angry cat.

Strategy Here's a good place to stop and visualize the pets in the story. What details help you picture them?

Skill Compare and contrast how Joe and Rita feel about their pets. What details tell you this?

Your Turn!

 Need a Review? See the *Envision It! Handbook* for help with compare and contrast and visualizing.

 **Ready to Try It?** As you read *I Wanna Iguana*, use what you've learned about compare and contrast and visualizing to understand the text.

Envision It! Words to Know

adorable

iguana

trophies

compassionate

exactly

mature

mention

Vocabulary Strategy for

Unfamiliar Words

Context Clues What do you do when you come across an unfamiliar word? Sometimes you can figure out what the word means by looking at the words and sentences around the word. They might have clues to help you figure out the meaning of the word.

1. Read the words and sentences around the word you don't know. Sometimes the author tells you what the word means.

2. If not, use the words and sentences to predict a meaning for the word.

3. Try that meaning in the sentence. Does it make sense?

Read "Choosing a Pet" on page 239. Use context clues to help you understand the meanings of the Words to Know or other unfamiliar words.

Words to Write Reread "Choosing a Pet." Write about a pet you would like to have. Explain what your reasons are for choosing that pet. Use words from the Words to Know list in your paragraph.

Choosing a Pet

Do you want a new pet? Some people want a pet that they think is adorable. They might want a tiny kitten or a puppy. Others may want a pet that is a little different, like an iguana or a tarantula. I've heard that there are those who just like to have a whole tank full of fish. Do you know what you want?

Maybe you want a mature animal that won't have to be trained. Maybe you want to have an animal that you can take to competitions. Would you like to win trophies? Or perhaps you want to be compassionate and rescue a pet from a shelter.

Did I mention that you should learn about your pet? It's important to be sensitive to the needs of this new member of your family. What kind of care will your new pet need? What will you feed your pet? Most animals don't eat spaghetti! Find out what you need to do to keep your pet healthy.

Choosing exactly the right pet is important. Your new pet can bring you years of happiness.

Your Turn!

Need a Review? For more information about using context clues to understand unfamiliar words, see *Words!*

Ready to Try It? Read *I Wanna Iguana* on pp. 240–255.

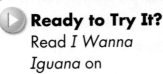

I Wanna

BY KAREN KAUFMAN ORLOFF
ILLUSTRATED BY DAVID CATROW

Genre

Realistic Fiction tells a made-up story that could really happen. Read this story to find out if Alex can persuade his mom to let him have an iguana.

Iguana

Question of the Week
**How do you know if a
solution is a good solution?**

Dear Mom,
I know you don't think I should have Mikey Gulligan's baby iguana when he moves, but here's why I should. If I don't take it, he goes to Stinky and Stinky's dog, Lurch, will eat it.

You don't want that to happen, do you?

Signed,
Your sensitive son,
Alex

243

Dear Mom,
Did you know that iguanas are really quiet and they're cute too. I think they are much cuter than hamsters.
Love,
Your adorable son,
Alex

Dear Alex,
Tarantulas are quiet too, but I wouldn't want one as a pet. By the way, that iguana of Mikey's is uglier than Godzilla. Just thought I'd mention it.
Love,
Mom

Dear Mom,
You would never even have to see the iguana. I'll keep his cage in my room on the dresser next to my soccer trophies. Plus, he's so small, I bet you'll never even know he's there.
Love and a zillion and one kisses,
Alex

Dear Alex,
Iguanas can grow to be over six feet long. You won't have enough space in your whole room, much less on your dresser (with or without your trophies).
Love,
Mom

Dear Alex,
How are you going to get a girl to marry you
when you own a six-foot-long reptile?
    Love,
Your concerned mother

Dear Mom,
Forget the girl.
I need a new friend now!
This iguana can be the brother I've always wanted.
   Love,
Your lonely child, Alex

Dear Alex,
You have a brother.
Love,
Mom

Dear Mom,
I know I have a brother but he's just a baby. What fun is
that? If I had an iguana, I could teach it tricks and things.
Ethan doesn't do tricks. He just burps.
Love,
Grossed-out Alex

Dear Alex,
How do I know
you're ready for a
pet? Remember
what happened when
you took home
the class fish?
Love,
Mom

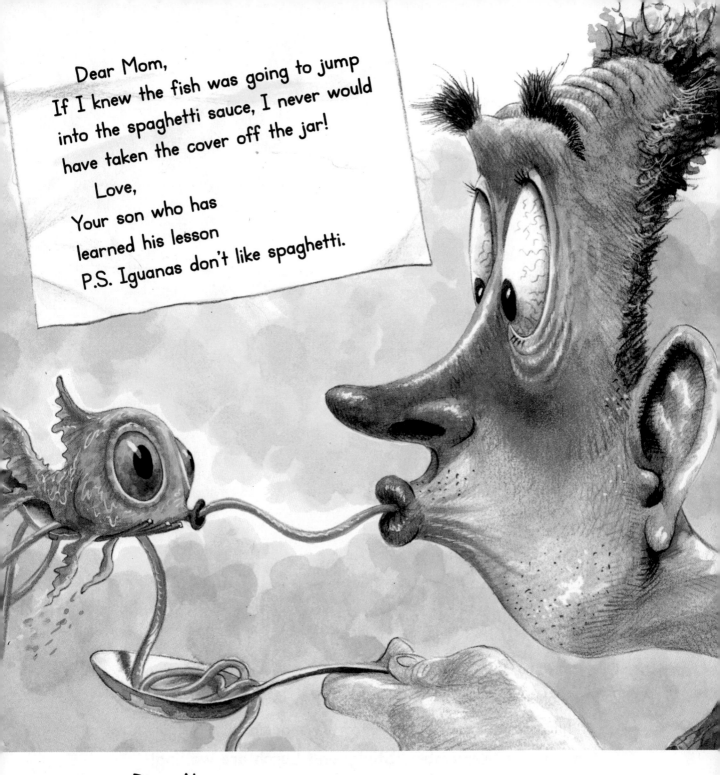

Dear Mom,
If I knew the fish was going to jump into the spaghetti sauce, I never would have taken the cover off the jar!
Love,
Your son who has learned his lesson
P.S. Iguanas don't like spaghetti.

Dear Alex,
Let's say I let you have the iguana on a trial basis.
What exactly would you do to take care of it?
Love,
Mom

Dear Mom,

I would feed him every day (he eats lettuce). And I would make sure he had enough water. And I would clean his cage when it got messy.

Love,
Responsible Alex
P.S. What's a trial basis?

Dear Alex,

A trial basis means Dad and I see how well you take care of him for a week or two before we decide if you can have him forever. Remember, Stinky and Lurch are waiting!

Love,
Mom

P.S. If you clean his cage as well as you clean your room, you're in trouble.

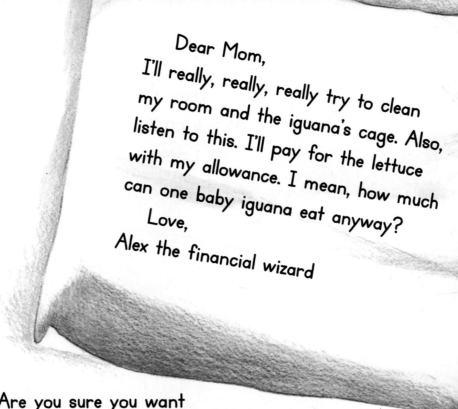

Dear Mom,
I'll really, really, really try to clean my room and the iguana's cage. Also, listen to this. I'll pay for the lettuce with my allowance. I mean, how much can one baby iguana eat anyway?
Love,
Alex the financial wizard

"Are you sure you want to do this, Alex?"

"Yes, Mom!
I wanna iguana. . .
Please!"

Dear Alex,
Look on your dresser.
Love,
Mom

"YESSSS!
Thank you!
Thank you!"

255

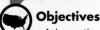

Envision It! | Retell

Think Critically

1. Throughout the story Alex uses a lot of different points to convince his mother that he should keep the iguana. What are some methods you have used to persuade someone to do something? **Text to Self**

2. The author uses persuasive writing between Alex and his mother to tell the story. How does this make the story more interesting to read? **Think Like an Author**

3. What comparisons does Alex make between an iguana and his baby brother, Ethan? **Compare and Contrast**

4. Throughout the story Alex tries to persuade his mother that an iguana would make a good pet. Think about some of the different scenes he imagines. What are some of the words that help you imagine the pet iguana? **Visualize**

5. **Look Back and Write** Look back at page 250. Alex's mother is concerned that he is not ready to have a pet. Do you think this is true? Provide details as evidence to support your answer.

TEST PRACTICE **Extended Response**

Meet the Author and the Illustrator

Karen Kaufman Orloff

Karen Kaufman Orloff is a children's book author and a columnist. She writes about life, kids, and families.

Ms. Orloff got the idea for writing *I Wanna Iguana* when her children wanted a pet dog, but her husband was allergic to dogs. So they discussed getting an iguana instead. She wasn't wild about the idea of a reptile, but her family did end up with two iguanas as family pets!

David Catrow

David Catrow is an illustrator, cartoonist, painter, and author. His cartoons appear in more than 900 newspapers in the United States and Canada, including the *New York Times*, *USA Today*, and the *Washington Post*. Mr. Catrow's work is often cited for its humor and imagination which are similar to the work of Dr. Seuss and Tedd Arnold.

If Mom Had Three Arms

We the Kids: The Preamble to the Constitution of the United States

Here are other books written by Karen Orloff or illustrated by David Catrow.

Reading Log

Use the Reader's and Writer's Notebook to record your independent reading.

Let's Write It!

Key Features of a Fairy Tale

● imaginary story that may include heroic acts

● often begin "Once upon a time…"

● often end "…and they lived happily ever after"

● characters are usually all good or all bad

READING STREET ONLINE
GRAMMAR JAMMER
www.ReadingStreet.com

Fairy Tale

A **fairy tale** is an imaginative story that often includes heroic deeds and exciting adventures. Fairy tales are usually written for children. The student model on the next page is an example of a fairy tale.

Writing Prompt Write a fairy tale with an iguana as a main character.

Writer's Checklist

Remember, you should …

☑ write an imaginative story.

☑ have a clear beginning, middle, and end.

☑ include details about the characters.

☑ build the plot to a climax.

☑ use singular and plural nouns correctly.

Maddie and the Iguana

Once upon a **time** in a faraway **land**, there lived a young **woman** named Maddie. All the **people** in her **village** knew that Maddie loved **nature**. She could often be found in the **woods** collecting **bugs** and **leaves**.

One **day** Maddie came upon a strange **animal**. "I wonder what this is," she said.

"I am an **iguana**," squeaked the animal.

"What is an iguana and why can you talk?" stuttered Maddie in a scared **voice**.

"An iguana is a kind of **lizard**, but I used to be Prince **Clayton**," announced the iguana. "Someone put a **spell** on me. Please cover me with three colorful leaves. Say three nice **words** and the spell will be broken."

Maddie had collected lots of colorful leaves. She put three of them over the iguana. Then she said, "please" and "thank you." The three nice words broke the spell.

The iguana turned into Prince Clayton. He and Maddie became **friends** and lived happily ever after.

Singular and plural nouns are used correctly.

Writing Trait Word Choice Vivid verbs help characters come to life.

Genre A **fairy tale** often ends with the words *happily ever after.*

Conventions

Singular and Plural Nouns

Remember A **singular noun** tells about one person, place, or thing. A **plural noun** tells about more than one person, place, or thing.

Objectives
• Understand how information changes when moving from one type of media to another type. • Compare how different writing styles are used for different kinds of information on the Internet.

21st Century Skills
INTERNET GUY

E-mail Texting is fun but e-mail can be even better. Share documents and work on a common project in school. E-mail skills get you ready for the world of work. Yes, e-mail can be pretty useful!

- The letter *e* in e-mail stands for "electronic." An e-mail is a message sent by computer over the Internet.

- E-mail lets you quickly communicate with people all over the world. Like letters, they can be formal or informal.

- Communication changes when you attach videos or photos.

- Read "The Big Soccer Game." Compare the language in these e-mails with the language you would read in a text message or a Web-based news article.

260

The Big Soccer Game

Francisco and José used to attend school together until José moved. They also played together on the soccer team. José knows Francisco needs some encouragement and support because he has a big soccer game coming up. Even though the two friends do not go to the same school anymore, they can keep in touch using e-mail.

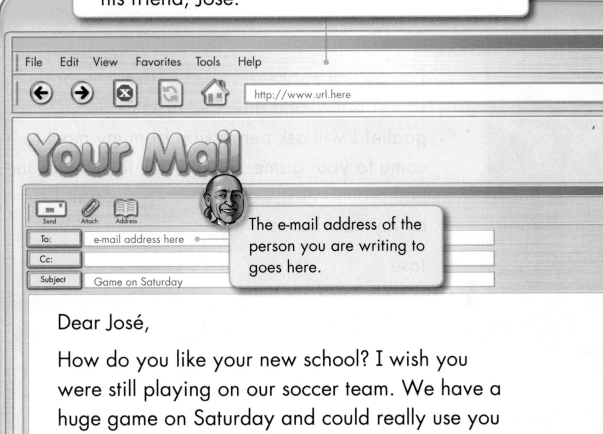

Francisco used his e-mail provider to write to his friend, José.

File   Edit   View   Favorites   Tools   Help

http://www.url.here

Your Mail

Send   Attach   Address

To: | e-mail address here
Cc:
Subject | Game on Saturday

The e-mail address of the person you are writing to goes here.

Dear José,

How do you like your new school? I wish you were still playing on our soccer team. We have a huge game on Saturday and could really use you as our goalie. Maybe you could come and cheer us on. We are playing our rival, the Jets.

Go Tigers!

Francisco

Sometimes, you are writing to a friend so your closing can be casual or less formal.

This message would have been shorter if Francisco had sent it as a text!

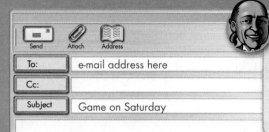

Notice the letter format, the informal language, and the other conventions in this e-mail. Compare this e-mail to the language and conventions used in Web-based news articles.

Send **Attach** **Address**

To: e-mail address here

Cc:

Subject Game on Saturday

Dear Francisco,

I really like my new school. I tried out for the soccer team, and guess what? I'm the new goalie! I will ask permission from my mom to come to your game. Would you like to kick the ball around next week? There's a soccer field by my new house.

José

Write **Reply** **Send** **Forward** **Delete** **Address** **Print**

From: (Sender's e-mail address appears here.)
Sent: Monday, July 22, 2005, 11:15 A.M.
To: (Receiver's e-mail address appears here.)
Subject: Re: Game on Saturday

Dear José,

Thanks for coming to my game on Saturday. The whole team appreciated it. If you had been our goalie, the Jets never would have scored. My mom took some photos of us celebrating after the game. I attached them to this e-mail.

Francisco

You can share photos or files by attaching them to an e-mail.

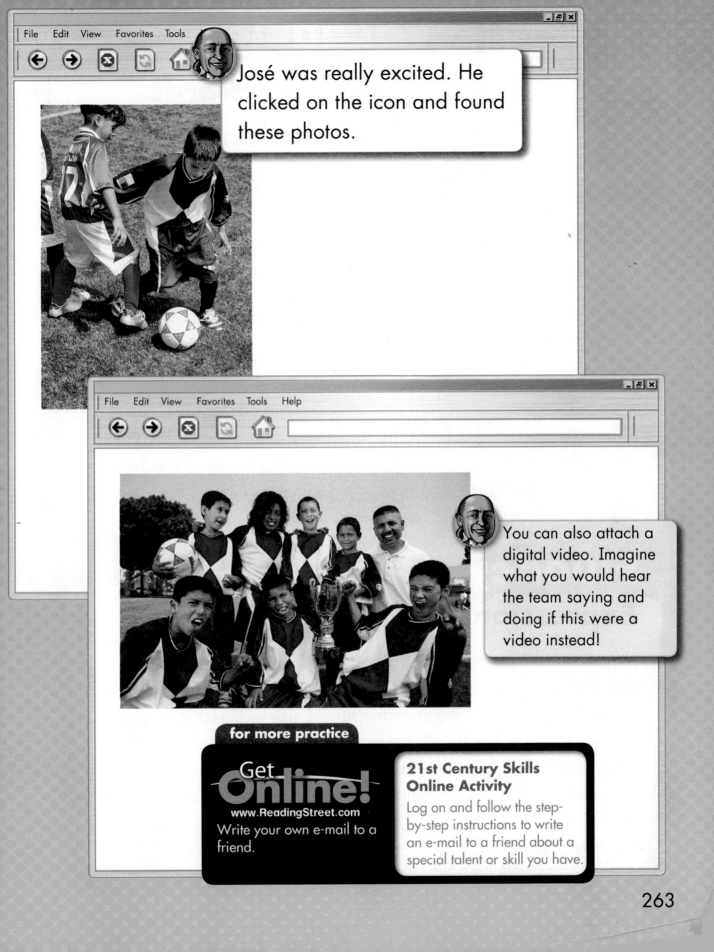

José was really excited. He clicked on the icon and found these photos.

You can also attach a digital video. Imagine what you would hear the team saying and doing if this were a video instead!

for more practice

Get Online!
www.ReadingStreet.com
Write your own e-mail to a friend.

21st Century Skills Online Activity

Log on and follow the step-by-step instructions to write an e-mail to a friend about a special talent or skill you have.

Objectives
● Listen closely when someone speaks, ask questions about the topic he or she is talking about, and comment about the topic. ● Speak clearly and to the point while making eye contact, changing how fast, loud, and clearly you speak to communicate your ideas. ● Read aloud and understand texts at your grade level.

Vocabulary

Unfamiliar Words

Context Clues Remember to use context clues to help you determine the meanings of unfamiliar words. If you come to a word you don't know, reread the words and sentences around it. They can help you find the correct meaning of the unfamiliar word.

Practice It! Choose a book from your classroom library or a book you are reading from your school library. Write down any unfamiliar words that you find. Use context clues to determine the meanings of the words. Check the dictionary to see if you are correct.

Fluency
Expression

When you are reading aloud you can use expression by changing the tone of your voice for each character. Use quotation marks to tell you when you should raise or lower your voice. Expression makes your reading easier to understand and more interesting for the listener.

Practice It! Practice reading aloud page 251. How should you use expression as you read these paragraphs? Does this help you to better understand the characters?

Listening and Speaking

Get Reddy For Middle School

When you give a speech, speak clearly and use expression in your voice.

Persuasive Speech

The purpose of a persuasive speech is to try and persuade an audience to agree with the speaker's opinion or point of view.

Practice It! Write a persuasive speech to talk a friend or relative into reading *I Wanna Iguana*. Give the speech to your class.

Tips

Listening ...

- Listen to identify the speaker's persuasive techniques.

- Ask relevant questions.

Speaking ...

- Use persuasive techniques.

- Have good posture.

- Use singular and plural nouns correctly.

Teamwork ...

- Ask and answer questions with appropriate detail.

265

Objectives
● Take part in discussions led by teachers and other students, ask and answer questions, and offer ideas that build on the ideas of others.

Oral Vocabulary

Let's Talk About

Finding Solutions

● Share ideas about finding solutions for something unexpectedly.

● Express opinions in teams about obstacles and solutions.

● Pose and answer questions about scientific problems and solutions.

READING STREET ONLINE
CONCEPT TALK VIDEO
www.ReadingStreet.com

266

Objectives
- Figure out the meaning of compound words by looking at the meaning of their parts.

Envision It! | **Sounds to Know**

football

compound word

READING STREET ONLINE
SOUND-SPELLING CARDS
www.ReadingStreet.com

Phonics

Compound Words

Words I Can Blend

shoelaces
wastebasket
repairman
downstairs
bookstore

Sentences I Can Read

1. Zack's shoelaces fell into the wastebasket by mistake.

2. The repairman went downstairs to fix the furnace.

3. I love to spend time in a bookstore.

I Can Read!

It's important to pay attention to the weatherman. Check before you leave the house each day. Find out if you will need to change your plans for riding your skateboard or playing basketball or softball.

What happens to your daytime activities if a weekend thunderstorm shows up? Will you need to wear a raincoat and carry an umbrella?

If raindrops do force you to stay inside, it's nice to know that at the end of the thunderstorm you may be treated to a beautiful rainbow.

You've learned

 Compound Words

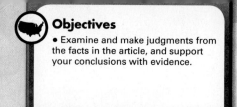

Envision It! | Skill Strategy

Skill

Strategy

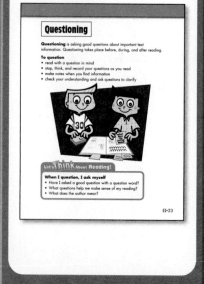

Comprehension Skill

Draw Conclusions

- A conclusion is a decision or opinion that makes sense based on facts and details.

- The details and facts you read and what you already know will help you to draw conclusions about the text.

- Use what you learned about drawing conclusions and the graphic organizer below as you read "Collecting Stamps." Draw conclusions about how you can collect stamps without spending money.

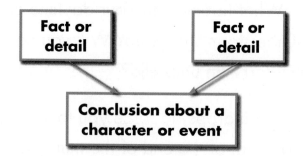

Comprehension Strategy

Questioning

Good readers ask themselves questions as they read. Literal questions such as *"Who is this character?"* help you understand what you are reading. Interpretive questions, such as *"Why is this happening?"* and evaluative questions, such as *"Do I agree with what the author is saying?"* help you connect to and think about the text.

Collecting

Collecting stamps is a fun and interesting hobby. Sometimes children and young people are interested in collecting stamps. But they might not have a lot of money to buy stamps. How can you get stamps without spending money?

There are a few ways you can solve that problem. One way is to ask people to give you stamps that they don't need. Start by telling your friends and your family that you are collecting stamps. Suppose your uncle gets a letter from France. He can save the stamp and give it to you!

Another way to get stamps is to trade them with other people. Once you start collecting, you might get more than one copy of the same stamp. Then you can use the copies to trade with other people for stamps that you don't have.

Asking people to save stamps for you and trading stamps are two good ways to get stamps. Before you know it, you'll have more stamps than you can count!

Strategy This is a good place to stop reading and ask a question, such as *What is the topic of this selection?*

Skill What conclusion can you draw about why you might get more than one copy of a stamp?

Your Turn!

Need a Review? See the *Envision It! Handbook* for help with drawing conclusions and questioning.

Ready to Try It? As you read *Prudy's Problem*, use what you've learned about drawing conclusions and questioning to understand the text.

butterflies

collection

shoelaces

enormous

scattered

strain

Vocabulary Strategy for

🎯 Compound Words

Word Structure If you read a long word you don't know, look closely at it. Is it made up of two small words? If it is, then that long word is a compound word. You may be able to use the two small words to help you figure out the meaning of the compound word. For example, *praiseworthy* describes someone or something that is worthy of praise.

1. Divide the compound word into its two small words.

2. Think of the meaning of each small word and put the two meanings together.

3. Try the new meaning in the context of the sentence to see if it makes sense.

Read "Get Organized" on page 273. Use the meanings of the small words in each compound word to help you figure out the meaning of the compound word.

Words to Write Reread "Get Organized." What do you collect? Write about your collection. Tell why you like to collect. Use words from the Words to Know list in your writing.

Get Organized

Are there enormous piles of stuff in your room? Are your things scattered everywhere? Is your closet clutter putting a strain on the door? Then it's time to take action!

First, realize that this will take time and work. Look at each thing. Ask yourself, "Do I use this? Will I ever use this?" For instance, you might need that extra button or pair of shoelaces sometime, but you'll probably never use that single sock with the big hole. So decide what to get rid of and what to keep. Take the things you are getting rid of. Are they in good shape? Give them to a charity. If not, throw them out.

Next, put the things you are keeping into groups. Put each group together in one place. Put all the books on a shelf or table. Hang the clothes in the closet or put them in drawers. Do you have a collection of objects, such as rocks, postcards, rare butterflies, or stamps? Display them together on a shelf, table, or wall.

Now vacuum and dust your room. Congratulations! You have a shiny, clean, and well-organized room.

Your Turn!

❚❚ Need a Review? For additional help with compound words, see *Words!*

▶ Ready to Try It? Read *Prudy's Problem and How She Solved It* on pp. 274–288.

273

Genre A **fantasy** includes make-believe events. Look for situations that could not happen.

Prudy's Problem

and How She Solved It

by Carey Armstrong-Ellis

Question of the Week
**When is it time
to find a solution?**

Prudy seemed like a normal little girl. She had a sister. She had a dog. She had two white mice. She had a mom and a dad and her own room at home.

Yes, Prudy seemed normal.

But Prudy collected things.

Now most kids collect something. Prudy's friend Egbert collected butterflies. So did Prudy.

Belinda had a stamp collection. So did Prudy.

Harold collected tin foil and made it into a big ball. So did Prudy.

All her friends had collections. And so did Prudy— but Prudy collected *everything*.

She saved rocks, feathers, leaves, twigs, dead bugs, and old flowers. She kept a box full of interesting fungi in the bottom drawer of her dresser. She saved every picture she had ever drawn and every valentine she had ever gotten. She saved pretty paper napkins from parties and kept them in her desk drawer. She had six hundred and fourteen stuffed animals in different unnatural colors.

277

She had collections of ribbons, shoelaces, souvenir postcards, flowered fabric scraps, pencils with fancy ends, pink scarves with orange polka dots, old calendars, salt and pepper shakers with faces, dried-out erasers, plastic lizards, pointy sunglasses, china animals, heart-shaped candy boxes with the paper candy cups still inside, tufts of hair from different breeds of dogs. . . .

She just could not throw anything away.

It drove her dad to distraction. He was a very tidy person who did not like clutter. He started saying unpleasant things as he tried to mow the lawn.

"Prudy, you have a problem," he said.

"What do you mean?" she asked, baffled.

"You just have too much stuff. Why don't we haul it all to the dump?" he suggested hopefully.

"I don't have too much stuff, Dad," Prudy said.

279

It even got to be too much for her mom, who did not mind clutter but could no longer navigate the living room.

"Maybe you could take all this to the thrift shop," she said. "Surely someone could use this old mushroom. . . ."

"I *like* that mushroom," Prudy said.

"Prudy, you have to face your problem," said her mother.

"I do not have a problem," said Prudy.

Prudy's little sister started putting together collections of her own.

"Uh–oh," said Egbert, eyeing Evie's little piles of pine twigs and used toothbrushes. "Prudy, how about if you packed everything all up and stuffed it into a rocket and sent it to Neptune?"

"Yeah, that would solve your problem!" agreed Harold and Belinda.

"There is no problem!" shouted Prudy.

But Prudy herself found that she could barely get to her desk to feed her mice.

She could not even get out of her room without setting off an avalanche of one thing or another.

And then one day while Prudy was walking home from school, something shiny caught her eye. It was a silver gum wrapper.

"I must take this home for my shiny things collection!" she thought.

She ran home and tried to squeeze it into her room.

Something started to happen. The walls started to bulge.

The door started to strain at the hinges.

The pressure was building higher . . . and higher. . . .

The room exploded with an enormous

BANG!

Bits and pieces of stuff flew everywhere.

"Holy smokes," said Prudy. "I guess maybe I do have a little problem."

For six weeks, everyone pitched in to gather Prudy's scattered collections.

"Now what, Prudy?" said her family.

"Now what, Prudy?" said her friends.

"I'm working on it!" said Prudy.

Prudy looked around for inspiration. She visited an art collection. She visited a fish collection. She visited a rock collection. She went to the library to find ideas.

At last, after many hours of scrutinizing stacks of books, she came up with a brilliant plan!

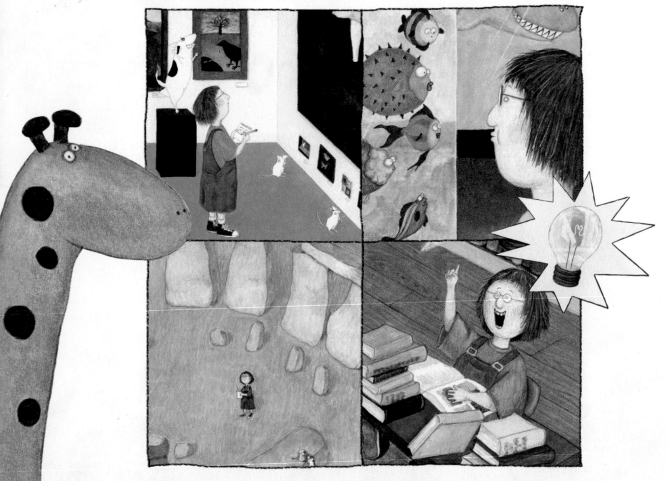

With saws whirring and hammers pounding, everyone set to work.

287

The Prudy Museum of Indescribable Wonderment was an amazing sight to behold.

Everyone wanted to go visit!

Within a year, it was the biggest tourist attraction in Prudy's town.

"Look at that, Egbert," said Belinda. "Did you ever realize how many kinds of gym socks there are?"

"I had no idea cheese rinds could be so fascinating!" said Prudy's mother.

"Can I go to the gift shop?" said Evie.

At last Prudy's collections were neat and orderly and appreciated by everyone. Now she could sit back and enjoy the museum and all her happy visitors. . . .

But she could never *really* stop collecting!

Envision It! Retell

Think Critically

1. Think about Prudy's collection. Do you have a collection? Did you use what you know about collecting things to help you understand Prudy's story? Explain your answer. **Text to Self**

2. This author seems to like lists. Why do you think the author uses lists?

   Think Like an Author

3. Look back at page 280. Prudy's mom told her she was going to have to face her problem. Why does she tell Prudy this? **Draw Conclusions**

4. What is a literal question you can ask and answer about this story? an interpretive question? an evaluative question? **Questioning**

5. **Look Back and Write** What made Prudy realize that she had a problem? Look at pages 284–286 to find out. Write about her creative solution. Use details from the story in your answer.

   TEST PRACTICE Extended Response

Carey Armstrong-Ellis

Carey Armstrong-Ellis collects snow globes and funny salt and pepper shakers. The shakers look like mushrooms, peanut-heads, fat chefs, and vegetables. Her daughters also collect things. They inspired her to write the story for *Prudy's Problem*.

Ms. Armstrong-Ellis painted the pictures for her book much later. She first had to take a special class. The class was on how to make art for children's books. It taught her the skills she needed.

Ms. Armstrong-Ellis also makes art with fabric, using her sewing machine to make animals, vegetables, and people. She sold her first flying pig in 1979. She has not stopped creating since.

Read more books about collecting.

Let's Go Rock Collecting
by Roma Gans

Collecting Baseball Cards
by Thomas S. Owens

Reading Log

Use the Reader's and Writer's Notebook to record your independent reading.

Let's Write It!

Key Features of an Advertisement

● tries to influence the attitudes or actions of people

● information is easy to read

● often includes photos or illustrations

● has a specific audience

READING STREET ONLINE
GRAMMAR JAMMER
www.ReadingStreet.com

Advertisement

An **advertisement** is a written message that tries to influence a specific group of people to do something. The student model on the next page is an example of an advertisement.

Writing Prompt Write an advertisement encouraging people to visit Prudy's museum.

Writer's Checklist

Remember, you should . . .

✓ include all important information visitors might need.

✓ establish a position and use supporting details.

✓ use language that will influence people to visit the museum.

✓ use irregular plural nouns correctly.

Come Visit Prudy's Museum of Indescribable Wonderment

The biggest tourist attraction in the city is now open for business! Come and walk through a unique museum filled with **shelves** of the most unusual collections: socks, **leaves, fish, scarves,** books, and so much more. Prudy's museum includes collections never before seen by the public!

Museum Hours:
Monday–Friday 10:00 AM–4:00 PM
Saturday and Sunday 12:00 PM–5:00 PM

Admission is ONLY 25 cents! **Children** under three get in free.

After you see all of Prudy's wonderful collections, browse the amazing gift shop. Take home a new collection of your own!

Writing Trait Focus The purpose for writing is clear.

Genre An **advertisement** tries to persuade people to do something.

Irregular plural nouns are spelled correctly.

Conventions

Irregular Plural Nouns

Remember Irregular plural nouns are not made plural by adding an -s to the end of the word; they have special forms. Examples include *foot/feet, mouse/mice, ox/oxen,* and *man/men.*

293

Social Studies in Reading

Genre
Interview

- An interview is a record of a conversation between two people.

- Interviews are often written like plays, using text features such as bold words and color to help readers follow the dialogue.

- An interview can provide interesting information about real people and their accomplishments or topics they know about.

- As you read "Meeting the Challenge of Collecting," look for the text features to help you understand the interview.

MEETING THE CHALLENGE OF COLLECTING

BY LISA KLOBUCHAR

The Field Museum of Natural History, in Chicago, is one of the world's biggest museums. Dr. Gary Feinman is the head of the Field Museum's anthropology department. Anthropology is the study of how people live. Anthropologists look at how people fit in with the places they live. They study how different groups of people are alike and different. Dr. Feinman explains how the museum puts together its anthropology collections. He also talks about some of the challenges of putting these collections on display and how the museum meets these challenges.

Dr. Gary Feinman

294

LISA KLOBUCHAR: What kinds of objects does the museum's anthropology department collect?

DR. FEINMAN: We have everything from tapestries to blow guns, from pottery to stone sculpture, from paintings to masks.

LK: That's quite a variety! How many objects does the museum own in all?

DR. F: Our department alone has over one million objects.

LK: Wow! How do you manage to display that many objects?

DR. F: Only a small part of the museum's anthropology collection is on display. We put out about one or two objects out of every one hundred. We don't have the space to display them all.

Incan pottery from Peru

Let's **Think** About...

Why does Dr. Feinman use the word "We"?
Interview

Let's **Think** About...

How does the author obtain information from Dr. Feinman?
Interview

295

Let's **Think** About...

What is the topic of this interview? How is it similar to the ideas in *Prudy's Problem and How She Solved It?*
Interview

LK: With so many interesting and unusual objects, how do you decide which to put on display?

DR. F: Our permanent displays all have certain themes. If an object fits in with that theme, we try to put it on display.

LK: Are there any objects that you would like to display but can't?

DR. F: Yes. Some objects are just too easily damaged. Some can be harmed by getting too hot or too cold. Others may be harmed by bright light or by air that is too moist or too dry. Moths or other insects can ruin cloth items and baskets.

Tapa bark cloth from Papua New Guinea

Woven basket of the Wappo Indians

LK: Sounds like a real problem. How do you protect these objects?

DR. F: We have a full-time staff to care for our collection. They make sure the objects are stored properly. The Field Museum is building an underground collections center. This center will allow the museum to store objects safely. Caring for the collection is like caring for one's health. It is better to avoid problems than to look for a cure after big problems arise.

Mask from Cameroon

Let's **Think** About...

What questions could Prudy have asked Dr. Feinman to help her solve her problem?
Interview

Let's **Think** About...

Reading Across Texts How are Prudy's museum and the Field Museum of Natural History alike? How are they different?

Writing Across Texts Create a Venn diagram to show how the two museums are alike and different.

297

Vocabulary

Compound Words

Word Structure When you are reading you may come across a long word made up of two smaller words. The word is probably a compound word. Remember to use the two smaller words to help you decode the meaning of the compound word.

Practice It! After you read *Prudy's Problem and How She Solved It*, work with a partner to make a list of four or five compound words from the story. Draw a line through each word to divide it into its two smaller words. Then write the meaning for each compound word. Use a dictionary to check your work.

Fluency

Rate

The rate at which you read depends on how well you know a text. You may have to slow down to read a new text. You can improve your rate by reading a selection more than once.

Practice It! With a partner, practice reading aloud page 282. Were there parts that slowed you down? Read it a second time with your partner. Did your rate improve?

Listening and Speaking

When you give a presentation on a problem, make appropriate contributions.

Presentation

When writing a problem-solution presentation, begin by stating the problem and explaining it. List details and examples of how the problem can be solved. Include your recommendations for which solution is best.

Practice It! With a small group, identify a problem you can research. Come up with possible solutions for the problem. Present your problem and possible solutions to the class. As a group, lead a class discussion about the topic.

Tips

Listening ...

• Listen and take notes on what the speaker says.

• Draw conclusions about what the speaker says.

Speaking ...

• Speak clearly about the topic.

Teamwork ...

• Take turns speaking during the discussion.

• Make suggestions that build on the ideas of others.

Objectives
• Speak clearly and to the point while making eye contact, changing how fast, loud, and clearly you speak to communicate your ideas. • Follow, retell, and give instructions to do an action in a particular way.

Let's Talk About

Fair Solutions

● Share ideas in teams about how you can make sure a solution is fair.

● Pose and answer questions about finding fair, equal, and honest solutions to situations.

● Discuss why fairness and respect are important.

READING STREET ONLINE
CONCEPT TALK VIDEO
www.ReadingStreet.com

Envision It! Sounds to Know

splash
3-letter blend

throw
3-letter blend

square
3-letter blend

strawberry
3-letter blend

Phonics

Consonant Blends
squ, spl, thr, str

Words I Can Blend

s q u **a r e**

s p l **i t**

t h r **e e**

s t r **e e t s**

s q u **a d**

Sentences I Can Read

1. A square split in half might be two rectangles or two triangles.

2. Peter lives three streets over from me.

3. Our basketball squad has practice today.

I Can Read!

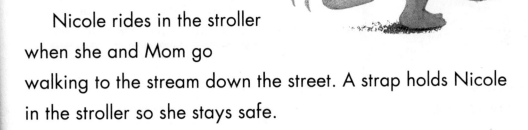

I am thrilled to have such a cute little sister. My sister Nicole is not even three. Mom splurged last year and got her a splendid new pink striped stroller.

Nicole rides in the stroller when she and Mom go walking to the stream down the street. A strap holds Nicole in the stroller so she stays safe.

When Nicole wants to get out of her stroller, she will stretch her arms up and start to squirm. If we don't get her out right away, look out! She might start to squeal.

303

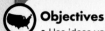
Skill

Strategy

Comprehension Skill

⊚ Author's Purpose

• The author's purpose is the reason an author writes something.

• There are many reasons for writing: to persuade, to inform, to entertain, or to express ideas and feelings.

• Use what you learned about an author's purpose and the graphic organizer below as you read "Salsa Garden."

Before You Read Read the title. For which reasons might the author write a piece with this title?

As You Read Think about the author's purpose.

After You Read Now what do you think the author's purpose was? Why?

Comprehension Strategy

⊚ Predict and Set Purpose

Before you read, set a purpose for why you are reading the text. What outcome, or result, do you want from reading? Then use ideas to predict what will happen and why. What do you think the story will be about? As you read, check your predictions and make new ones.

Salsa Garden

David saw the sign his father put on the garden fence. It said Salsa Garden.

"Salsa?" David read aloud. "Can you grow salsa?"

Dad replied, "Just watch and see what comes up."

Each time David helped by watering and pulling weeds, he looked at the green plants. They all looked different. Not one looked like salsa.

Finally, harvest time came. First, Dad dug in the ground and pulled out round white things that looked a lot like onions. Then, he pulled off pods hanging from a plant. They looked a lot like hot peppers. Next, he cut a green leafy plant that smelled spicy. Finally, Dad pulled round red balls from a fat vine. They sure looked a lot like tomatoes.

"Where's the salsa, Dad?" David asked as he followed his father to the kitchen.

Dad washed and cut everything up. He dumped his harvest into a machine with a sharp blade and turned it on. When he opened the lid, it was full of salsa!

Strategy Make a prediction and set a purpose before you read, using the title and photos. What do you think the story will be about? Confirm your prediction as you read.

Strategy Set a purpose before you read. What outcome do you want from reading this selection?

Skill What is the author's purpose? How do you know?

Your Turn!

Need a Review? See the *Envision It! Handbook* for help with author's purpose and predict and set purpose.

Ready to Try It? As you read *Tops & Bottoms*, use what you've learned about author's purpose and predict and set purpose.

Objectives
• Use context clues to figure out words you don't know or words that have more than one meaning.
• Identify words that are opposites.

Envision It! | Words to Know

bottom

crops

partners

cheated

clever

lazy

wealth

Vocabulary Strategy for

🎯 Antonyms

Context Clues Sometimes you read a word you don't know. The author may give you an antonym for the word. An antonym is a word that means the opposite of a word. For example, *empty* is the opposite of *full*. Look for a word in the words or sentences nearby that might be an antonym to help you understand the word you don't know.

1. Look at the words or sentences around the word you don't know. The author may have used an antonym.

2. Find a word that seems to mean the opposite of the word you don't know.

3. Use that word to help you figure out the word you don't know.

Read "Farming" on page 307. Look for antonyms to help you understand the meanings of the Words to Know and other words you don't know.

Words to Write Reread "Farming." Would you like to be a farmer? Why or why not? Write about your ideas. Use words from the Words to Know list in your writing.

Farming

Farming is not an occupation for lazy people. Farmers are always busy. In the spring they till, or turn up, the soil to prepare it for planting. Then they dig holes, put the seeds in the bottom of each hole, and cover them with soil. In the summer, farmers water and weed the growing crops. In the fall, it is time for harvesting. Then they cut or dig up the crops in the fields. In some countries, farmers use machines to do these things. In many countries, however, farmers still do many jobs by hand.

The weather can make any farmer look clever or foolish. Too much rain and the crops wash away; not enough rain and the crops die. The weather has often cheated farmers and ruined their crops. So farmers must be partners with the weather.

Most farmers do not make a lot of money. So why do they farm? Some farm to get the food they need. Many choose to be farmers because to them wealth is not as important as working with the land.

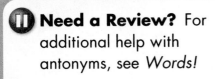

Your Turn!

⏸ **Need a Review?** For additional help with antonyms, see *Words!*

▷ **Ready to Try It?** Read *Tops & Bottoms* on pp. 308–325.

Genre

An **animal fantasy** is a story with animal characters that behave like people. Look for ways that Bear and Hare act like people.

Tops & Bottoms

adapted and illustrated by Janet Stevens

Question of the Week

What can we do to make sure solutions are fair?

Once upon a time there lived a very lazy
bear who had lots of money and lots of land.
His father had been a hard worker and a
smart business bear, and he had given all of
his wealth to his son.

But all Bear wanted to do was sleep.

Not far down the road lived a hare. Although Hare was clever, he sometimes got into trouble. He had once owned land, too, but now he had nothing. He had lost a risky bet with a tortoise and had sold all of his land to Bear to pay off the debt.

Hare and his family were in very bad shape.

"The children are so hungry, Father Hare! We must think of something!" Mrs. Hare cried one day. So Hare and Mrs. Hare put their heads together and cooked up a plan.

The next day Hare hopped down the road to Bear's house. Bear, of course, was asleep.

"Hello, Bear, wake up! It's your neighbor, Hare, and I have an idea!"

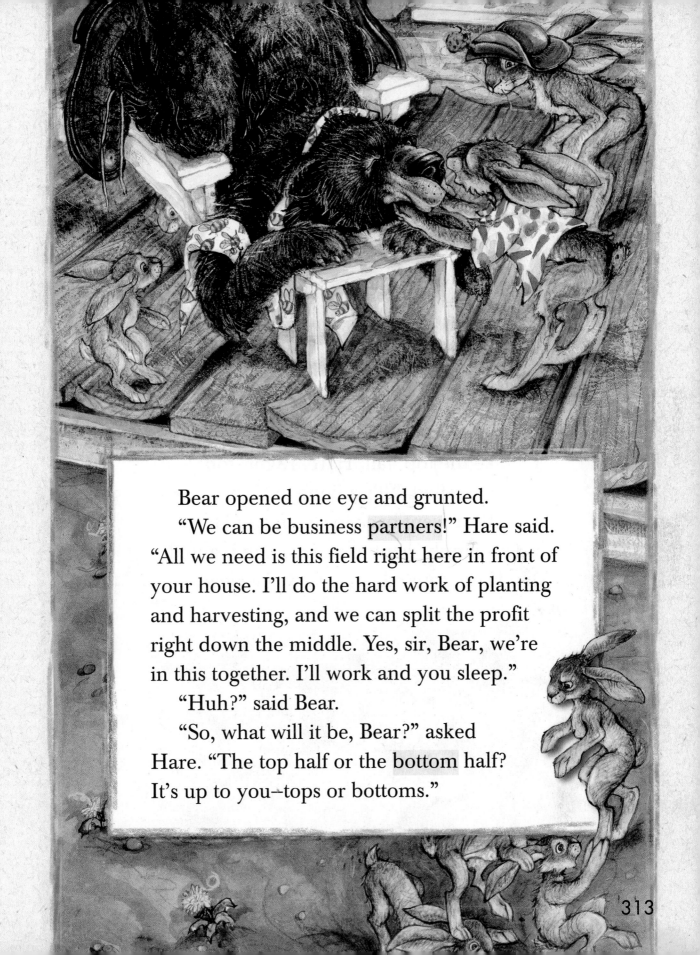

Bear opened one eye and grunted.

"We can be business partners!" Hare said. "All we need is this field right here in front of your house. I'll do the hard work of planting and harvesting, and we can split the profit right down the middle. Yes, sir, Bear, we're in this together. I'll work and you sleep."

"Huh?" said Bear.

"So, what will it be, Bear?" asked Hare. "The top half or the bottom half? It's up to you—tops or bottoms."

"Uh, let's see," Bear said with a yawn.
"I'll take the top half, Hare. Right—tops."
Hare smiled. "It's a done deal, Bear."
So Bear went back to sleep, and Hare
and his family went to work. Hare planted,
Mrs. Hare watered, and everyone weeded.

Bear slept as the crops grew.

When it was time for the harvest, Hare
called out, "Wake up, Bear! You get the tops
and I get the bottoms."

Hare and his family dug up the carrots, the radishes, and the beets. Hare plucked off all the tops, tossed them into a pile for Bear, and put the bottoms aside for himself.

Bear stared at his pile. "But, Hare, all the best parts are in your half!"

"You chose the tops, Bear," Hare said.

"Now, Hare, you've tricked me. You plant this field again—and this season I want the bottoms!"

Hare agreed. "It's a done deal, Bear."

So Bear went back to sleep, and Hare
and his family went to work. They planted,
watered, and weeded.

Bear slept as the crops grew.

When it was time for the harvest, Hare called out, "Wake up, Bear! You get the bottoms and I get the tops."

Hare and his family gathered up the lettuce, the broccoli, and the celery. Hare pulled off the bottoms for Bear and put the tops in his own pile.

Bear looked at his pile and scowled. "Hare, you have cheated me again."

"But, Bear," Hare said, "you wanted the bottoms this time."

Bear growled, "You plant this field again, Hare. You've tricked me twice, and you owe me one season of both tops and bottoms!"

"You're right, poor old Bear," sighed Hare. "It's only fair that you get both tops and bottoms this time. It's a done deal, Bear."

So Bear went back to sleep, and Hare and his family went to work. They planted, watered, and weeded, then watered and weeded some more.

Bear slept as the crops grew.

When it was time for the harvest, Hare called out, "Wake up, Bear! This time you get the tops and the bottoms!"

There in front of Bear's house lay a high field of corn. Hare and his family yanked up every cornstalk. Hare tugged off the roots at the bottom and the tassels at the top and put them in a pile for Bear. Then he carefully collected the ears of corn in the middle and placed them in his own pile.

Bear rubbed his eyes and watched.

"See, Bear? You get the tops and the bottoms. I get the middles. Yes, sir, Bear. It's a done deal!"

By now Bear was wide awake. "That's it, Hare!" he hollered. "From now on I'll plant my own crops and take the tops, bottoms, and middles!"

Hare and his family scooped up the corn and hopped down the road toward home.

Bear never again slept through a season of planting and harvesting. Hare bought back his land with the profit from the crops, and he and Mrs. Hare opened a vegetable stand.

And although Hare and Bear learned
to live happily as neighbors, they never
became business partners again!

Objectives
- Use ideas you get from different parts of a text to make predictions.
- Set a purpose for reading a text based on what you hope to get from the text.

Envision It! Retell

READING STREET ONLINE
STORY SORT
www.ReadingStreet.com

Think Critically

1. Look back through the story. Do you think Hare was fair to Bear? What can you learn from the way Hare acted? What can you learn from the way Bear did business? **Text to Self**

2. Janet Stevens must have had fun making the pictures. Pretend you can step into the picture on page 316. Look around. Tell everything you see, smell, and hear. **Think Like an Author**

3. Why do you think the author chose to use Hare as the main character in this story? **Author's Purpose**

4. What was your purpose in reading this story? Did you want to find out how Bear and Hare would treat each other? Did you predict that Bear would get nothing after the first harvest? **Predict and Set Purpose**

5. **Look Back and Write** Look back at page 320. Why does Bear think he has been cheated again? Provide evidence to support your answer.

TEST PRACTICE Extended Response

Meet the Author and Illustrator

Janet Stevens

Read more books by
Janet Stevens.

The Tortoise and
the Hare

When Janet Stevens began writing *Tops & Bottoms,* the words just would not come to her, so she started by drawing the pictures. "Drawing pictures first of Bear and Hare helped me get to know them. As I dressed them up and knew their personalities, they started to talk. Then I could write the story."

Ms. Stevens likes us to learn about the characters through her drawings. "When I draw characters, I like to exaggerate their personalities." You can see this in the very sleepy bear and the very energetic hare in *Tops & Bottoms.*

Coyote Steals
the Blanket

Reading Log

Use the Reader's and Writer's Notebook
to record your independent reading.

327

Objectives
● Write essays for a certain audience and reason. ● Use and understand how nouns work. ● Recognize and correctly use apostrophes in contractions and possessives.

Let's Write It!

Key Features of a Friendly Letter

● includes a date, salutation, and closing

● written in a friendly tone

● usually written to someone you know

READING STREET ONLINE
GRAMMAR JAMMER
www.ReadingStreet.com

Expository

Friendly Letter

A **friendly letter** is a letter that you write to a family member or friend. The student model on the next page is an example of a friendly letter.

Writing Prompt Write a letter from one of the characters in *Tops & Bottoms* to another.

Writer's Checklist

Remember, you should . . .

☑ put the date on the letter.

☑ include a salutation, and add a closing before you sign your name.

☑ keep a friendly tone.

☑ focus on your audience and purpose.

☑ use singular possessive nouns correctly.

October 4, 20__

Dear Bear,

   I know that I tricked you three times. I am sorry I kept all your crops. But, Bear, if it weren't for you, my family would have starved.

   Thanks to you, Mrs. Hare and I have had another wonderful season. Everyone thought our **farmstand's** vegetables were delicious. We made so much money that we were able to afford braces for all our little Hares.

   How are you doing? Do you get lonely at that big farm all by yourself? I heard your **tractor's** wheels fell off. Would you like me to run by and help you fix it?

   We would like you to come and visit us here at our new house. I know it is almost winter and a **bear's** sleep is very important. I hope you will join us for dinner before you start your winter nap. **Mrs. Hare's** carrot pies are the best you will ever eat!

                              Your friend,
                              Hare

Writing Trait Conventions of a letter include a date and salutation.

Genre A **friendly letter** has a pleasant tone.

Singular possessive nouns are used correctly.

Conventions

Singular Possessive Nouns

Remember A **singular possessive noun** shows that one person, place, or thing owns something. Add an apostrophe (') and the letter *s* to a singular noun to make it possessive.

Social Studies in Reading

Genre
Fable

● Animals are often the main characters in a fable.

● The theme or moral is the lesson of the fable and is supported by details in the story.

● The moral is often stated at the end of the fable, to stress its importance.

● Read the fable "The Hare and the Tortoise." Think about the theme or moral of the fable. What details in the fable support the theme?

The Hare and the Tortoise

by Aesop
illustrated by Michael Hague

One day a quick-footed Hare was making fun of a slow-moving Tortoise. Much to the Hare's surprise, the Tortoise began to laugh. "I challenge you to a race," said the Tortoise, "and I bet that I will win."

"Very well," said the Hare, "I will dance rings around you all the way."

It was soon agreed that the Fox would set the course and be the judge. The race began and the Hare ran so quickly that he soon left the Tortoise far behind. Once he reached the middle of the course, the Hare decided to take a nap.

While the Hare slept, the Tortoise plodded on and on, straight toward the finish line. When the Hare awoke from his nap, he was surprised that the Tortoise was nowhere in sight. Racing to the finish line as fast as he could, the Hare was shocked to find the Tortoise waiting for him with a smile on his face.

Slow and steady wins the race.

Let's **Think** About...

What is the moral the author wants you to learn from this story? **Fable**

Let's **Think** About...

Using details from "The Hare and the Tortoise," summarize the theme in your own words. How can you apply this lesson to your own life? **Fable**

Let's **Think** About...

Reading Across Texts Who were the winners and the losers in this fable and in *Tops & Bottoms*? Why did the winners win and the losers lose in each story?

Writing Across Texts Write a short paragraph that compares and contrasts the winners and losers from both stories.

331

Let's Learn It!

READING STREET ONLINE
ONLINE STUDENT EDITION
www.ReadingStreet.com

Vocabulary

Antonyms

Context Clues Antonyms are words
that have opposite meanings. When you
find an unfamiliar word in your reading,
look for words that might mean the
opposite. If you can find an antonym, it
will help you figure out the meaning of
the unfamiliar word.

Practice It! Select a book from your
classroom library. Work with a partner
to identify four antonyms from the book.
Write sentences using the antonyms as
context clues.

Fluency

Appropriate Phrasing

When you are reading,
group together words into
meaningful phrases so your
story will be more interesting
and understandable.

Practice It! Practice reading
aloud *Tops & Bottoms*, page
320. How should
you use phrasing
to make this page
sound interesting?

Media Literacy

Interview

In an interview, one person asks another person questions. The purpose is to find out what the person knows or has done.

Practice It! Give a radio interview with Bear from *Tops & Bottoms* for the class. With a partner, write questions and answers about Bear's experience with Hare. Choose one person to be the interviewer, and one to be Bear. Then discuss how your interview would be different if it were on TV instead of radio.

Tips

Listening ...

- Listen attentively to the speaker.

Speaking ...

- Express an opinion supported by accurate information.
- Speak with expression.

Teamwork ...

- Ask and answer questions with specific details.
- Understand that communication over radio uses only words and sounds.

Oral Vocabulary

Let's Talk About

Plant and Animal Adaptations

● Make and listen to comments about how plants and animals adapt.

● Ask relevant questions about animal habitats.

● Share what we can learn from plants and animals.

READING STREET ONLINE
CONCEPT TALK VIDEO
www.ReadingStreet.com

Envision It! | **Sounds to Know**

swing

ng

phone

ph

feather

th

chair

ch

shark

sh

Phonics

Consonant Digraphs
sh, th, ph, ch, ng

Words I Can Blend

th o s e

s h allow

g r a p h

c h apter

b r i n g

Sentences I Can Read

1. Remind those boys to stay in the shallow water.
2. The graph you need is in chapter five.
3. Can you bring the juice?

I Can Read!

Stephanie's favorite dish to make is a fish sandwich. She makes this choice whenever she is given the chance. Stephanie's mom furnishes her with those things she will need.

A young friend phoned. Stephanie shared this secret to a dish that will make her mouth water. A thick chunk of sharp cheddar cheese and a dash of relish finishes this dish.

Shortly, more friends will ring Stephanie for this charming dish.

You've learned

⊙ Consonant Digraphs
sh, th, ph, ch, ng

Envision It! | Skill Strategy

Skill

Strategy

Comprehension Skill

Main Idea and Details

- The topic is what a piece of writing is all about. The main idea is the most important idea about the topic.

- Details and facts are small pieces of information. They tell more about the main idea.

- Use what you learned about main idea and details and the graphic organizer below as you read "Do All Birds Fly?" Then write a short paragraph explaining whether all birds fly.

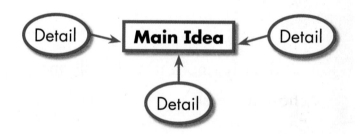

Comprehension Strategy

Text Structure

Good readers look for how a text is structured, or organized, to help them understand the information. A compare-and-contrast structure explains how things are alike and different. Other structures authors use include description, cause-and-effect, and question-and-answer formats.

338

Do All Birds Fly?

Birds are Alike

There are many different kinds of birds in the world. But all birds are alike in some ways. All birds lay eggs. All birds have feathers. And all birds have wings.

Penguins and Ostriches

Just because all birds have wings does not mean that all birds can fly. Penguins are birds but they do not fly. They use their wings to swim. Penguins are not the only birds that do not fly. Some large birds, like the ostrich, do not fly. They move about only by walking.

The Frigate

Some birds fly but hardly ever walk. The frigate is a bird that does not walk very well. It also does not swim. It gets from place to place only by flying.

Ducks

Most birds, however, combine flying with some kind of walking or swimming. Ducks can do three things. They can fly, walk, and swim. Perhaps that is why we sometimes say, "What a lucky duck!"

Strategy How do the headings better help you understand how the text is structured?

Skill What facts and details does this paragraph include about the frigate?

Your Turn!

Need a Review? See the *Envision It! Handbook* for help with main idea and details and text structure.

Ready to Try It? As you read *Amazing Bird Nests*, use what you've learned about main ideas and details and text structure to understand the text.

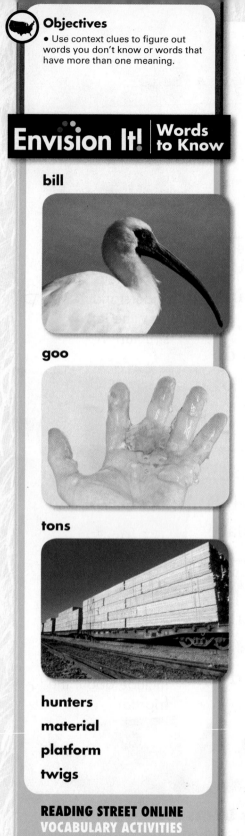

Objectives
● Use context clues to figure out words you don't know or words that have more than one meaning.

Envision It! | **Words to Know**

bill

goo

tons

hunters
material
platform
twigs

READING STREET ONLINE
VOCABULARY ACTIVITIES
www.ReadingStreet.com

Vocabulary Strategy for

◎ Unfamiliar Words

Context Clues If you come to an unfamiliar word, look at the words around it. Context clues, or the nearby words and sentences, can help you find the meaning of an unfamiliar word. Writers often give an example, a definition, or an explanation of a word you may not know.

1. Read the words and sentences around the word you don't know. Sometimes the author tells you what the word means in the context around a word.

2. If not, use the words and sentences to predict a meaning for the word.

3. Try that meaning in the sentence to see if it makes sense.

Read "Home Tweet Home" on page 341. Use context clues to find the meanings of unfamiliar words.

Words to Write Reread "Home Tweet Home." Make a list of the Words to Know and any unfamiliar words in alphabetical order. Beside each word, write the context clue that helped you understand its meaning.

Home Tweet Home

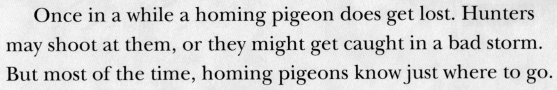

A homing pigeon is a kind of bird. It may look like other kinds of birds—with wings, a bill or beak, and feathers—but it can do something very special. A homing pigeon can find its way home from a drop-off point very far away.

Once in a while a homing pigeon does get lost. Hunters may shoot at them, or they might get caught in a bad storm. But most of the time, homing pigeons know just where to go.

Many people like to train homing pigeons. They keep their birds in their yard or on top of a roof. They may build a home with a platform where the birds can take off and land. Inside the home, the birds sleep on grass, twigs, and other kinds of material. The people must keep the pigeon's home clean, free of dirt and other kinds of goo.

Did you know that pigeons can be used to send messages? In France, there is a statue in honor of the pigeons used during World War I. It is a large statue that weighs several tons. It shows that pigeons carried messages that helped save the lives of many people.

Your Turn!

❚❚ Need a Review? For additional help with unfamiliar words, see *Words!*

▶ Ready to Try It? Read *Amazing Bird Nests* on pp. 342–353

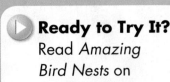

Amazing Bird Nests

by Ron Fridell

343

Robin feeding a worm to chicks.

A Safe Spot

Look up at the sky. A bird swoops low and lands on a tree branch.

It is spring, the season when birds build nests and lay eggs. The bird hops into its nest and sits gently on the eggs. The nest is their safe spot. It shelters the eggs from wind and rain. It also protects them from snakes, raccoons, and other hungry predators.

After the eggs hatch, the chicks no longer have the shell to protect them. Now the nest helps keep them warm and safe from harm. The parents feed the chicks until they grow bigger and stronger. Then everyone flies away, leaving an empty nest.

Gray Rat Snake raiding a bird's nest.

A Bald Eagle nest built in a tree.

A Hummingbird nest built on a pinecone.

Very Small and Very Big

Some birds build very small nests. Hummingbird nests are smallest of all. Some are just an inch across and an inch deep. Talk about small spaces! When the tiny female hummingbird sits on the eggs, her head sticks out one end of the nest and her tail out the other.

Some birds build very big nests. The nest of the American Bald Eagle can be ten feet across and twenty feet deep. It can weigh as much as two tons. That's more than most cars weigh! Eagles build their huge nests way high up at the tops of trees and mountains. That makes sense. Eagles are birds of prey. They are hunters. They spend their time high in the air, looking down for their next tasty meal.

All Kinds of Shapes

Birds should be proud of their nests. Each kind of bird builds its own special type of nest. Hummingbirds build little nests shaped like cups. Eagles build big, flat, platform nests. Woodpeckers build cavity nests by pecking holes in trees.

Which bird should win the prize for best nest-builder? How about the weaver bird? It uses its sharp bill like a needle to sew strips of fresh grass together. Then it weaves them into a nest. Weaver birds use a dozen kinds of knots to build their amazing home. It takes them about 500 trips to cut down and carry back all the grass to do the job.

A Sociable Weaver nest colony in a Quiver tree.

Ruppell's Weaver building a nest.

A Gila Woodpecker at its nest in a Saguaro cactus.

Kittiwakes nesting on the side of a bridge.

All Kinds of Places

Birds live in forests, deserts, grasslands, and wetlands. They live in the country and the city.

As cities take the place of forests and fields, birds must adapt to changing environments. City birds must build their nests in new and unusual places. Some use telephone poles, street lights, and mailboxes. Others build their nests in unused chimneys, flowerpots, and empty cans. Sometimes these city nests get in our way.

Watch Them Grow

Let's say a bird starts building a nest on the ledge outside your window. You could chase it away. Or, better, you could welcome the bird and watch it do its amazing work. Most birds take a week or two to build a nest.

Most bird eggs hatch in about three weeks. Baby birds usually spend another couple of weeks living in the nest. Watch them and you will see how the parents feed and care for their chicks. Keep watching as your bird family grows up and, finally, flies away.

One-day-old chicks.

All Kinds of Stuff

It's amazing how much strange stuff birds use to build their nests. Some birds use old snakeskin in their nests. Some birds use sticky spider silk to hold things together. To make the inside of the nest soft and warm, some birds use animal hair. Others line their nests with more than a thousand feathers!

Great Grey Bowerbird decorating its bower, or nest.

Raven chicks in nest built from barbed wire, plastic, garbage, and bones.

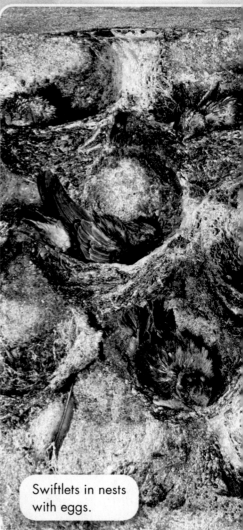

Swiftlets in nests with eggs.

Even More Stuff

City birds have lots of different materials to choose from. In some city nests you will find bits of paper and plastic wrap. In others you'll see paper clips, thumbtacks, hairpins, rubber bands, and barbed wire. One person even found money tucked away in a bird's nest—a five-dollar bill!

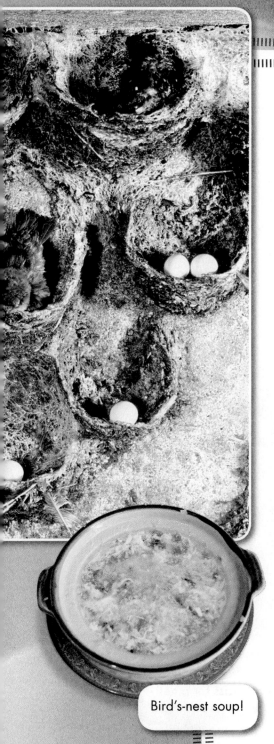

Bird's-nest soup!

The Strangest Nest

The strangest nest of all may be the white-nest swiftlet's. A swiftlet is a small bird that lives in Asian nations such as India and Thailand. What makes this bird's nest so strange?

A swiftlet nest is made of a goo that comes from the bird's mouth. That's right, the swiftlet spits out its nest! The goo comes out looking like long, wet noodles. The bird takes about a month to weave this sticky stuff into a cup-shaped nest. Soon, the goo dries out and becomes strong and sturdy.

Some people make soup from these nests. They really do! Workers use rope ladders to collect nests from cliffs and cave roofs. Then cooks make them into soup and serve it in restaurants.

Why would people eat bird's-nest soup? They believe that swiftlet goo will make them look and feel younger and healthier.

Amazing Birds

How do birds learn how to build these strange and amazing nests? Who teaches them?

No one. When a bird builds a nest for the first time, it has never seen one made before. The bird does not have to think about what it is doing. It just "knows" what to do. Just like you and I know how to breathe.

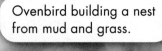

Ovenbird building a nest from mud and grass.

Atlantic Puffin collecting sticks and grass for a nest.

Northern Gannet using seaweed and algae to build nest.

But that doesn't mean that building a nest is an easy job. Far from it. Think about the 500 trips a weaver bird must make to bring back the grass to build its nest. Or the dozen different kinds of knots it uses to weave it.

And remember that birds must do nearly the whole job with their beaks, along with a little help from their feet. That would be like you using only a finger and thumb on one hand.

Try building a nest sometime from a pile of thin twigs, roots, and grass. Birds are amazing animals, and they build amazing homes!

Envision It! | Retell

READING STREET ONLINE
STORY SORT
www.ReadingStreet.com

Think Critically

1. What kinds of bird nests do you see in your neighborhood? Where are they? What are they made from?

Text to World

2. Throughout the selection the author used photos and captions. Why do you think he did that? How did the author draw your attention to each new topic? Did these text features help you to predict what the text was going to be about?

Think Like an Author

3. Look back at page 350. What is the main idea of this page? What details support the main idea?

Main Idea and Details

4. Look back at the selection. What stuff might a bird living in the country make a nest out of? How would the nest of a city bird be different? How did the structure of the selection help you find the answer? *Text Structure*

5. Look Back and Write Look back at the amazing bird nests. Choose one that you find interesting. Write a paragraph telling what makes that nest amazing. Be sure to include facts and details from the article to support your answer.

TEST PRACTICE | Extended Response

Meet the Author

Ron Fridell

Ron Fridell lives in Tucson, Arizona, where there are lots of birds. "While I was writing *Amazing Bird Nests,* it was spring—nest-building time. And right outside the kitchen window on a plant hanger, a hummingbird was building her nest." Mr. Fridell has also written about spiders, turtles, frogs, silkworms, scorpions, and snakes.

Use the Reader's and Writer's Notebook to record your independent reading.

Objectives
● Use and understand how nouns work. ● Use words that show a change in time or tell a reader he or she is near the end of a text.

Expository

Directions

Directions are a set of instructions that explain what to do, how to do something, or where to go. The student model on the next page is an example of directions.

Writing Prompt Write directions for something you know how to do well.

Let's Write It!

Key Features of Directions

● clearly explain how to do something

● use time-order words

● sometimes written as a numbered list

READING STREET ONLINE
GRAMMAR JAMMER
www.ReadingStreet.com

Writer's Checklist

Remember, you should . . .

☑ list steps in order.

☑ use sequence words such as *first*, *next*, and *then* as you list steps.

☑ reread your directions to make sure they are complete.

☑ use plural nouns correctly.

☑ use time-order and concluding transitions correctly.

How to Make the Best Kids' PB and J

First, make sure that you have peanut butter, jelly, two slices of bread, honey-roasted peanuts, a plate, a table knife (the kind with a rounded point), and a napkin.

Next, open the jars of peanut butter and jelly. Using the table knife, take peanut butter out of its jar and spread it on one side of one of the slices of bread. Then spread jelly onto one side of the other slice of bread. After that, open the package of honey-roasted peanuts and sprinkle them on the peanut butter-covered bread.

Then put the jelly-covered bread on the peanut butter-covered bread—jelly side down!

Last, sit down, grab your napkin, and take a bite of a sandwich that tastes like a professional sandwich makers' PB and J!

Writing Trait Organization
Separate paragraphs help make directions easier to follow.

Genre Directions explain how to do something.

Plural possessive nouns are used correctly.

Conventions

Plural Possessive Nouns

Remember A **plural possessive noun** shows that two or more people share or own something. Add an apostrophe (') to plural nouns that end in -s to make them possessive.

Science in Reading

Genre
Fairy Tale

● Fairy tales are folk tales that often have unbelievable characters and events.

● Many fairy tales begin with "Once upon a time in a land far away..." to show that the setting takes place long ago and far away.

● Many fairy tales end with "They lived happily ever after" to indicate a happy ending to the plot.

● As you read, locate the characteristics that make this story a fairy tale. Who are the characters? What is the setting? What events create the plot?

EXTRA! EXTRA!

Fairy-Tale News from Hidden Forest

by Alma Flor Ada
illustrated by Leslie Tryon

HIDDEN FOREST NEWS

VOLUME 203 NO.1   MARCH 3

Amazing Chick Sets Out to Visit Capital

MÉXICO—The unique Half-Chicken, born on a farm on the outskirts of Guadalajara with just one leg, one wing, and one eye, has set out to visit the capital city of México.

When asked by our reporter why he wanted to undertake such a long trip, he answered, "I have been told I'm unique. Everyone says the capital city is unique. I want to see what makes us alike."

Half-Chicken Stops Along the Way to Show His Kindness

MÉXICO—The reporter covering Half-Chicken's trip to the capital city of México reports that Half-Chicken is not only a unique-looking creature, but also a kind one. Although he is very intent on completing his trip and won't stop for sightseeing or recreation, he has made several stops along the way to come to the aid of Wind, Fire, and Water. They will surely not forget him.

WIND   FIRE   WATER

Cooperative Farming

Join us in establishing a Farming Co-op and a Farmers' Market. Working together, we will achieve greater results.

POTLUCK

Next Thursday at 6:00 P.M.

at Ms. Red Hen's house

Avenue of the Elms, Happy Valley

Child care with entertainment provided courtesy of Goldilocks and Little Red Riding Hood

Let's **Think** About...

How is Half-Chicken an amazing character? How is he like other fairy-tale characters? How is he different? Use details from the story to support your answer.
Fairy Tale

Let's **Think** About...

Where does the story take place? How is it like other fairy tales? How is it different?
Fairy Tale

HALF-CHICKEN EXPERIENCING TERRIBLE ORDEAL

MÉXICO—The reporter who has been shadowing Half-Chicken since the beginning of his trip witnessed the unique chicken disappearing through the back door of the viceroy's palace. Through the kitchen window our reporter saw Half-Chicken in the hands of the vice-royal cook, who seemed determined to throw him in a pot of boiling water. The reporter tried to enter the viceroy's palace, but he was refused admittance by the vice-royal guards.

This would be a terrible ending for such a brave, kind chicken.

Let's **Think** About...

Will this story have a happy ending? How do you know? What do you think will happen?
Fairy Tale

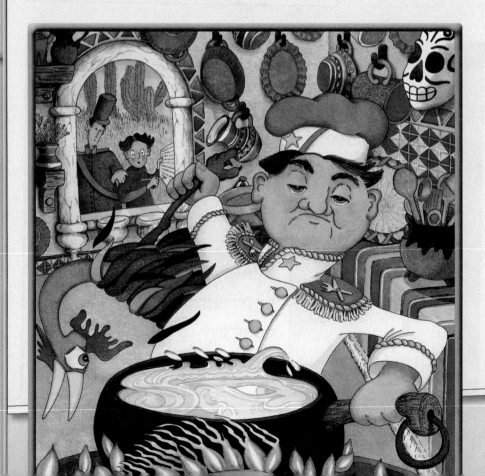

360

Listening and Speaking

When presenting a description, use words that help listeners picture what you are describing.

Description

When presenting a description, use words that help your listeners picture how something looks, tastes, sounds, feels, or smells.

Practice It! Work with a small group to give an oral presentation describing different types of bird nests. Use the information from *Amazing Bird Nests* and other research to prepare your speech. Present your speech to your class.

Tips

Listening ...

- Summarize what the speaker says.
- Listen to identify the speaker's effectiveness.

Speaking ...

- Speak at an appropriate pace.
- Determine your purpose for speaking.
- Use transition words.

Teamwork ...

- Provide suggestions that build on the ideas of others.

Poetry

- **Humorous poems** sometimes describe silly things that aren't real as if they were real.

- **Onomatopoeia** are words that sound the same as what the words mean, such as "beep" or "clang." These words can make a poem more playful.

- **Free verse** poems don't have **rhyme** or **rhythm** patterns, and they may arrange words in unusual ways or use **repetition**. Free verse poems can also be **humorous.**

- **Imagery** helps you to see, hear, feel, taste, and smell in your mind, or imagination, what is being described in the poem.

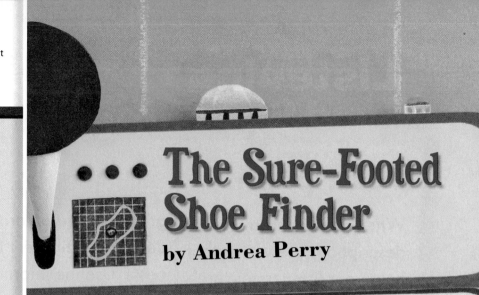

The Sure-Footed Shoe Finder

by Andrea Perry

How many times has this happened to you?
You're late for the school bus and can't find a shoe.
It might take you hours unless you have got
the Sure-Footed Shoe Finder there on the spot!

Just lift up the lever and open the gate,
then toss in the shoe that is missing its mate.
With a beep and a clang and a stagger and lurch,
the Shoe Finder's off on its shoe-finding search.

The powerful Foot-Odor-Sensitive Vent
tracks down your sneaker by matching its scent,
and mere seconds later the shoe is retrieved.
You won't miss the school bus! Now aren't
you relieved?

Most of our customers happen to choose
our standard shoe model for footwear they lose,
although the new jumbo Shoe Finder can trace
even those snow boots you children misplace!

Ants

by Marilyn Singer

One and one and one and one
    Dead leaves
    Dead crickets
One ant alone can't pick it
    up
    can't drag this meal to our busy nest
But one and one and one and one
    Together we tow
    Together we know
any time of day this is so:
One and one and one and one
    is the best way
    to get things done

Let's **Think** About...

How can you tell that "Ants" is a **free verse** poem? Describe the **rhyme**, **imagery**, and **repetition** used in the poem.

Let's **Think** About...

Which of the poems is a **humorous poem?** How do you know? Tell how the poem uses **imagery** and **onomatopoeia** as well as humor.

Third-Grade GENIUS

by Gary Soto

Me, I took two wires, a battery, and a bulb
And fit them nicely together in my hand.

Show and tell.

I said, "I know about electricity."
Then I walked up and down the aisles,
    showing my invention,
A flashlight of sorts. This on a rainy day,
With the battery of the sun gone dead.
This on a day when the headlights of cars
    came on at noon.

Me, I showed my friends about electricity,
The beam of my invention glinting off the
    teacher's glasses.
I beamed it at the hamster, whose eyes glowed
    red as berries.

I sat down, a magician who brought light
    to the classroom.
I kicked my legs, ropes hanging from
    the chair.
I was happy.

School ended.
The rain started to throw darts on our
    shoulders.
But I didn't worry. I had a baseball cap
And my invention in my hand,
The one-eyed headlight that brightened
    the sidewalk
On the way back home.

People
and *Nature*

How are people and nature connected?

Objectives
• Work together with other students.
Take part in discussions led by
teachers and other students, ask and
answer questions, and offer ideas that
build on the ideas of others.

Oral Vocabulary

Let's Talk About

Interacting with Nature

- Express ideas about how nature provides enjoyment.

- Pose and answer questions about the relationship between people and nature.

- Ask about what you can gain from nature.

READING STREET ONLINE
CONCEPT TALK VIDEO
www.ReadingStreet.com

371

Phonics

Contractions

Words I Can Blend

I'd

won't

they've

doesn't

we'll

Sentences I Can Read

1. I'd rather not go.

2. Won't you look at what they've done?

3. If it doesn't matter to you, we'll get a movie.

I Can Read!

I've always wanted to teach my cat, Muffin, to do tricks. Mom said, "That won't work. Most cats don't do tricks because they're too independent."

Dad said, "You can't teach a cat tricks, and, anyway, Muffin wouldn't be able to understand."

I'd heard enough. Muffin and I got to work. So far she's learned to sit on command and fetch when I throw her toy. I'm hoping she'll be able to roll over soon. It's amazing! My family is astounded. They've started bragging about her, and we've started calling her Muffin the Wonder Cat.

You've learned

- Contractions

Objectives

• Support your answers with details from the text. • Examine and make judgments from the facts in the article, and support your conclusions with evidence.

Envision It! Skill Strategy

Skill

Strategy

Comprehension Skill

Draw Conclusions

- A conclusion is a decision or an opinion that makes sense based on facts and details from the text.

- Use what you already know to draw conclusions. Support your conclusions with facts and details from the text.

- Use what you learned about drawing conclusions and the graphic organizer below as you read "Before It's a Raisin, It's a Grape!" Draw a conclusion about why so many grapes are grown in California, and support your conclusion with facts and details from the text.

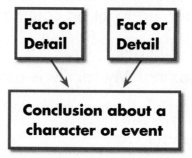

Comprehension Strategy

Important Ideas

When you are reading, look for the important ideas. These are the ideas the author explains or wants you to know. Understanding these ideas will help you understand the text as a whole.

Before It's a Raisin, It's a Grape!

Raisins come from grapes. Grapes have been grown in California for the past two hundred years. During the 1800s, men came looking for gold. Some of them ended up growing grapes instead.

Today most of the grapes we eat come from California. About 550 farmers grow grapes there. The warm, dry California weather helps grow sweet fruit.

Americans eat an average of about eight pounds of grapes a year. Most of them come from California. Many other countries enjoy grapes grown in the United States. People in Canada, Mexico, China, Taiwan, and Central American countries eat grapes grown in our country.

People in ancient China drank juice made from grapes mixed with snakes and frogs to feel better when they were sick. We can leave out the snakes and frogs! Grapes are good for us by themselves.

Skill What conclusion can you draw about the decision to grow grapes in California? Support your conclusion with details and facts from the text.

Strategy What important facts have you learned so far about grapes?

Your Turn!

⏸ **Need a Review?** See the *Envision It! Handbook* for help with drawing conclusions and important ideas.

Let's Think About..

▶ **Ready to Try It?** As you read *How Do You Raise a Raisin?* use what you've learned about drawing conclusions and important ideas to understand the selection.

area

grapevine

raisin

artificial

preservative

proof

raise

Vocabulary Strategy for

Homophones

Context Clues Homophones are words that sound the same but have different meanings and spellings, such as *write* (to make letters with a pen or pencil) and *right* (true, just, good). Context clues in the words and sentences nearby can help you figure out which meaning goes with which spelling of a homophone.

1. If a word you think you know doesn't make sense in the sentence, it may be a homophone.

2. Look at the words around it. Can you figure out the meaning?

3. Try the new meaning in the sentence. Does it make sense?

As you read "Baking with Aunt Millie" on page 377, look for homophones. Use context clues to help you figure out the meanings of the homophones and the Words to Know.

Words to Write Reread "Baking with Aunt Millie." Write about something special you like to do with a relative or a friend. Use homophones and words from the Words to Know list in your paragraph.

Baking with Aunt Millie

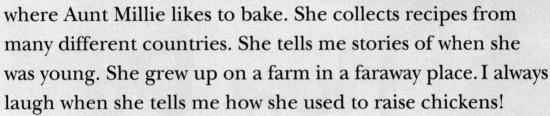

I love to visit my Aunt Millie. Her house is so pretty and it always smells so good.

There is a big grapevine wreath on the front door. She decorates it with an artificial flower and a bow.

Her kitchen has a special area where Aunt Millie likes to bake. She collects recipes from many different countries. She tells me stories of when she was young. She grew up on a farm in a faraway place. I always laugh when she tells me how she used to raise chickens!

Aunt Millie is a very good cook. She does not like to use any kind of preservative in her baking. Her ingredients are always natural. She always had fresh eggs when she was a girl on the farm. She still likes to use the best eggs.

We always make special oatmeal raisin cookies when I visit. I get to measure the flour, the oatmeal, and the sugar. I stir in the eggs and the raisins. Aunt Millie lets me take a big basket of cookies home. She always says, "Now you have proof you were at your Aunt Millie's house today!"

Your Turn!

❚❚ Need a Review? For additional help with homophones, see *Words!*

▶ Ready to Try It? Read *How Do You Raise a Raisin?* on pp. 378–393.

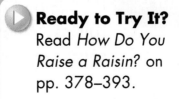

How Do You Raise a Raisin?

by Pam Muñoz Ryan
illustrated by Craig Brown

Genre This **expository text** asks questions using rhythm and rhyme. The answers tell all about raisins. What do you want to learn about raisins as you read?

Question of the Week
How do people and nature interact?

Let's
Think
About
Reading!

Let's Think About...

Why did the author write this text? How do you know?

⊙ Important Ideas

How do you raise a raisin?
Tell me so I'll know.
They're such peculiar little things.
How do they sprout and grow?
Do raisins grow on Earth, or other planets,
far away?
Do aliens collect them and space-shuttle
them our way?

Raisins are dried grapes. So far, there is no proof that raisins grow on other planets. Raisins ARE grown on Earth, in countries like Turkey, Iran, Greece, Australia, and the United States.

So who discovered raisins?
Were they here when Earth began?
Who WAS the first to nibble them—
dinosaur or man?

Raisins were probably discovered when someone or someTHING tasted grapes that had dried on the vine. Over the years people and animals figured out which grapes produced the sweetest, yummiest raisins.

Let's Think About...

How do grapes become raisins?
◉ **Important Ideas**

381

Let's Think About...

Why does the author include short poems in the text?

⊙ **Important Ideas**

Do raisins grow in **one** place,
like Raisin Creek or Raisin Hill?
Is there a special town called
Raisinfield or Raisinville?

Raisins grow best in areas with nice dirt, many days of hot weather, a dry climate, and plenty of water. Almost all of the raisins in the United States are grown in the San Joaquin Valley of California, near towns like Chowchilla, Dinuba, Kingsburg, Selma, Weedpatch, and even Raisin City! About 90 percent of the raisins sold in the United States come from the area around Fresno, California.

Do farmers plant some seeds
from the local garden shop?
And wait for raisin bushes
to produce a raisin crop?

Raisinville, USA

Farmers start a new crop of raisins by taking "cuttings" from an older grapevine. These pieces of stem are planted in sand until they sprout. Then, they are planted in the fields, next to a wooden stake.

Notice how the grapevines and the sprawling branches grow. Does a grapevine tamer train them into picture-perfect rows?

Grapevines are grown about eight feet apart. Fieldworkers hand-tie the sturdy branches, or "canes," to rows of wire. There are usually two sets of wire, a top set that is about six feet high, and a second wire that is three or four feet high.

Let's Think About...

How do farmers start and raise a new crop of raisins?
◎ Important Ideas

How long do raisins take to grow?
A week, a month, or a year?
How many hours must you wait
for a raisin to appear?

It takes at least three years until the vines
are old enough for the first crop of raisins.
That's 26,280 hours!

When grapes are ripe and ready,
how do farmers get them down?
Do they rent a burly giant
to shake them to the ground?

Let's Think About...

How does the short poem and the art compare and contrast with the real explanation?
⊚ **Important Ideas**

When grapes are ready, skilled grape-pickers snag the grape clusters from the vines using a sharp vine-cutter.

Most grapes are turned into raisins the same way they've been for thousands of years: they are left to dry naturally in the sun.

Let's Think About...

How are raisins dried?

◉ Important Ideas

What do raisins lie on
while they're basking in the sun?
Do they rest on little beach towels
until they're dried and done?

The grape clusters are laid on brown paper trays on the ground between the grapevine rows. This is called "laying the grapes down." The sun rises in the east and sets in the west. Most raisin growers plant their vineyards in east-to-west rows. This way, grapes drying between the rows receive the most sun. If they were drying in north-to-south rows, the grapes would be in the shade part of the day, and when it comes to raising raisins, the more sun the better.

Let's  About...

How is the placement of grapevine rows important?
◉ **Important Ideas**

How long do clusters lie around
to sweeten, dry, and bake?
How many weeks in the valley heat
does raising-making take?

Raisins bake in the sun for about two to
three weeks. Then, the paper trays are rolled
into bundles that look like burritos and are
left in the field for a few more days to make
sure that all the raisins are as dry.

Raisins do not look like grapes—
they're withered up and wrinkled!
Are they soaked inside a bathtub
until their skin is crinkled?

As grapes bake in the hot sun, their water evaporates. The more water they lose, the more the grapes shrivel, causing wrinkles.

How many grapes must a farmer dry
upon the valley ground?
To make a box of raisins
that weighs about one pound?

It takes about four and one-half pounds of fresh grapes to make one pound of raisins.

Let's Think About...

How does this art help you understand the text?
⊙ **Important Ideas**

How do the raisins get from fields
to the raisin factory door?
Does a vacuum cleaner suck them up
from the dusty valley floor?

Farmworkers toss the raisin bundles into a wooden trailer. The raisins are sent across a shaker that gets rid of the dirt and rocks. Then, raisins are taken to the factory and stored in big boxes, called bins, until they are ready to be packaged.

Let's Think About...

Can you imagine what is happening here? **Visualize**

Who puts raisins in the
boxes that keep them sweet and dried?
Do tiny fairy princesses stuff each one inside?

When they're needed, raisin bins are
brought into the factory for packaging. It
takes only 10 minutes from bin to package!
Workers and machines take off the stems and
capstems, sort, and wash the raisins. Then
the raisins are packaged in a variety of boxes
and bags.

Over the years, raising raisins flourished, but raisin seeds were a problem. When seeds were removed the raisins became a sticky, clumpy mess. Bakers and people who liked to eat raisins found this troublesome. They hoped for a seedless grape that would produce a yummy raisin.

In 1876, William Thompson introduced the Lady de Coverly grape to California. The green grapes were seedless, with thin skins, and produced a sweet and flavorful raisin. These grapes changed the raisin-producing industry forever and are still known today as Thompson Seedless grapes. Today 95 percent of the California raisin crop is Thompson Seedless grapes.

Let's Think About...

Why is the art of a man holding green grapes important? Who is the man?

Important Ideas

391

What's so great about raisins, anyway?

- They're nutritious. Raisins are rich in iron, calcium, potassium, and B vitamins and provide a good source of fiber.

- They make other foods taste better. Raisins have tartaric acid, a flavor-enhancer. Raisin juice and raisin paste are used in a variety of sauces such as pasta, barbecue, and steak sauces to boost their flavor.

- Raisin paste is sometimes used as filler in meatballs and meat pies to provide more servings.

- Raisins have a rich, natural color. Raisin juice is often added to frozen dairy desserts and baked goods as a color-enhancer, or food coloring.

- Ground raisins can be used instead of fat in fat-free baked goods like fat-free muffins, cookies, and brownies.

- Raisin paste and raisin juice concentrate are mold-inhibitors that prevent food from spoiling as easily. Bakers often use raisin products instead of artificial preservatives. Raisins extend the shelf life of bakery goods by several days over products without raisin products.

Let's Think About...

Why are raisins an important food?
Summarize

Follow These Steps

Ants on a Log

Spread celery
    pieces with peanut
    butter, cream cheese, or cheese spread.
Top with raisins.

Rats on a Raft

Spread cream cheese on graham crackers.
Dot raisins on top.

Super Balls

1 cup honey
1½ cups powdered milk
1 cup peanut butter
1½ cups graham cracker crumbs
1 cup raisins
¾ cup crushed cornflakes or dried coconut

Put crushed corn flakes or coconut in a dish.
In a mixing bowl, mix all other ingredients.
Shape into balls.
Roll balls in crushed
    cornflakes or coconut.

Let's **Think** About...

What can you
make with raisins?
⊙ **Important Ideas**

Think Critically

1. Raisins are added to many different foods as flavorings. What is one of your favorite ways to enjoy raisins? Why do you like it? Text to Self

2. This author asks questions and then gives the answers. Why do you think the author uses this method? Do you think it was helpful in understanding the information in the article? Think Like an Author

3. After reading the facts in the selection, what conclusion can you come to about why raisins are so popular?
Draw Conclusions

4. What important idea led to the growing of Thompson Seedless grapes? How did it change the raisin industry?
Important Ideas

5. **Look Back and Write** There is nothing wasted with raisins. Look back at page 392. Tell how raisins are used. Provide evidence to support your answer.

TEST PRACTICE | Extended Response

Meet the Author and the Illustrator

Pam Muñoz Ryan and Craig McFarland Brown

Pam Muñoz Ryan was born and raised in California's San Joaquin Valley. She is Spanish, Mexican, Basque, Italian, and Oklahoman. She has written more than twenty-five books for young people, including *Paint the Wind, Nacho and Lolita, When Marian Sang, Mice and Beans,* and *The Flag We Love.* Many of her books are also available in Spanish.

As a young girl, she spent many hot summers riding her bike to the library. The library became her favorite place to hang out because her family didn't have a swimming pool and the library was air-conditioned! That's how she got hooked on books and reading!

Craig McFarland Brown is an illustrator and author of children's books. Craig is also a muralist. Some of his paintings are on display as a mural in the children's museum in Pueblo, Colorado.

Here are other books by Pam Muñoz Ryan.

Mice and Beans

Nacho and Lolita

> **Reading Log**
> Use the Reader's and Writer's Notebook to record your independent reading.

Let's Write It!

Key Features of Fiction

- characters and events are imaginary

- setting may take place in the past, present, or future

- usually written in first or third person

Fiction

Fiction stories are made up of imaginary events, characters, and settings. The student model on the next page is an example of fiction.

Writing Prompt Imagine that you are a raisin farmer. Write a story about a day in your life.

Writer's Checklist

Remember, you should . . .

 write an imaginative story that builds the plot to a climax.

 include details about the characters and setting.

 use past, present, and future tense verbs correctly.

I Grow Raisins!

I **am** a raisin farmer, and today my grapes **are** ready to be turned into raisins! I like to **walk** out into the fields in the early morning and **look** out at my beautiful rows and rows of grapevines. My workers and I have **put** in many long hours of work over these last months.

"Let's get going," I **call** to the men and women who will help me **cut** the grapes today. We have **worked** long hours, but we are **excited** about the harvest. We are all very **tired** as we **lay** the grapes out to dry. But soon everyone is **singing** in celebration of all that we have accomplished.

We will have to **wait** weeks for the raisins to fully dry. I am not going to wait for my raisin treats, though. I am headed back to the house for a nice cool glass of milk and a big raisin cookie, and I am going to **invite** all the workers to come along with me!

Writing Trait Voice An engaging tone draws in readers.

Action and linking verbs are used correctly.

Genre Fiction tells an imaginary story.

Conventions

Action and Linking Verbs

Remember Action verbs are words that show action. **Linking verbs** such as *am, is, are, was,* and *were* do not show action. They link a subject to a word or words in the predicate.

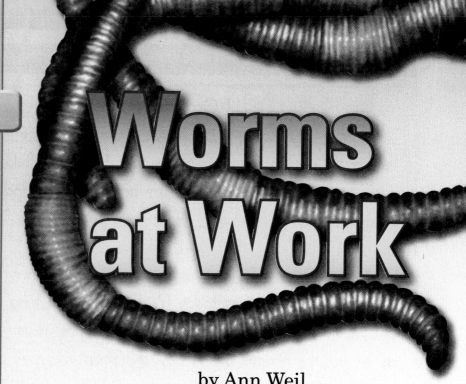

Science in Reading

Genre
Procedural Text

○ A procedural text explains multi-step directions about how to do or make something.

○ Many procedural texts use graphic features and text features to help the reader locate and use information in the text.

○ Before you read, look at the italicized word in the first paragraph. What does *compost* mean? Use the word to predict what the selection will be about. Verify your prediction after you read.

○ Read "Worms at Work." Follow the steps to create your own compost.

Worms at Work

by Ann Weil

Did you know that people all over the world keep worms to change their garbage into rich soil called *compost?* Worms eat food scraps. Two pounds of worms can eat a pound of garbage every day. That's a lot of trash.

Keeping worms is easy. It can also be a lot of fun. And while you're having fun taking care of the worms, you're also helping our environment by recycling trash into compost for houseplants and gardens.

Here's what you need to do.

You will need:

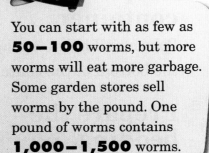

- Red worms ········O
  (also called
  red wigglers)

You can start with as few as **50–100** worms, but more worms will eat more garbage. Some garden stores sell worms by the pound. One pound of worms contains **1,000–1,500** worms.

- A large plastic
  container, about
  12 inches deep

12"

- Plastic bag or
  loose cover for
  the container

- Newspaper, leaves,
  and soil to make
  the bedding

- Water

- Food scraps ·······O

Feeding Dos
YES: Eggshells; coffee grounds and used tea bags; cooked rice, pasta, or potatoes; cereals; fruit and vegetable peelings; bread

Feeding Don'ts
NO: Meat and fish, dairy products. Worms would eat these, but they may make the worm bin smell bad and attract rats and flies.

Let's **Think** About...

What specific information about worms does this graphic feature tell you? How will this information help you set up a worm compost?
Procedural Text

Making Your Worm Bin

1 ## Prepare the container.
Poke small holes through the bottom of the container.

2 ## Prepare the bedding. ·············O
Fill the container about three-quarters full with small pieces of torn newspaper. (Do not use any colored or shiny newspaper.)

Add about a handful of soil. You can put in some dead leaves, too, if you like.

3 ## Pour water on the bedding. ·············O
Make sure all the bedding is damp, but not soaking wet.

4 ## Add the worms.
Gently move the worms into their new home.

5 ## Feed the worms. ····O
Bury the food scraps in the bedding.

6 ## Cover the bin.
Make sure air can still move in and around the bin.

Let's **Think** About...

If you were unsure of how small to make the pieces of newspaper, where could you locate an answer?
Procedural Text

Let's **Think** About...

Look at this illustration. What tool will help you with step 5?
Procedural Text

Maintaining Your Worm Bin

1 **Keep the bedding moist.**
Make sure the bedding does not dry out.

2 **Feed the worms.** ····o

Pay attention to how much the worms are eating. If they are not eating all the scraps, feed them less.

3 **Harvest the compost.** ··············o

Worms eat their bedding as well as their food. When the bedding is mostly gone, push what's left to one side and add fresh, damp bedding to the other side. Bury the food scraps in the new bedding. The worms will move to the food so you can harvest the compost without taking all the worms with it.

4 **Use the compost!**
Compost helps plants grow better. Add it to potted houseplants or to your outdoor flower or vegetable garden.

Let's **Think** About...

Reading Across Texts *How Do You Raise a Raisin?* and "Worms at Work" both explain how to do something. Which format makes following the directions easier?

Writing Across Texts Rewrite *How Do You Raise a Raisin* in the format of "Worms at Work." Summarize and explain the directions for making raisins in five steps.

401

Objectives
• Identify words that are opposites, words that are similar, words that have more than one meaning, and words that sound the same even though they mean different things.
• Speak clearly and to the point while making eye contact, changing how fast, loud, and clearly you speak to communicate your ideas.

Let's Learn It!

READING STREET ONLINE
ONLINE STUDENT EDITION
www.ReadingStreet.com

Vocabulary

Homophones

Context Clues Homophones are words that sound the same but have different meanings and spellings, like *pause* and *paws*. Context clues can help you determine the meaning of homophones.

Practice It! As you read *How Do You Raise a Raisin?*, make a list of three or four words that have homophones. Write both the word and its homophone. Then write down the definition of each homophone.

Fluency

Expression

Remember that when you read or speak aloud, you should change the volume, pitch, and rate of your voice to show emotion. This makes your reading more interesting.

Practice It! Practice reading aloud page 381. How should you use expression to make this page sound interesting?

Media Literacy

Use persuasive words that grab your audience's attention.

Commercial

The purpose of a commercial is to persuade your audience to buy your product. Use words that grab your audience's attention.

Practice It! In a small group, prepare a TV commercial to persuade your viewers to buy raisins. Include information from *How Do You Raise a Raisin?* and other research. Present your commercial to the class, using visual and sound aids. Discuss the impact of those aids on your message.

Tips

Listening ...

- Listen for persuasive techniques.
- Draw conclusions about what the speaker says.

Speaking ...

- Speak loudly enough to be heard.
- Use persuasive techniques.
- Use verbs correctly.

Teamwork ...

- Make relevant comments that build on the ideas of others.

Objectives

• Work with other students. Take part in discussions led by teachers and other students, ask and answer questions, and offer ideas that build on the ideas of others. • Listen closely when someone speaks, ask questions about the topic he or she is talking about, and comment about the topic.

Oral Vocabulary

Let's Talk About

Explaining Nature

- Share ideas about how people use myths to explain events in nature.

- Express opinions in teams about how people hand down stories.

- Pose and answer questions about the mysteries of nature.

READING STREET ONLINE
CONCEPT TALK VIDEO
www.ReadingStreet.com

Objectives
● Read aloud words that begin with common prefixes and end with common suffixes. ● Read aloud words with common spelling patterns.

Envision It! | **Sounds to Know**

unwrap

prefix un-

disappear

prefix dis-

replant

prefix re-

nonfiction

prefix non-

misplace

prefix mis-

READING STREET ONLINE
SOUND-SPELLING CARDS
www.ReadingStreet.com

Phonics

Prefixes *un-, re-, mis-, dis-, non-*

Words I Can Blend

unbelievable

reappear

misspelled

disbelief

nonstop

Sentences I Can Read

1. It seemed unreal that our dog could reappear after being missing for two weeks.

2. I saw with disbelief that I had misspelled two words.

3. We baked nonstop to get ready for the bake sale.

I Can Read!

My friend Landon says I have an unusual memory. "Nonsense," I disagree. "My memory is just as unreliable as anyone else's."

But I do know how to reconnect with unclear memories. Let's say I can't remember where I misplaced my math book. All I do is mentally retrace my steps from the time the book disappeared.

As I rerun the day nonstop in my mind, an unexpected picture pops up, and I'm reminded where the book is. I urged Landon to try my foolproof method.

You've learned

🎯 Prefixes
   un-, re-, mis-, dis-, non-

Envision It! | Skill Strategy

Skill

Strategy

Literary Elements: Character, Setting, and Plot

- A character is a person or animal in a story. Authors usually describe characters, and you can learn more about them, their relationships, and how they change from their actions and what they say.

- The setting is when and where a story takes place.

- The plot of a story includes what happens at the beginning, middle, and end. Earlier events usually influence the end.

- Use what you learned about these literary elements and the chart below as you read "An Up-and-Down Story."

Story Title		
Character	**Setting**	**Plot**

Comprehension Strategy

Inferring

As you read, use facts and details from the author and what you already know to come up with your own ideas. Inferring helps you connect to the story.

AN UP-AND-DOWN STORY

"Timber!" I heard Dad yell. I ran to my bedroom window and saw one of the trees in our backyard come crashing to the earth. It just missed hitting the garage.

Mom and I rushed outside. "What in the world are you doing now?" Mom asked.

Dad set down his axe and said, "I'm making a story pole!" Mom rolled her eyes.

Skill Who are the characters in this story? What is the setting?

Last summer we visited a place in Olympia, Washington, that had a story pole. Chief Shelton had carved animal figures into a cedar tree. The pole tells a story about Chief Shelton's Snohomish culture. He worked on it for five years. When he died in 1938, other people in the tribe finished the carvings. "Can I help?" I asked.

Skill What is the plot of the story?

"Sure, Billy!" Dad said.

"So, what kind of animal should we put at the top of our pole?" I asked.

"How about a mule?" Mom suggested.

Strategy How can you tell how Mom feels about Dad's project?

Pushing Up the Sky

Your Turn!

⏸ **Need a Review?** See the *Envision It! Handbook* for help with characters, setting, plot, and inferring.

▶ **Ready to Try It?** As you read *Pushing Up the Sky*, use what you've learned about characters, setting, plot, and inferring to understand the text.

Envision It! | Words to Know

antlers

languages

poked

imagined

narrator

overhead

Vocabulary Strategy for

🎯 Unknown Words

Dictionary/Glossary If you read a word you don't know, you can look it up in a dictionary or the glossary to find the correct meaning, how the word is divided into syllables, which syllables are stressed, and how to pronounce the word correctly.

1. Open the glossary in this book.

2. Find the entry for the word. Entries are in alphabetical order.

3. Use the pronunciation key and look at each syllable to pronounce the word.

4. Read all the meanings of the word. Then choose the one that makes the best sense in the sentence.

Read "The Class Play" on page 411. Use a dictionary or the glossary to find the meanings and pronunciations of the Words to Know.

Words to Write Reread "The Class Play." Imagine you are Ms. Chavez. What would you say to Jenna and Kate? Write your response. Use words from the Words to Know list.

The Class Play

"I have counted the votes," declared Ms. Chavez, waving a sheet of paper overhead. "Our play for Parents Night will be *Pushing Up the Sky*. Tryouts are tomorrow."

Jenna grinned and poked Kate in the shoulder. They both wanted to be Chiefs together. They had already learned the lines and planned their costumes.

The next day, Jenna tried out for the First Chief. That was scarier than she had imagined. She forgot several words.

When Kate tried out for the Seventh Chief's part, she didn't make a single mistake.

Later, Ms. Chavez announced the parts. Kate was the Narrator. She had a lot of lines, but she didn't get to wear a costume. "But I made such a beautiful cape," she wailed.

Jenna was the Elk. She didn't have any lines at all, and she had to wear brown paper antlers on her head. "Don't elks know *any* languages?"

Both girls were disappointed but glad to be in the play. Maybe next time they would get the parts they wanted.

Your Turn!

Need a Review? For additional help with unknown words, see *Words!*

Ready to Try It? Read *Pushing Up the Sky* on pp. 412–423.

Pushing Up

by Joseph Bruchac

illustrated by Teresa Flavin

Genre

A **drama** uses dialogue to present characters and plot. This drama is a myth about how something in nature came to be. Read to find out why the characters are pushing up the sky.

the Sky

Question of the Week
**How do people explain
things in nature?**

Snohomish

The Snohomish people live in the area of the Northwest that is now known as the state of Washington, not far from Puget Sound. They fished in the ocean and gathered food from the shore. Their homes and many of the things they used every day, such as bowls and canoe paddles, were carved from the trees. Like many of the other peoples of the area, they also carved totem poles, which recorded the history and stories of their nation. This story is one that was carved into a totem pole made for the city of Everett, Washington, by Chief William Shelton.

Characters

Speaking Roles

NARRATOR	**FIRST CHIEF**
TALL MAN	**SECOND CHIEF**
GIRL	**THIRD CHIEF**
MOTHER	**FOURTH CHIEF**
BOY	**FIFTH CHIEF**
	SIXTH CHIEF
	SEVENTH CHIEF

Non-speaking Roles

Animals and Birds—as many as group size will accommodate. Animals familiar to the Snohomish would include Dog, Deer, Elk, Mountain Goat, Bear, Mountain Lion, Rabbit, Weasel, Wolf, and Fox. Birds would include Hawk, Bald Eagle, Golden Eagle, Jay, Seagull, Raven, Heron, and Kingfisher.

Props/Scenery

The village can be suggested with a painted backdrop showing houses made of cedar planks among tall fir trees and redwoods, with the ocean visible in the background. Potted plants can be added around the stage to suggest trees if desired.

Bows and arrows held by Boy in Scene I can be from a toy set or made from cardboard.

The poles held by people and animals in Scene III can be rulers or long tubes of cardboard.

Costumes

People, including the **Narrator,** can wear blankets or towels. **Chiefs** wear them around their shoulders, and other humans wear them wrapped around their waists to suggest the robes often worn by people of the Northwest. Cone-shaped hats (worn by Snohomish women) may be worn by girls playing human characters.

Depending on their number and type, the **Animals** can be suggested by face paint or with decorated masks made from paper plates.

Scene I: A Village Among Many Tall Trees

(Tall Man, Girl, Mother, and Boy stand onstage.)

NARRATOR: Long ago the sky was very close to the earth. The sky was so close that some people could jump right into it. Those people who were not good jumpers could climb up the tall fir trees and step into the sky. But people were not happy that the sky was so close to the earth. Tall people kept bumping their heads on the sky. And there were other problems.

TALL MAN: Oh, that hurt! I just hit my head on the sky again.

GIRL: I just threw my ball, and it landed in the sky, and I can't get it back.

MOTHER: Where is my son? Has he climbed a tree and gone up into the sky again?

BOY: Every time I shoot my bow, my arrows get stuck in the sky!

ALL: THE SKY IS TOO CLOSE!

Scene II: The Same Village

(The seven chiefs stand together onstage.)

NARRATOR: So people decided something had to be done. A great meeting was held for all the different tribes. The seven wisest chiefs got together to talk about the problem.

FIRST CHIEF: My people all think the sky is too close.

SECOND CHIEF: The Creator did a very good job of making the world.

THIRD CHIEF: That is true, but the Creator should have put the sky up higher. My tall son keeps hitting his head on the sky.

FOURTH CHIEF: My daughter keeps losing her ball in the sky.

FIFTH CHIEF: People keep going up into the sky when they should be staying on the earth to help each other.

SIXTH CHIEF: When mothers look for their children, they cannot find them because they are up playing in the sky.

SEVENTH CHIEF: We are agreed, then. The sky is too close.

ALL: WE ARE AGREED.

SECOND CHIEF: What can we do?

SEVENTH CHIEF: I have an idea. Let's push up the sky.

THIRD CHIEF: The sky is heavy.

SEVENTH CHIEF: If we all push together, we can do it.

SIXTH CHIEF: We will ask the birds and animals to help. They also do not like it that the sky is so close.

SECOND CHIEF: The elk are always getting their antlers caught in the sky.

FOURTH CHIEF: The birds are always hitting their wings on it.

FIRST CHIEF: We will cut tall trees to make poles. We can use those poles to push up the sky.

FIFTH CHIEF: That is a good idea. Are we all agreed?

ALL: WE ARE ALL AGREED.

Scene III: The Same Village

(All the People, except Seventh Chief, are gathered together. They hold long poles. The Birds and Animals are with them. They all begin pushing randomly, jabbing their poles into the air. The sky can be imagined as just above them.)

GIRL: It isn't working.

BOY: The sky is still too close.

FIFTH CHIEF: Where is Seventh Chief? This was his idea!

SEVENTH CHIEF *(entering)*: Here I am. I had to find this long pole.

FIRST CHIEF: Your plan is not good! See, we are pushing and the sky is not moving.

SEVENTH CHIEF: Ah, but I said we must push together.

421

FIFTH CHIEF: We need a signal so that all can push together. Our people speak different languages.

SEVENTH CHIEF: Let us use YAH-HOO as the signal. Ready?

ALL: YES!

SEVENTH CHIEF: YAH-HOO.

(At the signal, everyone pushes together.)

ALL: YAH-HOO!

SEVENTH CHIEF: YAH-HOO.

(Again everyone pushes together.)

ALL: YAH-HOO!

TALL MAN: We are doing it!

MOTHER: Now my son won't be able to hide in the sky!

SEVENTH CHIEF: YAH-HOO.

(Again everyone pushes together.)

ALL: YAH-HOO!

BOY: It will be too high for my arrows to stick into it.

SEVENTH CHIEF: YAH-HOO.

(Again everyone pushes together.)

ALL: YAH-HOOOO!

FIRST CHIEF: We have done it!

NARRATOR: So the sky was pushed up. It was done by everyone working together. That night, though, when everyone looked overhead, they saw many stars in the sky. The stars were shining through the holes poked into the sky by the poles of everyone who pushed it up higher.

No one ever bumped his head on the sky again. And those stars are there to this day.

Think Critically

1. This play is also a myth. Think about another myth you have read. How is the setting like *Pushing Up the Sky*? How is it different? **Text to Text**

2. When does the narrator talk in this play? Does the narrator speak in first or third person? Why do you think the author includes a narrator? **Think Like an Author**

3. Describe the characters, their relationships, and the changes they undergo. What did they learn when they solved their problem? Paraphrase the details that support what they learned. **Literary Elements**

4. Why did people begin asking where the Seventh Chief was when their plan wasn't working? **Inferring**

5. **Look Back and Write** Look back through the play to find how the myth explains something in nature. Use details about the characters, setting, plot, and theme of the play to support your answer.

TEST PRACTICE Extended Response

Joseph Bruchac

Joseph Bruchac grew up in a small town in the mountains in New York. As a young boy he loved reading and nature. Often he would go off to read books deep in the forest. Bruchac worries that many people today do not notice nature. Some Native American tribes have stories to explain just about every part of nature. "Those stories tell us so much about nature and are a lot easier to remember than a bunch of facts."

Bruchac has traveled all over America to listen to the stories of different Native American tribes. He has always been a very careful listener. "The first thing I always tell young people is to listen. A good storyteller is a good listener first," he says.

Read more books by Joseph Bruchac.

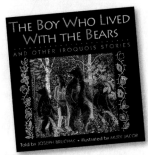

The Boy Who Lived with the Bears and Other Iroquois Stories

The Great Ball Game: A Muskogee Story

Use the Reader's and Writer's Notebook to record your independent reading.

425

Objectives
● Write stories that are creative, build to an ending, and include details about the characters and setting.
● Use and understand how verbs work.

Let's Write It!

Key Features of Plays or Skits

● includes a cast of characters

● often has a narrator to tell part of the story

● stage directions appear in parentheses

READING STREET ONLINE
GRAMMAR JAMMER
www.ReadingStreet.com

Play

A **play** is a story that is written to be performed. A **skit** is a short play. Plays and skits use dialogue and stage directions to tell a story. The student model on the next page is an example of a play.

Writing Prompt Write a play or skit about something occurring in nature.

Writer's Checklist

Remember, you should . . .

☑ include a cast of characters.

☑ give each character lines.

☑ include stage directions for the performers.

☑ build the plot to a climax.

☑ use past, present, and future tense verbs correctly.

426

Growing Vegetables

CHARACTERS

Narrator   Ms. Lee

Mr. Ruiz   Maddie

NARRATOR: Three people who live on Oakwood Street decided to create a vegetable garden.

MR. RUIZ: This vacant lot needs to be cleared. (He moves rocks.)

MS. LEE: I'm going to plant these vegetable seeds in neat rows. (She pokes holes and puts in seeds.)

MADDIE: My job **will be** to water the plants and pull the weeds. (She weeds.)

NARRATOR: After a few weeks, the vegetables are ready to be picked.

MR. RUIZ: (picking vegetables) I **will gather** the vegetables.

MS. LEE AND MADDIE: We'll cook a vegetable feast, and everyone **will have** a delicious meal!

Genre
A **play** or **skit** tells a story through characters.

Writing Trait Sentence variation helps dialogue sound natural.

Main and helping verbs are used correctly.

Conventions

Main and Helping Verbs

Remember A **verb phrase** is a verb that has more than one word. The **main verb** shows action. A **helping verb** shows the time of the action.

427

Social Studies in Reading

Genre
Myth

- Myths are old stories that have been told orally for generations.

- Myths often describe how things in nature came to be.

- The animal characters act like people.

- The author capitalizes each animal's name to represents all the animals of that kind.

- Myths usually have themes based on how the characters solve problems.

- Compare and contrast "Catch It and Run!" with other myths as you read.

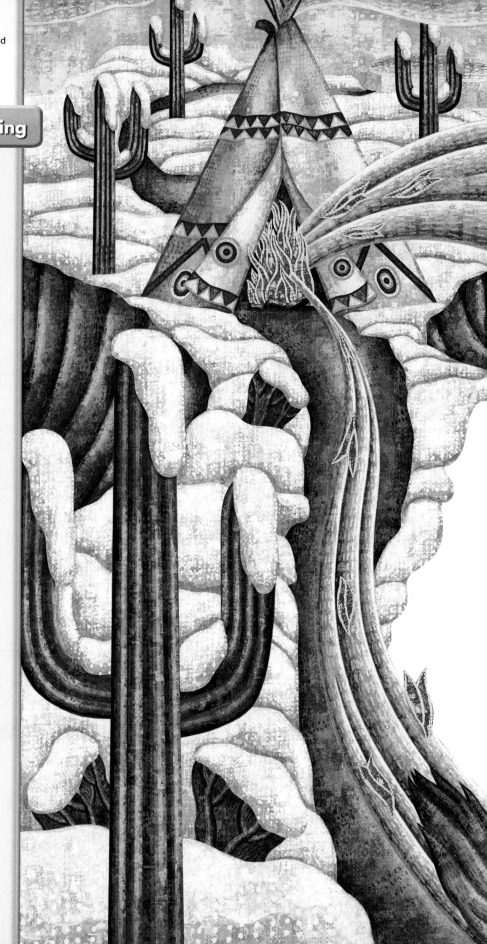

Catch It and Run!

from *When the World Was Young*
retold by **Margaret Mayo**
illustrated by **Richard Downs**

A long, long time ago, all fire belonged to
three Fire Beings who kept it hidden in their
tepee, high on a mountaintop. They would
not share the fire with anyone and guarded it
carefully, night and day. So, when winter came
and the fierce winds howled and snow covered
the earth, men, women, and children had no way
of warming themselves. No fire. No hot food.
Nothing at all.

Now Coyote, who is wise, knew about fire,
and one year, at winter's end, when he saw how
cold and miserable the people were, he decided
to steal some fire and give it to them. But how
would he do it?

Let's **Think** About...

How is the setting
in this myth like the
setting in "How the
Desert Tortoise Got
Its Shell"? How is it
different? **Myth**

429

Let's **Think** About...

What abilities do the animals in this story have that real animals do not have? **Myth**

Coyote thought hard.

He called a meeting of the animals, and he said, "Who will help me steal some fire and give it to the people?" And Bear, Deer, Squirrel, Chipmunk, and Frog offered to help.

Coyote thought again.

"Bear," he said, "you are big and strong, so you must come with me to the Fire Beings' tepee. Deer, Squirrel, and Chipmunk, you are fast runners, so you must wait beside the trail, ready to run."

"What about me?" asked Frog. "I'd like to help!"

"Fro-og," sighed Coyote, shaking his head, "you're such a squatty little thing. You can jump and swim. But you can't run. There's nothing you can do."

"I could wait by the pond and be ready," said Frog. "Just in case. . . ."

"You do that," said Coyote. "Wait and be ready. Just in case. . . ."

That made Frog happy. He squatted down by the pond, and he waited while the others set off along the trail through the forest that led to the Fire Beings' mountaintop.

On the way Coyote stopped from time to time and told one of the animals to wait beside the trail. First Squirrel, next Chipmunk, and then Deer were left behind, and at last Bear and Coyote walked on alone.

When they reached the tepee on top of the mountain, Coyote told Bear to wait in the shadows until he heard Coyote call *"Aooo!"* Then Bear must make a big, loud rumpus.

Let's Think About...

How are the animals described? How are they like all animals of their kinds? **Myth**

431

Coyote crept up to the tepee. He gave a soft bark, and one of the Fire Beings opened the flap and looked out.

Coyote sort of trembled and said in his quietest, most polite voice, "My legs are freezing cold. May I please put them inside your warm tepee?"

He was so exceedingly polite that the Fire Being said, "Ye-es, all right. . . ."

Coyote stepped in his front legs, then he stepped in his back legs, and then he whisked in his tail. He looked longingly at the great blazing fire in the center of the tepee, but he said nothing. He just lay down and closed his eyes as if he were going to sleep. But the next moment he gave a long Coyote call, *"Aooo-ooo!"*

From outside the tepee came the sound of a big, loud rumpus as Bear growled and stamped about.

The Fire Beings all rushed out shouting, "Who's that?" And when they saw Bear, they chased him.

Let's Think About...

How are the characters in this myth similar to the characters in the myth *Pushing Up the Sky?* Provide details from the myths to support your answer. **Myth**

Coyote was ready. He grabbed a piece of burning wood between his teeth and away he ran, out of the tepee and down the mountain.

As soon as the Fire Beings saw Coyote with the firebrand, they abandoned Bear and chased Coyote.

Coyote ran and ran. He was fast, but the Fire Beings were faster, and they came closer.

Then Coyote saw Deer. "Catch it and *run!*" he called and threw the firebrand.

Deer caught it and ran. But he ran so fast that the wind fanned the fire out behind him, and a flame jumped onto his long tail and burned most of it. So that's why Deer has a shortish tail, even today.

Deer was fast, but the Fire Beings were faster, and they came closer.

Let's **Think** About...

What happens to Deer that becomes the mythical reason that all deer have short tails? **Myth**

433

Then Deer saw Chipmunk. "Catch it and *run!*" he called and threw the firebrand.

Chipmunk caught it and ran. But the Fire Beings came closer and closer, until one of them reached out an arm and clawed his back and left three long black stripes. And that's why Chipmunk has stripes on his back, even today.

Then Chipmunk saw Squirrel. "Catch it and *run!*" he called and threw the firebrand.

Squirrel caught it and ran. But the firebrand had been burning fast, and it was now so short that its great heat made Squirrel's bushy tail curl up over his back. And that's why Squirrel has a curled-up tail, even today.

Squirrel came to the pond. The Fire Beings were right at his back. What could he do?

Then he saw small, squatty Frog, waiting and ready. Just in case. . . .

"Catch it and *jump!*" called Squirrel and threw the firebrand, which was now quite tiny.

Frog caught the firebrand, but as he jumped one of the Fire Beings grabbed his tail and pulled it off. And that's why Frog has no tail, even today.

Now when Frog jumped, he landed in the pond, and to save the flames from the water, he gulped down the tiny firebrand. He held his breath and swam over to the other side of the pond.

Let's **Think** About...

How does the story explain a chipmunk's stripes, a squirrel's tail, and a frog's missing tail? **Myth**

Then Frog saw a tree. "Catch it and *hide!*" he called and coughed up all that was left of the firebrand, just a few bright flames.

And the tree caught the fire and hid it.

The Fire Beings ran around the pond, and they looked for the fire. But it was hidden in the tree, and they didn't know how to get it out again, so they returned to their home, high on the mountaintop.

But Coyote, who is wise, knew how to get fire out of the tree. He knew how to rub two dry sticks together to make a spark that could be fed with pine needles and pine cones and grow into a fire. It was Coyote who taught the people how to do this so that they need not be cold, ever again, in wintertime. And it was Coyote who went around and gave some fire to all the other trees, so that fire lies hidden in every tree, even today.

Let's **Think** About...

Paraphrase the theme and supporting details in "Catch It and Run!" What can you conclude from how the characters solved problems?
Myth

Let's **Think** About...

Reading Across Texts Compare and contrast the settings in the two myths *Pushing Up the Sky* and "Catch It and Run!" How are they alike? How are they different?

Writing Across Texts Make a Venn diagram to compare and contrast the settings in each of these myths.

435

Objectives

● Follow, retell, and give instructions to do an action in a particular way.

● Read aloud and understand texts at your grade level. ● Use a dictionary or glossary to look up the meanings, syllable patterns, and ways to say words you do not know.

READING STREET ONLINE
ONLINE STUDENT EDITION
www.ReadingStreet.com

Vocabulary

Unknown Words

Dictionary/Glossary Use a dictionary or glossary to find the meanings of unknown words while you are reading. Words are listed in alphabetical order, followed by the definitions.

Practice It! Write the words *battery*, *bay*, and *bat* in alphabetical order. Look them up in a dictionary or glossary. Write the meanings of the words next to them, and a sentence for each meaning.

Fluency

Accuracy

The more accurately you read a selection, the more you will understand the story or subject. You may have to reread the text to improve your accuracy. Focus on reading each word correctly.

Practice It! With a partner, practice reading aloud a page from a book from your school library. Then reread the page. Did your accuracy improve?

436

Listening and Speaking

Speak in a tone that conveys the emotions of your character.

Drama

In a dramatization, people act out scenes from a story or play. A dramatization may show one or more events in the story.

Practice It! Work with your classmates to perform *Pushing Up the Sky*. Determine character assignments, memorize your lines, and choose an appropriate costume. Invite students from other classes to see your performance.

Tips

Listening ...

- Listen attentively.
- Listen for emotional clues.

Speaking ...

- Speak clearly, loudly, and at an appropriate pace.
- Use tone and emotion for characters' dialogue.

Teamwork ...

- Make suggestions to help improve the performance.
- Follow, restate, and give oral directions for staging the play.

437

Objectives

- Listen closely, ask questions about the topic he or she is talking about, and comment about the topic.
- Work with other students. Take part in discussions led by teachers and other students, and offer ideas that build on the ideas of others.

Oral Vocabulary

Let's Talk About

Investigating Nature

- Ask about what we can gain through investigating.

- Pose and answer questions about patterns in nature.

- Provide suggestions for what elements in nature we can learn more about through investigation.

READING STREET ONLINE
CONCEPT TALK VIDEO
www.ReadingStreet.com

438

Envision It! | Sounds to Know

giraffe

g

school

ch

cereal

c

lock

ck

kite

k

Phonics

Spellings of /j/, /s/, /k/

Words I Can Blend

g e r b i l

t w i c e

f l i c k e r

s c h o o l

c i t y

Sentences I Can Read

1. My pet gerbil has gotten loose twice.

2. The breeze made the candlelight flicker.

3. We attend the largest school in the city.

I Can Read!

My friend Chris and I were running on the track at school one nice day last spring. We had run around the track twice when Chris noticed a chrysalis on a big stick. I didn't even see it!

Chris is a science genius. She has a genuine interest in anything that has to do with science. Once she raced her pet mice through a maze to see how they learn.

Another time she stuck seeds in dirt to watch them grow. Like I said—she is a science genius.

You've learned

○ Spellings of /j/, /s/, /k/

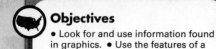

Objectives
• Look for and use information found in graphics. • Use the features of a text to guess what will happen next.

Skill

Strategy

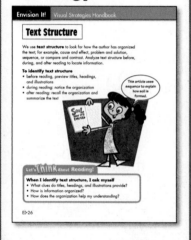

442

Comprehension Skill

🎯 Graphic Sources

- Graphic sources help you understand information that is in the text and give extra information.

- Maps, charts, illustrations, and captions make information easier to understand.

- Use what you learned about graphic sources and the chart below as you read "Patterns in the Sky." Then write a paragraph telling what you learned about constellations and how they were named.

Type of Graphic Source	What It Shows	How It Helps You Understand Information

Comprehension Strategy

🎯 Text Structure

Good readers look at the way information is organized, or structured, to help them understand what they read. Some selections are descriptions. Headings can help you know what is being described. Other structures are cause-and-effect, compare-and-contrast, and question-and-answer.

Patterns in the Sky

Constellations

Long ago, people looked up at the night sky and noticed patterns in the stars. They gave these patterns names, such as *Libra* and *Pisces*. Today we call these patterns *constellations*.

The Big Dipper

The Big Dipper is a star pattern that has inspired many stories. The seven stars of the Big Dipper are part of a constellation called *Ursa Major*. It is one of the most recognizable patterns in the sky. People have told stories about this group of stars for hundreds of years.

Other Names

Many of the names of the constellations come from old stories. *Hercules* is named after a brave hero from a Greek story. *Leo* is named for a lion with skin so strong that no weapon could harm it.

Where to Find Them

One reason that constellations were given names was for people to remember them. This helped people long ago understand how the movement of the Earth was connected to seasons.

Libra

Skill What does the photo show you that isn't in the text? Why is the caption needed?

Strategy Headings can help you figure out how the text is organized. What does this paragraph describe?

Seeing Stars

Your Turn!

⏸ **Need a Review?** See the *Envision It! Handbook* for help with graphic sources and text structure.

▶ **Ready to Try It?** As you read *Seeing Stars*, use what you've learned about graphic sources and text structure to understand the text.

Envision It! | Words to Know

ladle

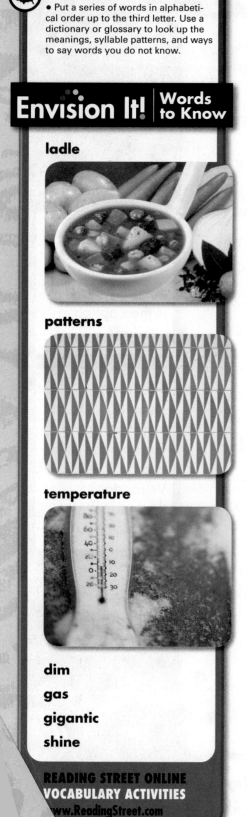

patterns

temperature

dim

gas

gigantic

shine

Vocabulary Strategy for

🎯 Unknown Words

Dictionary/Glossary When you read an unknown word, a glossary or an electronic dictionary can help you find out its meaning. A dictionary also gives you other information, such as the number of syllables, which syllables are stressed, parts of speech, history, and pronunciation of the word.

1. Look up the word in the glossary in the back of your book.

2. Use the pronunciation key, the syllable divisions, and stressed syllables to pronounce the word correctly.

3. Read the meanings for the word.

4. Choose the meaning that seems the best. Does it make sense in the sentence?

Read "A Letter from Far Away" on page 445. Use an electronic dictionary to find the meanings and pronunciations of the Words to Know.

Words to Write Reread "A Letter from Far Away." Write a letter to a friend about a real or an imaginary trip. Use words from the Words to Know list in your letter.

A Letter from Far Away

Dear Mom and Dad,

Grandpa and I are having a great time on our camping trip. We set up our tent right by the lake. I caught two fish today! The weather has been really hot. I hope the temperature goes down soon.

It's exciting to be so far away from the city. It is really dark here at night. I love the way the stars shine so brightly. These stars are nothing like the dim little dots we see in the city. Grandpa says that each star is a huge, gigantic ball of hot gas. That's amazing!

Grandpa and I like to look for patterns in the stars. Grandpa showed me some stars that form the shape of a ladle. I thought it looked more like a yo-yo than a big old spoon!

I'll mail this letter tomorrow, when we hike into town.

Love,
Darren

Your Turn!

❚❚ Need a Review? For additional help with unknown words, see *Words!*

▷ Ready to Try It? Read *Seeing Stars* on pp. 446–457.

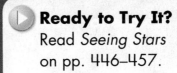

Seeing Stars

by Donna Latham

Question of the Week
**How can we learn about
nature by investigating?**

It's a perfect night for stargazing. Twinkling stars, more than you can count, dot the dark sky. They glow like fireflies. Stars, pinpoints of light, line up in patterns, or constellations.

Why do stars only come out at night? Do the stars look the same? Which one moves—a star or the Earth? How can you connect stars to draw pictures in the sky? Find out, as you take a close-up look at these far-off fireballs!

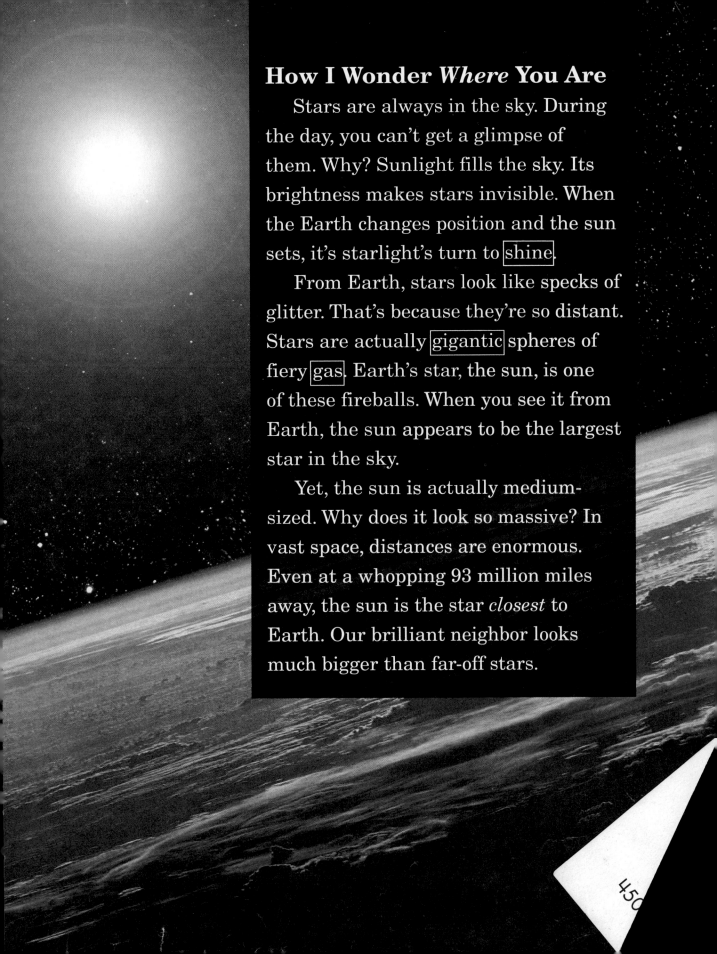

How I Wonder *Where* You Are

Stars are always in the sky. During the day, you can't get a glimpse of them. Why? Sunlight fills the sky. Its brightness makes stars invisible. When the Earth changes position and the sun sets, it's starlight's turn to shine.

From Earth, stars look like specks of glitter. That's because they're so distant. Stars are actually gigantic spheres of fiery gas. Earth's star, the sun, is one of these fireballs. When you see it from Earth, the sun appears to be the largest star in the sky.

Yet, the sun is actually medium-sized. Why does it look so massive? In vast space, distances are enormous. Even at a whopping 93 million miles away, the sun is the star *closest* to Earth. Our brilliant neighbor looks much bigger than far-off stars.

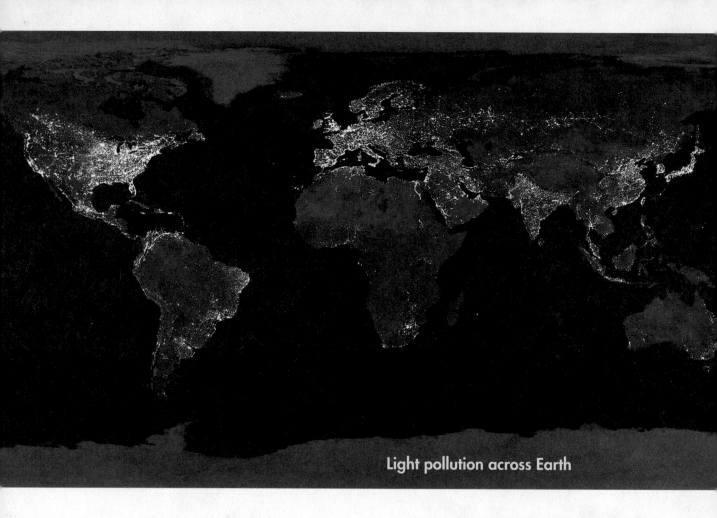

Light pollution across Earth

Do you live in a city or large suburb? There, stars appear super-far away. Why? You're probably familiar with water, air, and noise pollution. Have you ever heard of light pollution? This intense nighttime light makes twinklers tough to see. In urban areas, smog can also block your view of stars.

When you are away from the city, you can see several thousand stars—with your eyes alone. They're part of our galaxy, the Milky Way. These stars give the impression they're close. In the country, it feels as if you can reach up and touch them.

See Far!

Other stars are so far-flung you can't see them without help. A telescope is just what the astronomer ordered! The word *telescope* is made of two Greek roots, *tele* and *scope*. *Tele* means "far." *Scope* means "see." A telescope makes distant objects appear much closer. That's not all . . . with a telescope, you can gaze at *millions* of stars.

When you peek up, you see that some stars shine brightly. Others are dim. At first, they all look white, but they're actually blue, white, yellow, and red. We think of the sun as very hot, but it's yellow, and blue stars have the hottest temperature. Red stars have the coolest.

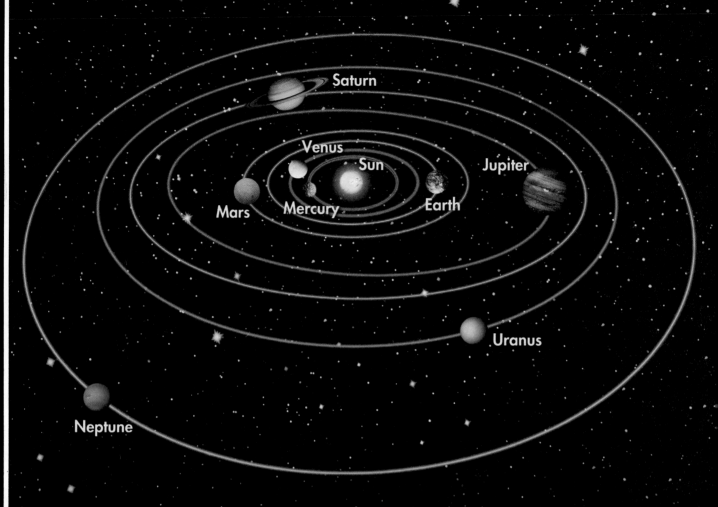

Moving Along

Have you ever noticed that stars appear to move?
You can track them with your eyes. Constellations drift
through the sky. From Earth, it looks like stars travel
around us. Yet, the opposite is true. The Earth moves.

You can't feel it, but right now you're riding a
huge merry-go-round. Earth spins through space as it
orbits the sun—and what goes around comes around!
Traveling at 1,000 miles per hour, it takes Earth
about 24 hours to spin completely. That makes the sky
change from day to night.

Connect the Stars

People have watched the stars for thousands of years. Stargazers in early times named constellations after animals, shapes, and characters from mythology. The stars have not changed locations since then. You can still gaze into the sky and connect stars to create the same shapes and patterns.

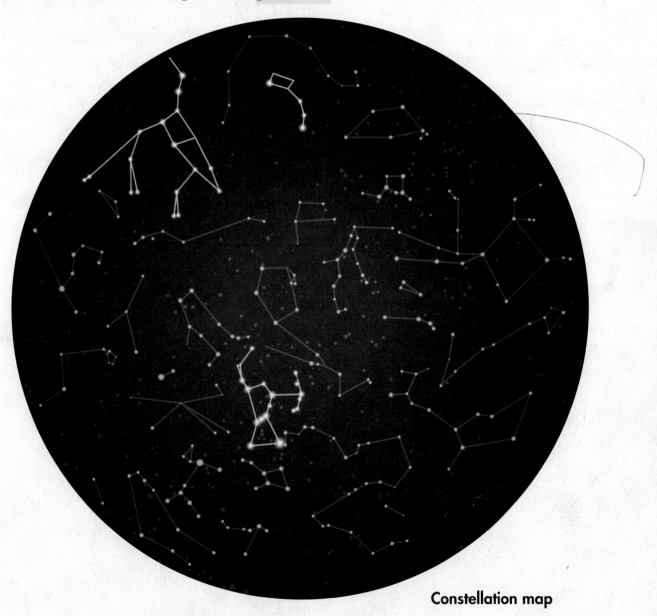

Constellation map

Hunt for Orion

People in different parts of the world can gaze at different constellations. Meet Orion, a gem of the Northern Hemisphere's winter sky, named after a boastful hunter from Greek mythology.

A sword swings from his belt, which is formed of three stars. He holds a starry shield. Orion has two of the sky's brightest stars. Betelgeuse, a gigantic red star, shines brilliantly at his shoulder. A scorching blue-white star called Rigel shines in Orion's left foot. Rigel is 50,000 times brighter than our sun!

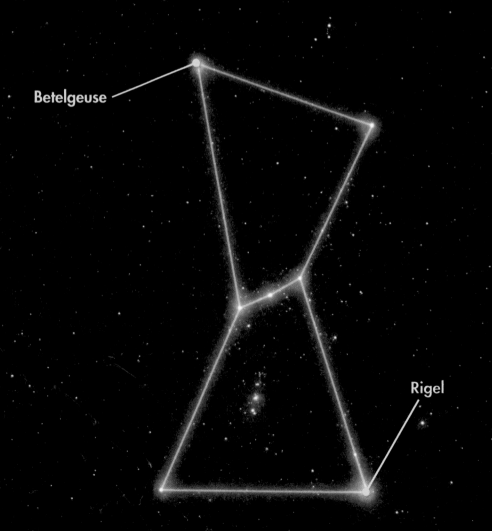

Betelgeuse

Rigel

Sirius, the Dog Star

Chase After Big Dog

Trotting after Orion is *Canis Major*, the Big Dog constellation. Big Dog has a head like a triangle and a perky tail. At its chest is blue-white Sirius, the Dog Star.

After the sun, Sirius is the brightest star we can see from Earth. That's because it's one of the stars closest to us even though it's nearly 6 trillion miles off! Its diameter is more than double the sun's.

In ancient times, people believed Sirius' bright light seared the Earth with summer heat. Today, the phrase "dog days of summer" describes the blistering period from July 3 to August 11. During this time, Sirius rises and sets with the sun.

Scoop Up the Big Dipper

The Big Dipper is a dazzler of the northern sky. It looks like a giant ladle. Connect the stars to see the Dipper's handle and bowl—but don't stop there! The Big Dipper is part of the *Ursa Major,* or Great Bear, constellation. The handle of the Dipper forms the bear's tail. The bowl is part of its body.

Because of Earth's movement, the Big Dipper's handle tips in different directions. The handle faces down in the winter. During the summer, it's up.

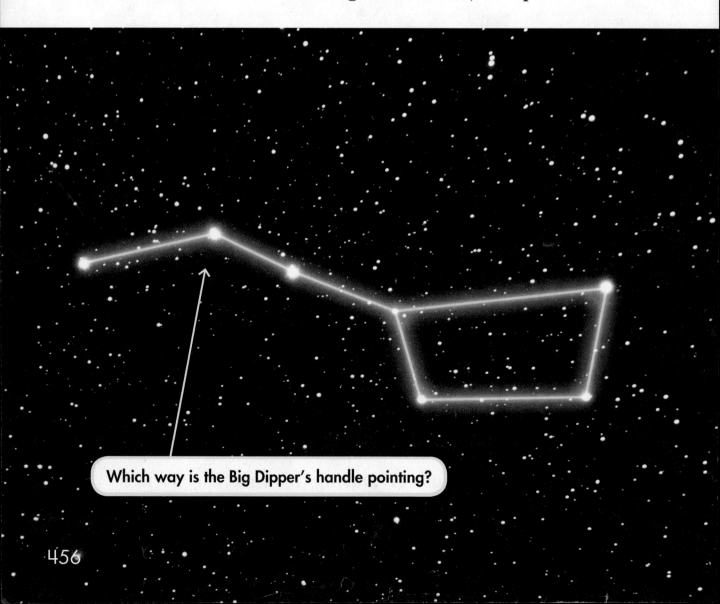

Which way is the Big Dipper's handle pointing?

So Vast It Needs a New Word to Describe It!

Oh, my stars, the universe is ginormous! It appears to sprawl forever. How many stars does it hold altogether? No one knows for sure. NASA believes there are zillions. Astronomers claim that to tally all the stars would be as hard as counting grains of sand on a beach. It could take eons . . .

For now, keep seeing stars!

Objectives
● Use the features of a text to guess what will happen next. ● Look for and use information found in graphics.

Envision It! Retell

Think Critically

1. On page 453, you learned that people have watched the stars for "thousands of years." What do we know about stars now that people did not know thousands of years ago? **Text to World**

2. This author uses photographs to show the stars. Look back and find a photograph of a constellation. Why did the author use lines on the photo?
Think Like an Author

3. How does the chart on page 452 show you that the Earth moves through the sky? **Graphic Sources**

4. The heading on page 451 is "See Far!" What did you learn about telescopes on this page? Do the italics help you to clarify information on this page?
Text Structure

5. Look back at page 454. Why do you see different constellations depending on where you live? Provide evidence to support your answer.

TEST PRACTICE **Extended Response**

Donna Latham

When she isn't connecting stars to make pictures in the sky, Donna Latham is writing. Her book *Fire Dogs* received the ASPCA Henry Bergh Children's Book Award. Ms. Latham can usually be found with her Lhasa Apso, Nikki, by her side. Her other books include *Ellen Ochoa: Reach for the Stars!* and *Hurricane! The 1900 Galveston Night of Terror.*

Reading Log

Use the Reader's and Writer's Notebook to record your independent reading.

Let's Write It!

Key Features of a Formal Letter

● has a polite tone

● has a specific purpose and audience

● includes the 5 parts of a letter

READING STREET ONLINE
GRAMMAR JAMMER
www.ReadingStreet.com

Formal Letter

A **formal letter,** sometimes called a business letter, is written to a specific person for a specific purpose.

Writing Prompt Think about something in nature that you would like to investigate. Now write a formal letter to a scientist asking the questions you would like to have answered.

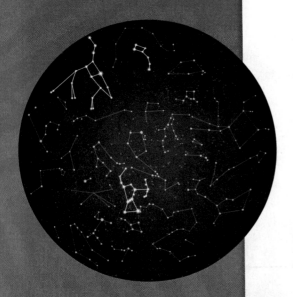

Writer's Checklist

Remember, you should . . .

☑ know your audience and purpose for writing.

☑ include all 5 parts of a letter.

☑ write in cursive using proper word spacing.

☑ capitalize official titles of people.

☑ make sure your sentences show subject-verb agreement.

March 8, 20___

Professor M. Duncan

University of California

Los Angeles, CA 90095

Dear Professor Duncan,

My **name is** Darnell Williams, and **I am** interested in stars. My teacher told me you are a scientist who studies astronomy, so I am writing to ask you some questions.

Which star is farthest away from Earth? Why do stars twinkle? How many stars are there? Do **you have** a telescope at home? I would also like to know how astronomy helps people.

Thank you for reading my letter. I hope you will write me back.

Sincerely,

Darnell Williams

Writing Trait Conventions Commas and capitalization are used correctly.

Genre A **formal letter** has a polite tone.

Subjects and **verbs** must agree in number.

Conventions

Subject and Verb Agreement

Remember A sentence with a singular **subject** should have a singular **verb**. A sentence with a plural subject should have a plural verb.

461

Objectives
● Identify and use fun word games.
● Describe different forms of poetry and how they create images in the reader's mind. ● Identify words that paint a picture in your mind and appeal to your senses.

Science in Reading

Genre
Poetry

● Poetry is a creative expression of language that usually uses rhyme, rhythm, and imagery.

● Some poems are riddles that require the reader to guess what the poem is describing.

● Riddles are playful uses of language that use different or unusual meanings of words and phrases to provide clues and create images.

● As you read "Scien-Trickery," try and guess who or what in science the riddles are about.

SCIEN-TRICKERY
Riddles in Science

by J. Patrick Lewis
illustrated by Frank Remkiewicz

Revealing Ceiling

When we go into hiding,
Most nights are unexciting,
But that will change providing
You let us entertain.

Delighting you, igniting
Way up here by highlighting!
We thank you for inviting
Us through your windowpane.

ANSWER: Stars, starlight, or constellations

Stars are actually hot spheres of gas, and they shine because of the energy produced by chemical reactions. In the night sky you can see several dozens of stars, but the universe contains trillions of them.

POLARIS

URSA MINOR

URSA MAJOR

Let's Think About...

Locate examples of playful uses of language in the riddle. What makes it playful? **Poetry**

463

Gee!

It keeps you from flying
Off into space.
It's what makes you fall
Flat on your face.
And if it could talk
Like you and I do,
I think it would say,
"I'm pulling for you."

ANSWER: Gravity

Gravity is simply the force that draws bodies toward the earth.

Go, Moon, Glow!

"I'll hide my face!" says Moon, says she,
"Sun will think I'm gone."
"Now where is Moon," says Sun, says he,
"to shine my light upon?"

Several minutes then go by . . .
How soon will Moon appear?
Says Moon, "How I enjoy this dark
Celestial atmosphere!"

It's all because the earth has flown
Between the moon and sun.
But wait a second! There's a slice
Of Moon for everyone.

ANSWER: Lunar eclipse

Let's **Think** About...

Compare the three riddles in this selection. Describe how they are different and how they are the same. **Poetry**

Let's **Think** About...

Reading Across Texts *Seeing Stars* was written to give the reader information. What is the purpose of the "Scien-Trickery" riddles?

Writing Across Texts Use what you have learned to write your own riddle about science.

When the earth blocks the sun's light to the moon, there is a lunar eclipse. When the moon blocks the sun's light to the earth, there is a solar eclipse. Lunar eclipses are more common but can only occur when the moon is full.

Let's Learn It!

Vocabulary

Unknown Words

Dictionary/Glossary You may come to a word you don't know when you are reading. Use a dictionary or glossary to find the meaning of the word. You can also find out how to pronounce the word by using the pronunciation key and looking at each syllable.

Practice It! Choose two or three glossary words and copy the pronunciations shown in parentheses. Exchange pronunciations with a partner and use the pronunciation key to identify each other's words.

Fluency

Appropriate Phrasing

When you are reading, pause slightly after reading a group of words that go together. This will make your reading flow.

Practice It! Read aloud *Seeing Stars*, page 448. How should you use phrasing to make your reading flow and the information sound more interesting?

Listening and Speaking

Speak clearly and include all important information.

Voice mail

When you leave a voice mail message, remember to speak clearly and include all important information for your listeners.

Practice It! Listen to oral directions about how to leave a voice mail for a friend. Restate the directions to make sure you understand them, tell the directions to your partner, and then follow the directions.

Tips

Listening ...

- Determine your purpose for listening.
- Restate oral directions.

Speaking ...

- Use appropriate pace and volume.
- Give clear oral directions.
- Use subject-verb agreement.

Teamwork ...

- Follow the oral directions for leaving a voice mail.

Oral Vocabulary

Let's Talk About

Helping Animals

● Share ideas about how people help animals.

● Make and listen to pertinent comments about ways to rescue animals.

● Ask what people can learn from studying and helping animals.

READING STREET ONLINE
CONCEPT TALK VIDEO
www.ReadingStreet.com

You've learned
1 2 7
Amazing Words
so far this year!

Objectives
● Read aloud words that begin with common prefixes and end with common suffixes. ● Read aloud words with common spelling patterns.

Envision It! Sounds to Know

adorable

suffix -able

toothless

suffix -less

cheerful

suffix -ful

convertible

suffix -ible

kindness

suffix -ness

loudly

suffix -ly

Phonics

Suffixes -ly, -ful, -ness, -less, -able, -ible

Words I Can Blend

patiently

usable

fondness

cheerful

responsible

countless

Sentences I Can Read

1. If you wait patiently, I'll find a camera that's usable.

2. My family has a fondness for our cheerful puppy.

3. The team's coach was responsible for countless victories.

I Can Read!

Things that are responsible for bringing the most happiness are invisible. The goodness of family and friends is capable of giving us countless reasons to be thankful.

Sometimes we suffer from illness or sadness. The cheerful visit of a close friend can quickly help us to feel hopeful again. Nearly everyone feels comfortable and forgets their shyness around those who know them best.

Take the time to show others how grateful you are for these incredible blessings.

You've learned

- Suffixes -ly, -ful, -ness, -less, -able, -ible

Objectives
● Describe how characters relate to each other and the changes that happen to them. ●Tell in order the main events of a story. Explain how they will affect future events in a story.

Envision It! | Skill Strategy

Skill

Strategy

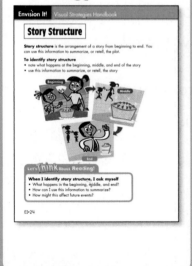

Comprehension Skill

Generalize

- When you read about how several things are alike in some way, you can make a general statement about them.

- Clue words such as *most, many, all,* or *few* signal generalizations.

- Use what you learned about generalizing and the graphic organizer below as you read "Songbirds of the Sea." What generalization can you make from the story?

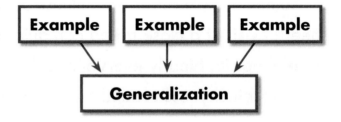

Comprehension Strategy

Story Structure

As you read, think about the events that happen at the beginning, middle, and end of the story, including how earlier events might influence the end and how a character might change. Using the structure of a story can help you retell the story in your own words and improve your comprehension.

Songbirds of the Sea

Dad always wanted to see beluga whales in the wild. I wasn't very excited about going to Canada for our vacation. "Sam, I think you might enjoy learning about the songbirds of the sea," Dad said.

"Songbirds? I thought whales lived in the water," I said.

"Many people call beluga whales songbirds because they are always making beautiful sounds," Dad said. "That's how they communicate and find food."

So, we traveled by boat on the Churchill River in late July. This river has the most beluga whales in the world.

After an hour on the boat, we spotted a pod of twenty belugas. It was incredible! They were huge. Everyone was really excited. This was more fun than I thought it would be. In fact, I would say it was the most fun I ever had on vacation! I guess learning can be fun.

Skill What clue words in this sentence signal a generalization?

Skill What generalization does the author make in this paragraph?

Strategy How do Sam's feelings change from the beginning to the end of the story?

Your Turn!

⏸ **Need a Review?** See the *Envision It! Handbook* for help with generalizing and story structure.

▶ **Ready to Try It?** As you read *A Symphony of Whales*, use what you've learned about generalizing and story structure to understand the story.

Envision It! | Words to Know

bay

blizzards

surrounded

anxiously	melody
channel	supplies
chipped	symphony

Vocabulary Strategy for

⊙ Unfamiliar Words

Context Clues Sometimes when you are reading, you come across an unfamiliar word. How can you figure out what the word means? Look for context clues. Context clues are in the words and sentences around the word. They can help you figure out the meaning of the word.

1. Read the words and sentences around the word you don't know. Sometimes the author tells you what the word means.

2. If not, use the words and sentences to predict a meaning for the word.

3. Then try that meaning in the sentence. Does it make sense?

Read "Breaking the Ice" on page 475. Use context clues to help you understand the meanings of the Words to Know and other unfamiliar words.

Words to Write Look at the pictures in *A Symphony of Whales*. Choose a picture to write about. Use words from the Words to Know list in your description.

Breaking the Ice

Josh is a sailor on a Canadian icebreaker. An icebreaker is a ship with a heavy steel bow, or front, that it uses to break through ice. Sometimes a ship, surrounded on all sides by ice, becomes trapped and can't move. The icebreaker cuts a channel through the ice so that the ship can sail to safety.

Josh likes helping people. One winter, a waterfront village on a bay in the far north had been buried by blizzards. The people were running out of food and other supplies. No one could get to the village over land, so the villagers called the icebreaker for help.

The ship had to cut a path through the ice on the bay. The people were nervous and watched the ship anxiously. They chipped away the ice around the dock so that the ship could get close enough to unload the supplies. As the ship sailed away, the villagers began to sing a song. Josh did not know the melody, or tune, but he enjoyed the symphony of voices saying thank you.

Your Turn!

⏸ **Need a Review?** For additional help with unfamiliar words, see *Words!*

▶ **Ready to Try It?** Read *A Symphony of Whales* on pp. 476–491.

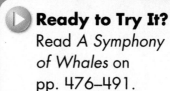

A Symphony of

Whales

by Steve Schuch
illustrated by Wendell Minor

Fiction sometimes tells a story based on events that really did happen. Look for parts you think are true.

Question of the Week
**How can people help
animals in danger?**

From the earliest time she could remember, Glashka had heard music inside her head. During the long, dark winters, blizzards sometimes lasted for days. Then her family stayed indoors, close to the small fire. Glashka heard the songs calling to her out of the darkness, beyond even the voice of the wind.

The old ones of her village said, "That is the voice of Narna, the whale. Long has she been a friend to our people. She was a friend of our grandparents' grandparents; she was a friend before we saw the boats of strange men from other lands. But it is long now

since one of us has heard her. It is a great gift you have."
And Glashka would fall asleep, wrapped in her sealskin
blanket, remembering their words.

The sea gave life to Glashka's village. The seals gave
meat and warm furs to protect against the winter cold. In
summer the people caught salmon and other fish, then
salted them to keep for the hard times to come. And from
Narna, the whale, the people received food for themselves
and their sled dogs, waterproof skins for their parkas and
boots, and oil for their lamps in the long winter darkness.

One year the snows came early. For three days a
blizzard bore down on the village. When it finally stopped,
Glashka's family needed supplies from the next village.
Glashka asked if she might help drive the sled dogs. "It is
not so easy to drive the sled," her parents said. "The dogs
will know if you are uncertain of the way. But you will
know the way home. Perhaps on the way back, you may
try. Now go to sleep."

That night in her dreams, Glashka drove the dogsled. But the dogs did not follow her commands. Instead they led her to open water surrounded by ice. Glashka heard the singing of Narna, louder than she had ever heard it before. She awoke in the darkness of her sealskins, wondering what the dream had meant.

The morning was clear and cold as the family set out. The dogs made good time to the neighboring village. Before starting back, Glashka's parents packed the supplies into the sled. Glashka checked the dogs' feet for cuts. She rubbed their ears and necks. Glashka's parents gave her the reins. "We'll follow behind you. If your heart

and words are clear, the dogs will listen and take you where you wish to go."

They set off. Across the ice, snow swirled as the wind began to pick up. Suddenly the sled dogs broke from the trail, yelping and twitching their ears. "What is it?" Glashka's parents shouted.

"I think they hear something," Glashka called back.

The sled dogs pulled harder. Their keen ears could pick up high-pitched notes that most humans couldn't hear. But Glashka, if she turned just right, could make out the eerie moans and whistles that grew louder until even her parents could hear them.

The dogs stopped short. They were right at the edge of a great bay of open water, surrounded on all sides by ice and snow.

Everywhere Glashka looked, the water seemed to be heaving and boiling, choked with white whales. Her father came up beside her. "Beluga whales," he said softly.

Glashka stared. "There must be more than a thousand of them."

The cries of the whales rose and fell on the wind as they swam slowly about. The dogs whined and pawed anxiously at the ice. "Let's hurry to the village," cried Glashka. "We'll get help!"

Glashka's father, though, knew there was no help. "They must have been trapped when they came here last fall looking for food," he said quietly. "There's nothing we can do to free them. When the last of the water freezes over, the whales will die."

But Glashka's mother remembered that an icebreaker, several winters ago, had rescued a Russian freighter trapped in the sea ice. "Could we call on the emergency radio? Maybe an icebreaker can clear a channel for the whales," she said.

Glashka and her parents raced back to their village. They gathered everyone together and told them what had happened. Glashka's father got on the emergency radio and put out a distress call. "Beluga whales, maybe thousands of them, trapped. We need an icebreaker. Can anyone hear me?"

Far out at sea, a great Russian icebreaker named the *Moskva* picked up the faint signal. "We read you," the captain radioed back. "We're on our way, but it may take us several weeks to reach you. Can you keep the whales alive until then?"

Some of the people from Glashka's village started setting up a base camp near the whales. Others set out by dogsled to alert the surrounding settlements.

Everyone came—young and old, parents, grandparents, and children. Day after day they chipped back the edges of the ice, trying to make more room for the whales to come up to breathe. "Look," said Glashka's grandmother. "See how the whales are taking turns, how they give the younger ones extra time for air."

483

As Glashka took her turn chipping back the ice, the song of Narna filled her ears again. She sang to the whales while she worked, trying to let them know help was on the way. Each day, Glashka looked anxiously for a ship. But each day, a little more water turned to ice. Each day, the whales got weaker from hunger.

Glashka knew how it felt to be hungry. The year before, her village had caught barely enough fish to make it through to spring. Sometimes the memory still gnawed at her. Even so, she gave the whales part of the fish from her lunch. The other villagers noticed and began to feed some of their own winter fish to the whales too.

One morning Glashka awoke to the sounds of excited voices and barking dogs. The icebreaker had broken through the main channel during the night. "Hurry,

Glashka," her parents called. Glashka pulled on her boots and parka and ran down the path to the water.

Everyone was gathered. Off to one side, the old ones stood, watching. They beckoned Glashka to join them. "Now," they said, "let us see what the whales will do."

The whales crowded together in fear, keeping as far from the icebreaker as possible. On board the ship, the captain gave orders. He hoped the whales would see the pathway cleared through the ice and follow the ship to safety. The icebreaker slowly turned around and faced back out to sea.

But the whales wouldn't follow the ship. "They may be afraid of the noise of our engines," the captain radioed to shore. "I've heard that trapped whales will sometimes follow the singing of other whales. We'll try playing a recording of whale songs."

Glashka felt a shiver down her back. "Narna's songs," she whispered to the sled dogs. "They're going to play Narna's songs."

485

Then the songs of the whales echoed over the water—deep moans and high whistling calls, ancient sounds from another world.

But the whales would not go near the ship. Again and again, the captain inched the giant icebreaker closer to the whales, then back toward the sea. But the whales stayed as far away as they could.

"It's no use," the captain radioed in despair. "And we can't stay beyond tomorrow. Already the channel is starting to refreeze!"

Glashka was near tears as she asked the old ones what could be done now. "Wait," they said. "Let us see what tomorrow brings."

That night the song of Narna came to Glashka again. Only this time it was different. She heard the music and voices of whales, but she heard other music too . . . melodies she'd never before. . . . While it was still dark, Glashka woke her parents. "I've heard Narna again," she said. "And I've heard other music too!"

"You have to tell the old ones," Glashka's parents said.

The old ones of the village listened carefully as Glashka told them what she had heard. "So, it is other music Narna is asking for," they said thoughtfully. "Long is the time, but once, it is said, humans and whales made music together. Perhaps the time has come again. Let us speak with the captain!"

487

Quickly Glashka and the old ones radioed the ship. "Have you any other music, people music, to play for the whales?" they asked. The captain said he would see what his crew could find.

First, they tried playing rock and roll. The electric guitars and drums boomed, but the whales would not follow the ship.

Next, the crew tried Russian folk music. It was softer, with many voices singing together. The whales swam a little closer, but still they would not follow the ship.

On shore, Glashka ran back to the radio transmitter. She had to talk with the captain. "I *know* there's other music that will work. Please keep trying!" she told him.

The crew found some classical music. First the sweet sounds of violins and violas, next the deeper notes of the cellos and, deepest of all, the string basses . . . and way up high, a solo violin. . . .

Everyone fell silent as the melody carried over the water. The whales grew quiet, too, listening.

489

A few whales started to sing back to the ship and to each other. Gradually more whales joined in.

Then . . . they began to swim toward the ship!

Cautiously the captain started the huge engines and headed slowly out to sea. One whale followed, then another, then a few more. Soon all the whales were following the ship through the narrow channel, past the broken chunks of ice, back to the safety of the open ocean.

On shore, people laughed and cried and hugged each other. The sled dogs jumped up and barked, trying to lick the noses and faces of anyone they could reach. Glashka buried her wet face in the fur of the dogs' necks. "Such good, good dogs," she told them over and over. "Such good dogs. Now the whales are going home!"

On board the ship, the captain and his crew raised every flag. The music played as the captain radioed to say the whales were safe. He and his crew were finally going home too.

Glashka and her family looked out to sea. They waved to the icebreaker and the disappearing whales. "And do you hear Narna singing now?" her grandmother asked.

"Yes," Glashka said, "but it isn't just Narna I hear now. It's something bigger than that . . . something like a whole symphony of whales!"

491

Envision It! | Retell

READING STREET ONLINE
STORY SORT
www.ReadingStreet.com

Think Critically

1. In the story, Glashka and her village worked together to save the whales. Think of a time you worked as part of a team. What did you do? What was the outcome? **Text to Self**

2. The author begins his story with Glashka hearing music inside her head. How does the beginning get you ready for the rest of the story? **Think Like an Author**

3. Think about the lives of the villagers and the lives of the whales. What does that say about how people and nature are connected? **Generalize**

4. Think about the beginning, middle, and end of the story. Using story structure, retell it in your own words. **Story Structure**

5. **Look Back and Write** The old ones talk about "other music." What is the "other music," and why is it important? Use story details to support your answer.

TEST PRACTICE | **Extended Response**

492

Meet the Author and the Illustrator

Steve Schuch and Wendell Minor

Read more books illustrated by Wendell Minor.

Steve Schuch first became interested in whales when a scientist who was also a musician came to his college. The musician played his cello along with recordings of whale songs. "That evening forever changed how I heard music and thought about whales," says Mr. Schuch.

Before writing *A Symphony of Whales*, Mr. Schuch composed music by playing his violin over real whale sounds. The music is called "Whale Trilogy."

Fire Storm by Jean Craighead George

Wendell Minor travels all over the world to research his books. When working with Jean Craighead George on *Snow Bear and Arctic Son*, he went to Barrow, Alaska. Barrow is near the Arctic Circle. His experiences helped him to paint the pictures for *A Symphony of Whales*.

Rachel: The Story of Rachel Carson by Amy Ehrlich

Mr. Minor loves the outdoors. He says, "What gives me satisfaction is bringing the world of nature to children."

Reading Log

Use the Reader's and Writer's Notebook to record your independent reading.

Objectives
• Establish a main idea in a topic sentence. • Include sentences that support your ideas with simple facts, details, and explanations. • Write essays that have a clear ending.

Let's Write It!

Key Features of a News Article

- begins with a headline
- describes a current event
- includes all important information about the event

READING STREET ONLINE
GRAMMAR JAMMER
www.ReadingStreet.com

News Article

A **news article** is a nonfiction retelling of a real-life event. The student model on the next page is an example of a news article.

Writing Prompt Think about an event that took place in your town or neighborhood. Now write a news article about it that answers the 5 Ws (Who, What, Where, When, Why) and How. Make sure you give your article a headline.

Writer's Checklist

Remember, you should . . .

☑ establish a central idea, and use facts, details, and explanations to support that idea.

☑ answer the questions who, what, when, where, why, and how.

☑ end with a concluding statement.

☑ use verbs correctly.

Hollywood Comes to Cherrydale

Last week, something unusual **happened** in Cherrydale. A Hollywood crew **came** to shoot Town Square, a movie about a small town in the 1800s. They **thought** the buildings on Main Street **had** just the right old-fashioned look.

The movie **takes** place in winter, so the snowy street **was** perfect. About 100 local men, women, and children **performed** as extras. They **dressed** in 19th-century costumes and **walked** or **rode** horses up and down Main Street. Are you excited about seeing Cherrydale 100 years ago? Then **go** see the movie next summer.

Genre A **news article** includes the who, what, when, where, why, and how.

Past, present, and future verb tenses are used correctly.

Writing Trait Sentences are clear and to the point.

Conventions

Verb Tenses

Remember **Present tense** tells about an action that is happening now. **Past tense** tells about an action that has already happened. **Future tense** tells about an action that will happen in the future.

495

Science in Reading

Genre
Magazine Article

● Magazine articles give details and facts that support the main idea about a topic and use many illustrations.

● Ideas in illustrations, titles, and topic sentences help readers make and confirm predictions.

● The text features help readers predict, locate, and verify information, and graphic sources show information visually.

● Use ideas and text features to predict what "He Listens to Whales" will be about. Find details and facts to verify your predictions as you read.

He Listens to Whales

from *Ranger Rick*

by E. Shan Correa

Joe Mobley, marine biologist

Humpback whales chatter and call to each other—and they sing songs for hours. What does all this humpback "hollering" mean? Here's one scientist who's trying to find out.

Joe Mobley lives near the island of Maui in Hawaii. (*Maui* rhymes with "*zowie*.") It's the perfect place for a scientist who studies how humpback whales behave. The whales hang out near Maui all winter long.

Joe has lots of questions about these huge mammals. How do they know where to go when they travel through the ocean? How do they find each other? How do groups stay together? Joe thinks clues to these mysteries are held in the sounds that these whales make. To collect clues, he listens to the humpbacks.

Let's  About...

Read the title and introduction. What do you predict the topic and main idea will be? Verify your predictions as you read. **Magazine Article**

497

Whale Chatter

"Humpbacks make three main types of sounds," Joe explains. "Both the males and the females call loudly when they're hungry or eating. Males 'talk' when they're hanging out in groups. And males sing during mating time."

Joe first heard the whales' feeding calls from a tape that another scientist had made. The whales were feeding in their summer home off the coast of Alaska. All were scooping up small fish and shrimp-like krill with their enormous mouths. And they seemed to call to each other while they ate. "You can imagine how noisy they were!" Joe says with a laugh. "They eat all the time during the summer," he continues, "but they almost never eat during the winter."

To listen to whales in winter, Joe doesn't have to go far. He just heads to their winter home in the ocean around Maui. That's when he hears the second kind of whale sound, which he calls "talking."

This scientist is listening for whale calls.

Let's Think About...

Read the first sentence. What do you predict will be explained? Verify your predictions as you keep reading.
Magazine Article

Let's Think About...

Look at the photos and captions. How do scientists hear the whale sounds?
Magazine Article

These scientists are recording humpback whale songs.

Joe explains what the sounds may mean: "Whales hang out in groups called *pods*. While they're in pods, the male whales make strange clicks, creaks, roars, and whines. Some of them seem to be signaling to females, as if they were saying, 'Hey, I'm over here!' Or they might be saying to other males, 'This is my mate, so stay away.' So far, no one has heard females or young whales 'talking' in this way."

Long Songs

Whale songs are the third kind of sound that Joe studies. You may have heard them on records. Some parts of a whale's song sound sad, like children crying. Some parts are high squeaks. And some rumble like thunder.

"These songs are beautiful, but *loud*!" Joe says. "They're much louder than any other animal sound, louder even than rock music. Our boat shakes when a singing whale is close by."

A humpback's song has parts that are repeated over and over. One song can last 30 minutes. Then the whale might repeat the whole song. Sometimes a humpback sings for more than 20 hours without stopping!

Let's Think About...

What are pods? How did the author make it easy to locate the answer? **Magazine Article**

Let's Think About...

Reading Across Texts *A Symphony of Whales* and "He Listens to Whales" both are about whales. How are the ideas in these selections alike? Support your answer with evidence from the texts.

Writing Across Texts Create a Venn diagram to compare and contrast the two selections.

Objectives

• Speak clearly and to the point while making eye contact, changing how fast, loud, and clearly you speak to communicate your ideas. • Listen closely when someone speaks, ask questions about the topic he or she is talking about, and comment about the topic. • Use context clues to figure out words you don't know or words that have more than one meaning.

Let's Learn It!

READING STREET ONLINE
ONLINE STUDENT EDITION
www.ReadingStreet.com

Vocabulary

Unfamiliar Words

Context Clues Use context clues to find the meanings of unfamiliar words while you are reading. The words or sentences around the unfamiliar word may provide clues to its meaning.

Practice It! Select three Words to Know words. Read *A Symphony of Whales*. Use context clues to determine the meaning of each word. Write the meaning of each word as it is used in the story. Record the words or phrases you used as context clues.

Fluency

Rate

The rate at which you read a selection can depend on your background knowledge and interest in the subject. The more familiar you are with the subject and the more you like it, the more likely you will be able to read the text at an appropriate rate with good comprehension.

Practice It! With a partner, practice reading aloud page 490. Did your rate slow down at certain parts? Read it a second time with your partner. Did your rate improve?

500

Listening and Speaking

Description

When giving a description, include as many sensory details—how it looks, feels, sounds, smells, and tastes—as possible. Try to create a picture or image in your listeners' minds.

Practice It! Work with a partner to use information from the textbook and other research to describe how whales look, sound, and feel. Read your description aloud to the class.

Tips

Listening ...

- Listen attentively and respond with questions and comments.

- Picture in your mind what is being described.

Speaking ...

- Determine your purpose for speaking.

- Speak at an appropriate pace and loudly enough to be heard.

- Use past, present, and future tense verbs correctly.

Teamwork ...

- Give suggestions that build on each other's ideas.

Objectives
● Ask questions about the topic and comment about the topic. ● Take part in discussions led by teachers and other students, and offer ideas that build on the ideas of others.

Let's Talk About

Observing Nature

● Share ideas about how people observe nature.

● Ask what we can observe in different environments.

● Share comments about the importance of observing nature.

READING STREET ONLINE
CONCEPT TALK VIDEO
www.ReadingStreet.com

503

Objectives
● Decode words with two consonants that make one sound.

Envision It! | **Sounds to Know**

knight

kn

sign

STOP

wrench

gn

wr

whistle

comb

st

mb

Phonics

Consonant Patterns
wr, kn, gn, st, mb

Words I Can Blend

knew
wrinkle
crumbs
whistle
gnawing

Sentences I Can Read

1. Kayla knew her shirt would wrinkle in the rain.

2. The ducks ate bread crumbs in the park.

3. Whistle for the puppy gnawing on the bone.

I Can Read!

Yesterday I was outside when I heard something rustling in a bunch of thistles. I bent down on one knee and peered in. Nestled in the midst of a small wreath of brush was a tiny wren.

The bird hopped onto my thumb and began to speak. "Many birds have a gnawing hunger. Please give us bread crumbs and seeds to right this wrong."

Birds don't talk! A gnat could have knocked me over! I built a feeder to feed that wren and all of its friends.

You've learned

Consonant Patterns
wr, kn, gn, st, mb

READI
ENVISI
www.Re

Objectives

• Identify the cause and effect relationships among ideas in the text. • Set a purpose for reading a text based on what you hope to get from the text.

Envision It! | Skill Strategy

Skill

Strategy

Comprehension Skill

◎ Cause and Effect

• A cause tells why something happened.

• An effect is what happened.

• Words such as *because* and *so* are clues that can help you figure out a cause and its effects.

• Use what you learned about cause and effect and the graphic organizer below as you read "Winter Blooms." Then write a paragraph that explains why you have to keep plants indoors to grow in the winter.

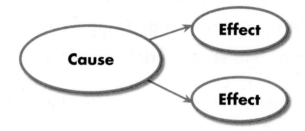

Comprehension Strategy

◎ Predict and Set Purpose

When you read, it is important to think about why you are reading. Ask yourself what it is you want to find out. Make predictions about what you think will happen. Stop and check to see if your predictions are correct.

Winter Blooms

Have you ever wanted to grow plants in the winter? During winter months, the Earth tilts away from sun, so there is less sunlight and less heat. Plants need sunlight in order to grow.

But wait! You can still grow plants inside, even during the coldest days of the year. Place your plants in front of a window that faces south or west because they will get more direct light. You can tell if a plant is not getting enough light by how it grows. If a plant leans toward a window, it wants more sunlight!

Plants are like people. They also need water. If the leaves on your plants begin to shrivel up or fall off, it is because you aren't giving them enough water. But be careful, you can also over water plants.

If you learn the secrets to growing indoor plants, you too can have winter blooms.

Skill Which clue word in this paragraph shows a cause-and-effect relationship?

Skill What is the cause of a plant that leans toward a window?

Strategy Predict what reasons the author will give to explain why plants are like people.

AROUND ONE CACTUS

Your Turn!

⏸ **Need a Review?** See the *Envision It! Handbook* for help with cause and effect and predicting and setting a purpose.

▶ **Ready to Try It?** As you read *Around One Cactus,* use what you've learned about cause and effect and predicting and setting a purpose to understand the text.

507

Vocabulary Strategy for

Prefixes and Suffixes

Word Structure When you see a word you don't know, look closely at it. Does it have a prefix at the beginning or a suffix at the end? The prefix *un-* makes a word mean "not _____" or "the opposite of _____." For example, *unhappy* means "not happy." The suffix *-ing* tells that the verb is an ongoing action, such as *running,* or turns a verb into an adjective, as in *"running* shoes."

1. Does a word you don't know have a prefix or a suffix? If so, put your finger on it.

2. Look at the base word. Do you know what the base word means?

3. Now use the prefix or suffix to figure out the meaning of the whole word.

4. Try your meaning in the sentence. Does it make sense?

Read "A Trip to Death Valley" on page 509. Look for words with prefixes or suffixes, and use them to figure out the meanings of the words.

Words to Write Reread "A Trip to Death Valley." Write a short paragraph about life in the desert. Use words with prefixes and suffixes and from the Words to Know list.

A Trip to Death Valley

Have you ever been to the desert? It is an incredible place. Some people like to go hiking in Death Valley National Park in the spring. Before they go, they need to know how to be survivors in this noble, waterless land.

Hikers need to make sure they have plenty of water. They should wear cool, loose fitting clothing. Good hiking boots are a must.

It is probably best to go with a guide. The guide will know all about the topic of desert life. Park rangers take tour groups to see some wonderful desert sights.

Desert travelers will want to search for unseen animals among the Joshua trees and sand dunes. Will they see a stinging scorpion? There may be a coyote or a bobcat nearby. There are some man-made sights too. A lofty thermometer sits 135 feet high near the desert town of Baker, California!

If you decide to go on a desert adventure, don't go unprepared! You will see a very special place.

Your Turn!

⏸ **Need a Review?** For additional help with prefixes and suffixes, see *Words!*

▶ **Ready to Try It?** Read *Around One Cactus* on pp. 510–527.

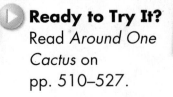

AROUND ONE CACTUS

Owls, Bats and Leaping Rats

by Anthony D. Fredericks
illustrated by Jennifer DiRubbio

Genre

Narrative nonfiction tells about real things using elements of stories. As you read, think about how the facts have been arranged.

511

Dear Two-Legged Adventurer,

Welcome to my hot and rocky home! You may think that this place is lifeless and dull, but it's not. In fact, the more you learn about the desert the more amazing it becomes. I think the desert is a topic you can really sink your teeth into. Get it?

The desert is filled with amazing creatures and incredible plants. Some of us are friends, some of us aren't. But that's OK, because we have all learned to adapt to our special environment. That means that we can survive and reproduce. It also means that there are many kinds of neighbors who like to live in the same place. Some neighbors may be dangerous, like me. And some, like the bat, may spend the whole night sticking its face into flowers. We're all special.

Many of us live in and around the saguaro cactus— it's really a sharp place to be! Some live high above in lofty apartments. Others hide between rocks on the ground. And a few live underground where it's cool.

I hope you enjoy visiting our unique home. We're an unusual band of neighbors—some fly, some slither, some hop and a few even dance in the moonlight. Look around, but be careful where you walk!

Warm regards,

W. D.

(Western Diamondback Rattlesnake)

This is the desert, wild and free,
A place of sun-baked majesty,
With shifting dunes and rocky edges
And bushes gripping ancient ledges.
Here stands a cactus, tall and grand,
A haven for creatures in
a waterless land.

This is the cactus.

513

The prickly cactus with arms raised high
Was watched by a boy with a curious eye.
"Who could be living on this arid ground?"
He asked as the breeze tumbled all around.

514

He observed the giant in the fading light,
But the critters were resting far from sight.
So he turned and slowly walked away.
Then the creatures woke to play and prey.

515

A leaping rat builds a cozy nest
(A sheltered place for her young to rest)
Beside the cactus tall and grand,
A haven for creatures in a waterless land.

A tiny owl with perfect sight,
Who sleeps by day and hunts by night,
Lives high above her neighbor's nest
(A special place for young to rest)
Beside the cactus tall and grand,
A haven for creatures in a waterless land.

A long-nose bat flies to this tower
And spreads the pollen from flower
to flower,
Above the owl with perfect sight,
Who sleeps by day and hunts by night,
Who lives above her neighbor's nest
(A special place for young to rest)
Beside the cactus tall and grand,
A haven for creatures in a waterless land.

A rattlesnake with deadly teeth
Slip-slides across the ground beneath
The long-nose bat upon the tower,
Who spreads the pollen from flower to flower,
Above the owl with perfect sight,
Who sleeps by day and hunts by night,
Who lives above her neighbor's nest
(A special place for young to rest)
Beside the cactus tall and grand,
A haven for creatures in a waterless land.

Some scorpions with stinging tails
Dance along on unseen trails,
Past rattlesnakes with deadly teeth
Slip-sliding on the ground beneath
The long-nose bat upon the tower,
Who spreads the pollen from flower to flower,
Above the owl with perfect sight,
Who sleeps by day and hunts by night,
Who lives above her neighbor's nest
(A special place for young to rest)
Beside the cactus tall and grand,
A haven for creatures in a waterless land.

A den of foxes starts to stir.
They clean and groom their light brown fur,
While eyeing scorpions with stinging tails
Who dance along on unseen trails,
Past rattlesnakes with deadly teeth
Slip-sliding on the ground beneath
The long-nose bat upon the tower,
Who spreads the pollen from flower to flower,
Above the owl with perfect sight,
Who sleeps by day and hunts by night,
Who lives above her neighbor's nest
(A special place for young to rest)
Beside the cactus tall and grand,
A haven for creatures in a waterless land.

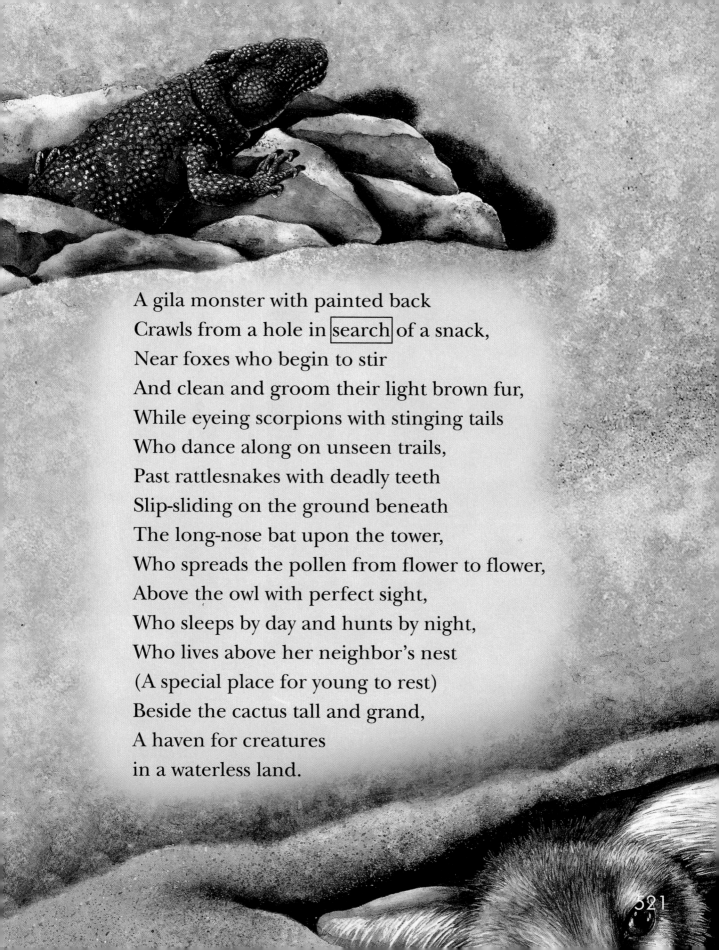

A gila monster with painted back
Crawls from a hole in search of a snack,
Near foxes who begin to stir
And clean and groom their light brown fur,
While eyeing scorpions with stinging tails
Who dance along on unseen trails,
Past rattlesnakes with deadly teeth
Slip-sliding on the ground beneath
The long-nose bat upon the tower,
Who spreads the pollen from flower to flower,
Above the owl with perfect sight,
Who sleeps by day and hunts by night,
Who lives above her neighbor's nest
(A special place for young to rest)
Beside the cactus tall and grand,
A haven for creatures
in a waterless land.

522

A world of survivors in a sun-baked land
Are sheltered and harbored by a cactus grand.
The spiny plant with its weathered face
Is a noble guard in this busy place.

Field Notes:

All of the animals described in this book are found in the Sonoran desert of the southwestern United States and Mexico. The specific species illustrated are all nocturnal: they sleep during the day and come out in the cool of night to hunt and feed. These creatures can all be found in or around a Saguaro cactus.

Saguaro Cactus

The Saguaro (suh-WAR-oh) Cactus lives in the Sonoran desert. The Saguaro provides food, shelter and moisture for a wide variety of desert animals. It thrives in rocky areas. It requires very little water and can go for two years without rain. Surprisingly, about 75 to 95 percent of the cactus's weight is water.

Fantastic Fact:
Saguaros can grow as tall as 56 feet, weigh as much as an African elephant, and live to be over 200 years old.

Kangaroo Rat

This animal's name comes from the fact that it hops over the ground like a kangaroo. Kangaroo rats reach an overall length of nine to 14 inches (including the tail) and are often pale in color with shades of tan, cream and off-white. Their hind feet are large with hairy soles that aid in jumping in loose, soft sand. They live in underground burrows shaped like the letter U. They primarily eat seeds which they gather from various plants at night. Their life span is less than five years.

Fantastic Fact:
Kangaroo rats are so efficient at converting the dry seeds they eat into water that they need no other water source.

Elf Owl

Elf owls live in the abandoned nests of gila woodpeckers. Their nests are 15 to 35 feet above the ground. Because of the moisture stored in the cactus and the thick lining of the nest, an elf owl stays cool even when the air temperature is over 100 degrees. Elf owls are tiny birds with rounded heads, yellow eyes, a greenish-yellow bill and white eyebrows. They eat insects, spiders, and other small animals such as lizards and centipedes. They can be easily identified by their high-pitched squeaky whistle.

Fantastic Fact:

The elf owl is the world's smallest owl. Adults grow to a length of just five inches and a total weight of one and a half ounces.

Lesser Long-Nose Bat

This creature rests in caves during the day and feeds at night. Its eyes are best for seeing in the dark. It plays a critical role in the life of the saguaro. When the saguaro blossoms in May, the long-nose sips the nectar inside the flowers. As it drinks, pollen sticks to the bat's face and is carried to the next flower. This is one way the saguaro cactus is pollinated.

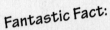

Rattlesnake

Rattlesnakes belong to a group of poisonous snakes known as pit vipers. These snakes have small depressions, or pits, on both sides of their faces. These pits are used as temperature detectors to help them locate prey in the dark. The rattle at the end of a rattlesnake's tail is made of dry, horny rings of skin that interlock with each other. They never shake the rattle when hunting—that would spoil the hunt. When they shake it they are announcing their presence, warning that they are dangerous, and asking to be left alone. The rattlesnake's venom, or poison, is produced in a large gland behind the eyes. When a rattlesnake bites, its fangs enter and leave the victim in less than a second. The poison is injected into the victim through both fangs. Their diet may include small warm-blooded animals such as rodents and rabbits, birds, and lizards.

Fantastic Fact:
A rattlesnake's fangs are "folded" back into its mouth when not in use.

Scorpions

There are more than 1,300 species of scorpions worldwide. Although some species have as many as twelve eyes, scorpions have very poor eyesight. They have sense organs on their bellies to detect chemical trails of their own species. In addition, they rely on their sense of touch to locate prey. Often, a scorpion walks around with its claws spread apart until it bumps into a tasty spider or insect. Only then does it capture its victim!

Fantastic Fact:
A scorpion's stinger is a hollow tube connected to a poison gland near the end of its tail.

Kit Fox

Kit foxes live throughout the desert regions of North America. Adults have a slender body, narrow skull, long nose and a long bushy tail. Their pale color makes them nearly invisible against light-colored desert sands. The soles of their feet are hairy, which helps them walk on loose sand. They also have large ears that stand up straight in the air. When the desert breeze blows over them, it cools the blood inside. Then the blood circulates, cooling the rest of the body. They feed on rodents, squirrels, rabbits, insects and birds. When running, they can reach speeds of up to 25 miles per hour.

Gila Monster

A Gila monster has black, orange, pink or yellow splotches and spots on its body. It also has small bead-like scales across its back. This lizard's diet consists of eggs, lizards, birds and mice. An adult Gila monster grows to 18 inches in length. It prefers to live in rocky desert areas hiding among rock ledges. It has a poisonous bite; however they are not aggressive toward humans.

Fantastic Fact:
The Gila monster and the Mexican Beaded Lizard are the only two poisonous lizards in the world.

Envision It! Retell

READING STREET ONLINE
TORY SORT
ww.ReadingStreet.com

Think Critically

1. You learned what it is like for many different animals to live in a hot, dry land. What do you think it would be like if you and your family had to live in a desert? **Text to Self**

2. On page 514, the author writes, "The prickly cactus with arms raised high." How does the author use words to create an image of the cactus? **Think Like an Author**

3. According to the Field Notes, why don't kangaroo rats need to drink water? **Cause and Effect**

4. What did you want to learn about the cactus and desert animals? Did you make some predictions about how the animals behaved? Did the Field Notes help you clarify your predictions? Were your predictions correct? **Predict and Set Purpose**

5. Look back at page 521. Which animals do you think are dangerous? Provide evidence to support your answer.

TEST PRACTICE **Extended Response**

Meet the Author and the Illustrator

Anthony D. Fredricks and Jennifer DiRubbio

Anthony D. Fredricks used to be a classroom teacher and reading specialist. He is the author of more than 20 children's books. Most of his books are about nature and science. He and his wife live on a mountainside in Pennsylvania with a variety of critters!

Jennifer DiRubbio is a wildlife illustrator and is active in the conservation of endangered species.

Anthony and Jennifer have worked together on a series of books about exploring various natural habitats: *Under One Rock, In One Tidepool, Around One Cactus, Near One Cattail,* and *On One Flower.*

Read other books by Anthony D. Fredricks.

Near One Cattail: Turtles, Logs and Leaping Frogs

In One Tidepool: Crabs, Snails and Salty Tails

Use the Reader's and Writer's Notebook to record your independent reading.

Reading Log

Objectives
● Establish a main idea in a topic sentence. ● Include sentences that support your ideas with simple facts, details, and explanations. ● Write essays that have a clear ending.

Let's Write It!

Key Features of a Compare-and-Contrast Composition

● shows how two things are similar and different

● includes supporting facts, details, and explanations

● ends with a concluding sentence or paragraph

**READING STREET ONLINE
GRAMMAR JAMMER
www.ReadingStreet.com**

Compare-and-Contrast Composition

A **compare-and-contrast composition** is nonfiction that shows how two or more people, things, or ideas are the same and different. The student model on the next page is an example of a compare-and-contrast composition.

Writing Prompt Write a composition that compares and contrasts two different animals.

Writer's Checklist

Remember, you should . . .

☑ make sure your central idea is in the topic sentence.

☑ explain how the animals are alike and different using supporting facts, details, and explanations.

☑ end with a conclusion.

☑ use verbs correctly.

The Scorpion and the Gila Monster

The scorpion and the Gila monster **are** two different animals that have some similarities. For example, both live in the desert. Both animals can look very scary, but in different ways. Some scorpions look scary because they **have** twelve eyes. The Gila monster is scary because it is scaly and has black, orange, pink, or yellow spots on its body.

Each animal hurts its prey in different ways. The scorpion uses its claws or its stinger to capture its prey and likes to **eat** spiders and insects. The Gila monster **has** a poisonous bite and likes to eat eggs or lizards. These two animals can also be very different in size. The smallest scorpion is only two tenths of an inch long, and the largest is more than eight inches long. On the other hand, a Gila monster can grow as long as eighteen inches. But even with all their differences, both of these animals use their special talents to survive in the hot and rocky desert.

Writing Trait Word Choice Words such as *very*, *different*, and *both* are used to compare and contrast.

Genre A **compare-and-contrast composition** shows how things are alike and different.

Irregular Verbs are used correctly.

Conventions

Irregular Verbs

Remember Regular verbs usually add *-ed* to show past tense. **Irregular verbs** change in other ways. Examples include *are/were*, *has/had*, and *is/was*.

Objectives

● Find and use information by following and explaining a set of written directions with many steps.
● Compare how different writing styles are used for different kinds of information on the Internet.

21st Century Skills

INTERNET GUY

Search Engine Use quotes in a search engine. "Capital of Minnesota" only finds pages with all the words together. Capital of Minnesota finds every page with at least one of the words.

● A search engine helps you find Web sites on the Internet using keywords typed into the search engine window. Click on the SEARCH button to see the results. Each item on the list is a Web site that contains your keyword.

● As you read "The Water Cycle," compare the written conventions used for search engines, Web sites, and Web-based news articles.

The Water Cycle

You just learned how water is recycled again and again. If you want to learn more about how the water cycle works, you could try searching the Internet.

You type the keywords *"water cycle"* into a search engine and click SEARCH.

File   Edit

Search Engine | "water cycle"   search

File

You might find results such as the following.

1. The **Water Cycle**. A Bibliography. This bibliography lists books about the water cycle.

2. A diagram demonstrating the **Water Cycle**. This diagram shows how water enters the atmosphere through evaporation and comes back to the earth through condensation.

3. The **Water Cycle** is a constant action in nature. You can see the water cycle at work by doing this experiment at home.

If the second link seems interesting to you, click on it.

Your keywords are bold. Read the text surrounding them for a summary of each Web site.

533

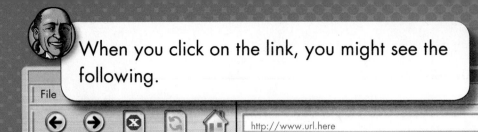

When you click on the link, you might see the following.

http://www.url.here

The Water Cycle

The water cycle is a continuous action happening in nature. Whether you realize it or not, all water is part of the water cycle. The water that comes out of your faucet has a role just as important in the water cycle as the ocean does.

- Bodies of Water
- Diagrams
- Experiments
- Recycling Water
- **Steps in the Water Cycle**
- Weather

 If you click on Steps in the Water Cycle, this is what you might find.

File   Edit   View   Favorite

Steps in the Water Cycle

The water cycle consists of 3 main steps. Water found on land or in water warms up and turns to water vapor through evaporation. Water vapor cools and condenses. When it condenses, it turns into precipitation. The water returns to land as rain, snow, sleet, or fog. The water on land returns to a river or lake, and finally the ocean where the water cycle begins again.

If you go back and click on <u>Diagrams</u>, this is what you might find.

File   Edit   View   Fav

http://www.url.here

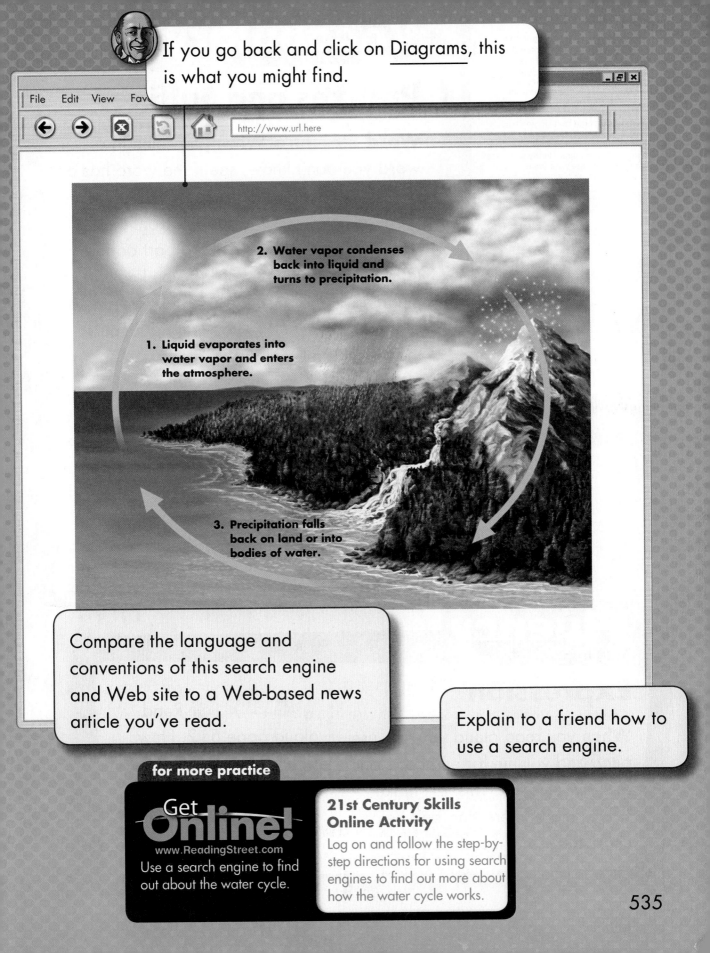

2. Water vapor condenses back into liquid and turns to precipitation.

1. Liquid evaporates into water vapor and enters the atmosphere.

3. Precipitation falls back on land or into bodies of water.

Compare the language and conventions of this search engine and Web site to a Web-based news article you've read.

Explain to a friend how to use a search engine.

for more practice

Get **Online!**
www.ReadingStreet.com
Use a search engine to find out about the water cycle.

21st Century Skills Online Activity
Log on and follow the step-by-step directions for using search engines to find out more about how the water cycle works.

Let's Learn It!

READING STREET ONLINE
ONLINE STUDENT EDITION
www.ReadingStreet.com

Vocabulary

Prefixes and Suffixes

Word Structure When you come to a word you don't know, see if the word has a prefix or suffix added to the base word. A prefix is a word part added in front of the base word. A suffix is a word part added to the end of a base word. If you know the meaning of the base word and the meaning of the prefix or suffix, you can figure out the meaning of the word.

Practice It! Choose two words from *Around One Cactus* that have either a prefix or a suffix. Write the meaning of the base word, the suffix or prefix, and the whole word. Then write sentences that use the whole words and just the base words.

Fluency

Expression

When you read aloud you can use pitch and volume for emphasis and to show emotion. This will make stories more interesting and help characters to come alive.

Practice It! Read aloud page 512. How should you use expression to make your reading sound more interesting?

536

Listening and Speaking

Get Ready For Middle School

Oral Report

In an oral report, a speaker talks about a topic in front of an audience. The purpose is to inform people about the topic.

Practice It! Prepare a presentation about one of the animals from *Around One Cactus*. Think of a question about the animal, and then research the answers. Give an oral report on that animal to your class.

Tips

Listening . . .

- Face the speaker.
- Restate the speaker's ideas.
- Ask questions and make comments about the topic.

Speaking . . .

- Speak clearly, loudly, and at a good rate.
- Organize your ideas.

Teamwork . . .

- Ask and answer questions with detail.

Poetry

- **Lyrical poems** often express strong emotions or describe nature using few words, but much imagination. They usually focus on only one thing.

- Lyrical poems often use **rhyme** and **cadence,** or **rhythm,** that repeats itself.

- **Free verse poems** may also express strong emotions, but they have little or no **rhyme** and **rhythm.** In some free verse poems the lines do not start with a capital letter.

- Poems use **imagery,** or sensory language and comparisons, to help the reader picture the way something looks, sounds, feels, tastes, and smells.

538

Cloud Dragons
by Pat Mora

What do you see
in the clouds so high?
What do you see in the sky?

Oh, I see dragons
that curl their tails
as they go slithering by.

What do you see
in the clouds so high?
What do you see? Tell me, do.

Oh, I see *caballitos*
that race the wind
high in the shimmering blue.

LEMON MOON

by Beverly McLoughland

On a hot and thirsty summer night,
The moon's a wedge of lemon light
Sitting low among the trees,
Close enough for you to squeeze
And make a moonade, icy-sweet,
To cool your summer-dusty heat.

Hurt No Living Thing

by Christina Rossetti

Hurt no living thing;
   Ladybird, nor butterfly,
   Nor moth with dusty wing,
Nor cricket chirping cheerily,
Nor grasshopper so light of leap,
   Nor dancing gnat, nor beetle fat,
   Nor harmless worms that creep.

Let's **Think** About...

Can you see how all three poems on these two pages are considered **lyrical poems?** Explain the image that each poet created for the reader.

Let's **Think** About...

What words help you know how something looks? tastes? feels? sounds?

539

Springtime

by Nikki Giovanni

in springtime the violets
grow in the sidewalk cracks
and the ants play furiously
at my gym-shoed toes
carrying off a half-eaten peanut
butter sandwich i had at lunch
and sometimes i crumble
my extra graham crackers
and on the rainy days i take off
my yellow space hat and splash
all the puddles on Pendry Street and not one
cold can catch me

540

Laughing Boy

by Richard Wright

In the falling snow
A laughing boy holds out his palms
Until they are white.

How to Use This Glossary

This glossary can help you understand and pronounce some of the words in this book. The entries in this glossary are in alphabetical order. There are guide words at the top of each page to show you the first and last words on the page. A pronunciation key is at the bottom of the following page. Remember, if you can't find the word you are looking for, ask for help or check a dictionary.

The entry word is in dark type. It shows how the word is spelled and how the word is divided into syllables.

The pronunciation is in parentheses. It also shows which syllables are stressed.

Part-of-speech labels show the function or functions of an entry word and any listed form of that word.

a·dore (ə dôr′), VERB. to love and admire someone very greatly: *She adores her mother.* ❑ VERB. **a·dores, a·dored, a·dor·ing.**

Sometimes, irregular and other special forms will be shown to help you use the word correctly.

The definition and example sentence show you what the word means and how it is used.

Aa

a·dor·a·ble (ə dôr′ə bəl), ADJECTIVE. attractive; delightful: *What an adorable kitten!*

ant·ler (ant′lər), NOUN. a bony, branching growth on the head of a male deer, elk, or moose. Antlers grow in pairs and are shed once a year. ❑ PLURAL **ant·lers.**

antlers

anx·ious·ly (angk′shəs lē), ADVERB. uneasily; with fear of what might happen: *We looked anxiously at the storm clouds.*

ar·e·a (âr′ē ə), NOUN. **1.** the amount of surface; extent: *The rug covers a large area.* **2.** a level, open space: *a playground area.*
❑ PLURAL **ar·e·as.**

ar·range (ə rānj′), *VERB.* to put things in a certain order: *She arranged the books on the library shelf.* ❑ *VERB* **ar·rang·es, ar·ranged, ar·rang·ing.**

ar·ti·fi·cial (är′tə fish′əl), *ADJECTIVE.* made by a person or machine; not natural: *Plastics are artificial substances that do not occur in nature.*

Bb

bat¹ (bat), *NOUN.* a small, flying mammal that comes out at night to feed, often on mosquitoes: *Bats have sensitive ears.*

bat² (bat), *NOUN.* a piece of wood or metal used for hitting the ball in baseball or softball.

bat 1.

bat·ter·y (bat′ə rē), *NOUN.* a container filled with chemicals that produces electrical power: *We needed a battery for the flashlight.*

bay (bā), *NOUN.* a part of a sea or lake partly surrounded by land.

bill (bil), *NOUN.* the beak of a bird.

bill

blew (blü), *VERB.* past tense of *blow.*

bliz·zard (bliz′ərd), *NOUN.* a blinding snowstorm with very strong, cold winds. ❑ *PLURAL* **bliz·zards.**

blow (blō), *VERB.* **1.** to make air come out of your mouth. **2.** to move in the wind: *The leaves blew around the yard.* ❑ *VERB* **blows, blew, blow·ing.**

a in *hat*	ėr in *term*	ô in *order*	ch in *child*	ə = a in *about*
ā in *age*	i in *it*	oi in *oil*	ng in *long*	ə = e in *taken*
â in *care*	ī in *ice*	ou in *out*	sh in *she*	ə = i in *pencil*
ä in *far*	o in *hot*	u in *cup*	th in *thin*	ə = o in *lemon*
e in *let*	ō in *open*	ù in *put*	ᴛH in *then*	ə = u in *circus*
ē in *equal*	ò in *all*	ü in *rule*	zh in *measure*	

bot·tom (bot′əm), *NOUN.* the lowest part: *These berries at the bottom of the basket are crushed.*

bulb (bulb), *NOUN.* a round, underground part from which certain plants grow. *Onions and tulips grow from bulbs.* ❏ *PLURAL* **bulbs.**

bun·dle (bun′dl), *NOUN.* a number of things tied or wrapped together. ❏ *PLURAL* **bun·dles.**

but·ter·fly (but′ər flī), *NOUN.* an insect with large, often brightly colored wings: *Her flower garden attracted many butterflies.* ❏ *PLURAL* **but·ter·flies.**

butterfly

Cc

car·pen·ter (kär′pən tər), *NOUN.* someone whose work is building and repairing things made of wood.

carpenter

car·pet·ma·ker (kär′pit māk ər), *NOUN.* A person who makes carpets and rugs for floors: *The carpetmaker sold us a blue carpet.*

chan·nel (chan′l), *NOUN.* a body of water joining two larger bodies of water: *The small channel was too narrow for the boat's passage.*

cheat (chēt), *VERB.* to deceive or trick someone; to do business or play in a way that is not honest: *I hate to play games with someone who cheats.* ❏ *VERB* **cheats, cheat·ed, cheat·ing.**

chip (chip), *VERB.* to cut or break off a small thin piece of something: *I chipped the cup when I knocked it against the cupboard.* ❏ *VERB* **chips, chipped, chip·ping.**

clev·er (klev′ər), *ADJECTIVE.* bright; intelligent; having a quick mind: *She is a clever girl to have solved that math problem.*

col·lec·tion (kə lek′shən), NOUN. a group of things gathered from many places and belonging together: *Our library has a large collection of books.*

collection

com·pas·sion·ate (kəm pash′ə nit), ADJECTIVE. Wishing to help those who suffer; full of compassion: *The compassionate doctor treated people who could not afford to pay her.*

con·serve (kən sėrv′), VERB. to save something from loss or waste: *Fixing a leaky faucet helps to conserve water.* ❏ VERB **con·serves, con·served, con·serv·ing.**

crop (krop), NOUN. plants grown for food: *Wheat, corn, and soybeans are major crops in the United States.* ❏ PLURAL **crops.**

cud·dle (kud′l), VERB. to lie close and comfortably; to curl up: *The two puppies cuddled together in front of the fire.* ❏ VERB **cud·dles, cud·dled, cud·dling.**

Dd

dan·ger·ous·ly (dān′jər əs lē), ADVERB. not safely: *The car drove dangerously close to the wall.*

dim (dim), ADJECTIVE. somewhat dark; not bright: *The light from the candle was too dim for reading.*

Ee

e·nor·mous (i nôr′məs), ADJECTIVE. very, very large; huge: *Long ago, enormous animals lived on the Earth.*

enormous

er·rand (er′ənd), NOUN. a short trip that you take to do something: *She has errands to do downtown.* ❏ PLURAL **er·rands.**

ex·act·ly (eg zakt′lē), ADVERB. without any error; precisely: *I know exactly where I put the keys.*

ex·cit·ed·ly (ek sī′tid lē), ADVERB. with strong, lively feelings: *My heart beat excitedly as I opened the old trunk.*

Ff

flip·per (flip′ər), *NOUN.* one of the broad, flat body parts used for swimming by animals such as seals and penguins. ❑ *PLURAL* **flip·pers.**

flippers

fro·zen (frō′zn), *ADJECTIVE.* hardened with cold; turned into ice: *frozen sherbet.*

fu·el (fyü′əl), *NOUN.* something that is used as a source of heat or energy, such as gasoline, coal, or wood: *The car wouldn't run because it was out of fuel.*

Gg

gas (gas), *NOUN.* a substance, such as air, that is neither a solid nor a liquid: *Sometimes balloons are filled with a gas called helium.*

gear (gir), *NOUN.* the equipment or clothing needed for a particular activity: *Their camping gear included tents, sleeping bags, and flashlights.*

gi·gan·tic (jī gan′tik), *ADJECTIVE.* huge or enormous: *The gigantic footprints must have been made by an elephant.*

goo (gü), *NOUN.* a sticky or messy substance: *Wash that goo off your hands.*

grape·vine (grāp′vīn), *NOUN.* **1.** a vine that grapes grow on. **2.** way that news and rumors are mysteriously spread: *We heard it on the grapevine.*

Hh

hatch (hach), *VERB.* to come out of an egg: *One of the chickens hatched today.* ❑ *VERB* **hatch·es, hatched, hatch·ing.**

hatch

hun·ter (hun′ tər), *NOUN.* an animal or person who goes after animals for food or sport: *Owls and eagles are hunters.* ❑ *PLURAL* **hun·ters.**

hunter

Ii

i·guan·a (i gwä′nə), *NOUN.* a large lizard found in tropical America that has a row of spines along its back. ❑ *PLURAL* **i·guan·as.**

i·mag·ine (i maj′ən), *VERB.* to make a picture or idea of something in your mind: *We can hardly imagine life without cars.* ❑ *VERB* **i·mag·ines, i·mag·ined, i·mag·in·ing.**

in·cred·i·ble (in kred′ə bəl), *ADJECTIVE.* **1.** impossible to believe; unbelievable: *the hurricane's power was incredible.* **2.** very good: *what an incredible day it is!*

Kk

knowl·edge (nol′ij), *NOUN.* what you know: *Gardeners have great knowledge of flowers.*

Ll

la·dle (lā′ dl), *NOUN.* a large spoon with a long handle and a deep bowl: *Dad used a ladle to serve the soup.*

ladle

lan·guage (lan′gwij), *NOUN.* human speech, spoken or written: *Civilization would be impossible without language.* ❑ *PLURAL* **lan·guag·es.**

547

laun·dry (lȯn′drē), **1.** NOUN. clothes, towels, and other such items that need to be washed or have just been washed: *One of my chores is folding the laundry.* **2.** ADJECTIVE. used for doing laundry: *The laundry basket was full of dirty clothes.*

laundry

la·zy (lā′zē), ADJECTIVE. not willing to work or move fast. *He lost his job because he was lazy.*

lof·ty (lȯf′tē), ADJECTIVE. **1.** very high: *lofty mountains.* **2.** proud; haughty: *He had a lofty contempt for others.*

Mm

mar·ket·place (mär′kət plās′), NOUN. a place where people meet to buy and sell things: *The marketplace was very crowded.*

ma·te·ri·al (mə tir′ē əl), NOUN. the substance from which something is made: *The Three Little Pigs used different materials to build their houses.* ❑ PLURAL **ma·te·ri·als.**

ma·ture (mə chŭr′ or mə tŭr′), ADJECTIVE. **1.** ripe or full grown: *Grain is harvested when it is mature.* **2.** mentally or physically like an adult: *He is very mature for someone so young.*

mel·o·dy (mel′ə dē), NOUN. a pleasing or easily remembered series of musical notes; tune.

men·tion (men′shən), VERB. tell or speak about something: *I mentioned your idea to the group, and they liked it.* ❑ VERB **men·tions, men·tioned, men·tion·ing.**

mer·chant (mėr′chənt), NOUN. someone who buys and sells goods for a living: *Some merchants do most of their business with foreign countries.*

Nn

nar·ra·tor (nar′āt ər), NOUN. the person who tells the story or tale: *I was the narrator in the school play.*

no·ble (nō′bəl), ADJECTIVE. **1.** showing greatness of mind and character; good: *a noble person.* **2.** excellent; fine; splendid; magnificent: *Niagara Falls is a noble sight.*

Oo

o·ver·head (ō′vər hed′), *ADVERB.* over the head; on high; above: *The stars twinkled overhead.*

Pp

par·ka (pär′kə), *NOUN.* a warm, heavy jacket with a hood: *If you go out in this cold weather, you should wear your parka.*

parka

part·ner (pärt′nər), *NOUN.* a member of a company or firm who shares the risks and profits of the business. ❑ *PLURAL* **part·ners.**

pat·tern (pat′ ėrn), *NOUN.* an arrangement or design: *The birthday cake was decorated with a pattern of balloons.* ❑ *PLURAL* **pat·terns.**

peck (pek), *VERB.* to strike with the beak: *The baby sparrow pecked its egg.* ❑ *VERB* **pecks, pecked, peck·ing.**

plat·form (plat′fôrm), *NOUN.* a flat, raised structure or surface: *He stepped up on the platform to give his speech.*

plen·ty (plen′tē), *NOUN.* a full supply; all that you need; a large enough number or amount: *You have plenty of time to catch the train.*

plug (plug), *NOUN.* a device at the end of a wire that is put into an outlet to make a connection with a source of electricity: *A plug has metal prongs.*

poke (pōk), *VERB.* to push with force against someone or something; jab: *He poked me in the ribs with his elbow.* ❑ *VERB* **pokes, poked, pok·ing.**

preen (prēn), *VERB.* to smooth or arrange the feathers with the beak. ❑ *VERB* **preens, preened, preen·ing.**

preen

pre·serv·a·tive (pri zėr′və tiv), *NOUN.* any substance that will prevent decay or injury: *Paint is a preservative for wood surfaces.*

549

proof (prüf), NOUN. a way or means of showing that something is true: *Do you have proof of what you are saying?*

Rr

raise (rāz), **1.** VERB. to lift something up; put up: *We raised the flag. Raise your hand if you know the answer.* **2.** NOUN. an increase in amount, especially in wages, salary, or allowance: *He was happy with his raise.* ◻ VERB **rais·es, raised, rais·ing.** PLURAL **raises.**

rai·sin (rā′zn), NOUN. a small, sweet, dried grape.

Ss

scat·ter (skat′ər), VERB. to separate and go in different directions: *The chickens scattered in fright when the truck honked at them.* ◻ VERB **scat·ters, scat·tered, scat·ter·ing.**

search (sėrch), 1. VERB. to look through; examine; try to find something by looking for it. **2.** NOUN the act of searching: *She found her book after a long search.* ◻ VERB **search·es, searched, search·ing.**

sec·tion (sek′shən), NOUN. a part or division of something: *We visited the children's section of the library.*

shelf (shelf), NOUN. a horizontal board on a wall or in a cupboard, used for holding or storing things: *Meg placed the books on the shelves.* ◻ PLURAL **shelves.**

shine (shīn), VERB. to give off light or reflect light; glow: *The candles on the cake shone for a moment before Rebecca blew them out.* ◻ VERB **shines, shone, shin·ing.**

shoe·lace (shü′lās), NOUN. a string or cord used for fastening a shoe: *The kindergartners practiced tying their shoelaces.* ◻ PLURAL **shoe·la·ces.**

snug·gle (snug′əl), VERB. to lie closely and comfortably together; nestle; cuddle: *The kittens snuggled together in the basket.* ◻ VERB **snug·gles, snug·gled, snug·gling.**

snuggle

splen·did (splen′did), ADJECTIVE. very good; excellent: *James and his family had a splendid vacation in Colorado.*

spoil (spoil), VERB. **1.** to become bad or not good to eat: *The fruit spoiled because I kept it too long.* **2.** to injure the character or disposition of: *They spoiled her by always giving her what she wanted.* □ VERB **spoils, spoiled, spoil·ing.**

sprout (sprout), VERB. to produce new leaves, shoots, or buds; begin to grow: *Tulips sprout in the spring.* □ VERB **sprouts, sprout·ed, sprout·ing.**

sprout

stead·y (sted′ē), ADJECTIVE. firmly fixed; firm; not swaying or shaking: *This post is as steady as a rock.*

sting (sting), **1.** VERB. to pierce or wound with a sharp point: *The wasp will sting you if you're not careful.* **2.** NOUN. a sharp pain: *Our team felt the sting of defeat.* □ VERB **stings, stung, sting·ing.**

store (stôr), **1.** NOUN. a place where things are sold: *grocery store, toy store.* **2.** VERB. to put things away until they are needed: *We always store comforters in the closet during the summer.*

strain (strān), VERB. to draw tight; stretch too much: *The weight strained the rope.* □ VERB **strains, strained, strain·ing.**

stray (strā), VERB. to lose your way; wander; roam: *Their dog has strayed off somewhere.* □ VERB **strays, strayed, stray·ing.**

sup·plies (sə plīz′), NOUN PLURAL. the food and equipment necessary for an army exercise, camping trip, and so on.

sur·round (sə round′), VERB. to shut something in on all sides; encircle; enclose: *A high fence surrounded the field.* □ VERB **sur·rounds, sur·round·ed, sur·round·ing.**

sur·vi·vor (sər vī′vər), NOUN. someone or something that survives: *There were two survivors from the plane crash.* □ PLURAL **sur·vi·vors.**

sym·pho·ny (sim′fə nē), *NOUN.* a long, complicated musical composition for an orchestra.

Tt

tem·per·a·ture (tem′pər ə chər), *NOUN.* The degree of heat or cold in something, usually measured by a thermometer: *The water temperature was too cold for swimming.*

term (tèrm), *NOUN.* a definite or limited time: *The U.S. President's term in office is four years.*

thou·sand (thou′znd), *NOUN* or *ADJECTIVE.* ten hundred; 1,000. ❏ *PLURAL* **thou·sands.**

thread (thred), *NOUN.* a very thin string made of strands of cotton, silk, wool, or nylon, spun and twisted together. *She fixed the sweater with cotton thread.*

thread

ton (tun), *NOUN.* a unit of weight equal to 2,000 pounds: *A small car weighs about one ton, and a minivan weighs about two tons.* ❏ *PLURAL* **tons.**

top·ic (top′ik), *NOUN.* a subject that people think, write, or talk about: *Newspapers discuss the topics of the day.* ❏ *PLURAL* **top·ics.**

trade (trād), *VERB.* to exchange one thing for another: *Rita traded her blue crayon for a red one.* ❏ *VERB* **trades, tra·ded, tra·ding.**

tro·phy (trō′fē), *NOUN.* **1.** an award, often in the form of a statue or cup, given as a symbol of victory. **2.** a prize in a race or contest. ❏ *PLURAL* **tro·phies.**

twig (twig), *NOUN.* a small, thin branch of a tree or other woody plant: *The children collected small shells and twigs to decorate their sandcastles.* ❏ *PLURAL* **twigs.**

twitch (twich), *VERB.* to make small, jerky movements: *The cat's tail twitched as he watched the bird outside the window.* ❏ *VERB* **twitch·es, twitched, twitch·ing.**

Uu

un·seen (un sēn′), *ADJECTIVE.* not seen; unnoticed: *An unseen error caused the plane crash.*

un·wrap (un rap′), *VERB.* to open: *She unwrapped the gift.* ❏ *VERB* **un·wraps, un·wrapped, un·wrap·ping.**

Vv

va·ri·e·ty (və rī′ə tē), *NOUN.* a selection of different things: *This market sells a wide variety of fruits and vegetables.*

vis·ion (vizh′ən), *NOUN.* the ability to think ahead and plan: *Our group needs a leader with vision.*

Ww

wa·ter·less (wȯ′tər lis), *ADJECTIVE.* **1.** containing little or no water. **2.** needing no water: *waterless cooking.*

wealth (welth), *NOUN.* riches; many valuable possessions; property: *people of wealth, the wealth of a city.*

wil·low (wil′ō), *NOUN.* a tree with narrow leaves and thin branches that bend easily: *She liked to sit under the curved branches of the willow.*

willow

wob·ble (wob′əl), *VERB.* to move unsteadily from side to side; shake; tremble: *The baby wobbled when she began to walk alone.* ❑ *VERB* **wob·bles, wob·bled, wob·bling.**

Yy

yank (yangk), *VERB.* to pull with a sudden, sharp movement: *Keith yanked open the heavy door.* ❑ *VERB* **yanks, yanked, yank·ing.**

Unit 1

When Charlie McButton Lost Power

English	Spanish
bat	murciélago
battery	* batería
blew	estalló
fuel	combustible
plug	enchufe
term	duración
vision	* visión

What About Me?

English	Spanish
carpenter	* carpintero
carpetmaker	alfombrista
knowledge	conocimiento
marketplace	mercado
merchant	comerciante
plenty	mucho
straying	descarriando
thread	hilo

Kumak's Fish

English	Spanish
gear	aparejos
parka	* parka
splendid	* espléndido
twitch	tirón
willow	sauce
yanked	arrastró

Supermarket

English	Spanish
laundry	lavandería
section	* sección
shelves	estantes
spoiled	echada a perder
store	tienda
thousands	miles
traded	intercambiaban
variety	* variedad

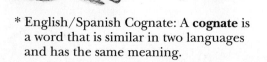

* English/Spanish Cognate: A **cognate** is a word that is similar in two languages and has the same meaning.

554

My Rows and Piles of Coins

English	Spanish
arranged	ordené
bundles	paquetes
dangerously	peligrosamente
errands	recados
excitedly	con emoción
steady	estable
unwrapped	desenvolví
wobbled	me tambaleé

Unit 2

Penguin Chick

English	Spanish
cuddles	se arrima a
flippers	aletas
frozen	congelada
hatch	salir del cascarón
pecks	picotea
preen	atusa
snuggles	se acurruca

I Wanna Iguana

English	Spanish
adorable	* adorable
compassionate	* compasivo
exactly	* exactamente
iguana	* iguana
mature	maduro
mention	* mencionar
trophies	* trofeos

Prudy's Problem and How She Solved It

English	Spanish
butterflies	mariposas
collection	* colección
enormous	* enorme
scattered	desparramadas
shoelaces	cordones de zapatos
strain	doblarse

Tops & Bottoms

English	Spanish
bottom	parte de abajo
cheated	engañaste
clever	listo
crops	cosechas
lazy	perezoso
partners	socios
wealth	riqueza

Amazing Bird Nests

English	Spanish
bill	pico
goo	baba
hunters	cazadoras
material	* materiales
platform	* plataforma
tons	toneladas
twigs	ramitas

Unit 3

How Do You Raise a Raisin?

English	Spanish
area	* área
artificial	* artificial
grapevine	parra
preservative	* preservativo
proof	graduación
raise	cultivar
raisin	pasa

Pushing Up the Sky

English	Spanish
antlers	cuernos
imagined	* imaginar
languages	idiomas
narrator	* narrador
overhead	por arriba
poked (holes)	hechos a empujones

Seeing Stars

English	Spanish
dim	opacas
gas	* gas
gigantic	* gigantescas
ladle	cucharón
patterns	figuras
shine	brillar
temperature	* temperatura

A Symphony of Whales

English	Spanish
anxiously	ansiosamente
bay	bahía
blizzards	ventiscas
channel	canal
chipped	picaron
melody	* melodía
supplies	suministros
surrounded	rodeada
symphony	* sinfonía

Around One Cactus: Owls, Bats and Leaping Rats

English	Spanish
incredible	* increíble
lofty	elevado
noble	* noble
search	búsqueda
stinging	pinchadura
survivors	sobrevivientes
topic	tema
unseen	invisible
waterless	desérticoe

557

366: "Third-Grade Genius," from *Fearless Fernie: Hanging Out with Fernie & Me* by Gary Soto, copyright © 2002 by Gary Soto. Used by permission of G.P. Putnam's Sons, A Division of Penguin Young Readers Group, A Member of Penguin Group (USA) Inc., 345 Hudson Street, New York, NY 10014. All rights reserved.

378: "How Do You Raise a Raisin?" by Pam Munoz Ryan. Text copyright © 2003 by Pam Munoz Ryan. Illustrations copyright © 2003 by Craig Brown. Used with permission by Charlesbridge Publishing, Inc.

412: "Pushing Up the Sky," from *Pushing Up the Sky* by Joseph Bruchac, copyright © 2000 by Joseph Bruchac. Used by permission of Dial Books for Young Readers, A Division of Penguin Young Readers Group, A Member of Penguin Group (USA) Inc., 345 Hudson Street, New York, NY 10014. All rights reserved.

428: "Catch It and Run!", reprinted with the permission of Simon & Schuster Books for Young Readers, an imprint of Simon & Schuster Children's Publishing Division. From *When the World Was Young* by Margaret Mayo, illustrated by Louise Brierly. Text copyright © 1995 Margaret Mayo. Illustrations copyright © 1995 Louise Brierly.

462: From Scien-trickery: Riddles in Science by J. Patrick Lewis, illustrated by Frank Remkiewicz. Text copyright © 2004 by J. Patrick Lewis. Illustrations copyright © 2004 by Frank Remkiewicz. Used by permission of Houghton Mifflin Harcourt Publishing Company. All rights reserved.

476: *A Symphony of Whales*, text copyright © 1999 by Steve Schuch, reprinted by permission of Harcourt, Inc.

496: Reprinted from "He Listens to Whales" by E. Shan Correa, from the May 1991 issue of *Ranger Rick* ® magazine, with the permission of the publisher, The National Wildlife Federation ®. Copyright © 1991 by the National Wildlife Federation.

510: From "Around One Cactus: Owls, Bats and Leaping Rats" by Anthony D. Fredericks. Copyright © 2003 by Anthony D. Fredericks. Illustrations copyright © 2003 Jennifer DiRubbio Lubinsky. Used by permission.

538: "Cloud Dragons" from *Confetti: Poems for Children.* Text copyright © 1996 by Pat Mora. Permission arranged with Lee & Low Books, Inc., New York, NY 10016.

539: "Lemon Moon" by Beverly McLoughland, originally appeared in *Ranger Rick* ® magazine, November 1990. Reprinted by permission of the author, who controls all rights.

540: "Springtime" from *Spin a Soft Black Song, Revised Edition*, by Nikki Giovanni, illustrated by George Martins. Copyright © 1971, 1985 by Nikki Giovanni. Reprinted by permission of Hill and Wang, a division of Farrar, Straus and Giroux, LLC.

541: "Laughing Boy," original title "In the Falling Snow," by Richard Wright. Copyright © 1973 by Richard Wright. Reprinted by permission of John Hawkins & Associates, Inc.

Note: Every effort has been made to locate the copyright owner of material reproduced on this component. Omissions brought to our attention will be corrected in subsequent editions.

Illustrations

Cover: Leo Timmers
EI•1–EI•15 Mike Lester
EI•16–EI•25, 118, 119 Jim Steck
50, 52, 53 Dean MacAdam
76–81 Robbie Short
307 Janet Stevens
364 Sachiko Yoshikawa
398–401 Jeff Mangiat
412–422 Teresa Flavin
423 Richard Downs
428–434 Shonto Begay
476–490 Wendell Minor
539 Paul Perreault
W•2–W•15 Nomar Perez.

Photographs

Every effort has been made to secure permission and provide appropriate credit for photographic material. The publisher deeply regrets any omission and pledges to correct errors called to its attention in subsequent editions.

Unless otherwise acknowledged, all photographs are the property of Pearson Education, Inc.

Photo locators denoted as follows: Top (T), Center (C), Bottom (B), Left (L), Right (R), Background (Bkgd)

18 (C) ©SW Productions/Getty Images
20 (BL) ©Paul Edmondson/Corbis
21 (BR) ©Jose Luis Pelaez, Inc./Corbis, (T) ©Paul Edmondson/Corbis

WORDS! | Vocabulary Handbook

Antonyms

Synonyms

Base Words

Prefixes

Suffixes

Context Clues

Related Words

Compound Words

Multiple-Meaning Words

Homographs

Homonyms

Homophones

Dictionary

Thesaurus

Antonyms

Antonyms are words that have opposite meanings. *Same* and *different* are antonyms.

Same

Antonyms can be used to contrast two things. Antonyms help readers understand differences.

Different

Synonyms

Synonyms are words that have the same meaning or similar meanings. *Loud* and *noisy* are synonyms.

Loud

Knowing and using synonyms can help make your writing more interesting. Look in a thesaurus to find synonyms.

Noisy

Base Words

A base word is a word that cannot be broken down into smaller words or word parts. *Cover* and *motion* are base words.

Knowing the meaning of a base word can help you understand the meanings of longer words.

Prefixes

A prefix is a word part that can be added to the beginning of a base word. In the word *uncover, un-* is a prefix.

Cover

Uncover

Knowing the meaning of a prefix can help you figure out the meaning of a new word.

Common Prefixes and Their Meanings

un-	not
re-	again, back
in-	not
dis-	not, opposite of
pre-	before

Suffixes

A suffix is a word part added to the end of a base word. In the word *motionless*, *-less* is a suffix.

Motion

Motionless

Common Suffixes and Their Meanings

-able	can be done
-ment	action or process
-less	without
-tion	act, process

> Knowing how a suffix changes a word can help you figure out the meaning of a new word.

Context Clues

Read the words before and after a word that you don't know to help you make sense of it.

I couldn't decide what to wear! The red, blue, green, or fuchsia dress?

Related Words

Related words are words that have the same base word. *Sign*, *signal*, and *signature* are related because they all have the base word *sign*.

Sign

Welcome to TOWN

Signature

Signal

If you know the base words, you may be able to figure out the meanings of words related to it.

Compound Words

Compound words are words made of two smaller words. *Sandbox* and *ladybug* are compound words.

 **+** **=**

sand **box** **sandbox**

Look for smaller words that you already know in unfamiliar words.

+ **=**

lady **bug** **ladybug**

Multiple-Meaning Words

Multiple-meaning words are words that can have different meanings depending on how they are used.

Homographs

Homographs are words that are spelled the same but have different meanings. They may be•pronounced the same way or differently.

Read the words before and after a homograph to discover its meaning and pronunciation. Check a dictionary to be sure.

Homophones

Homophones are words that sound the same, but they
are spelled differently and they have different meanings.

Homonyms

Homonyms are words that are spelled the same and
sound the same, but they have different meanings.

Seal

Seal

You can figure out
the meaning of a
homonym by reading
the words around it.

Homophones

Homophones are words that sound the same, but they are spelled differently and they have different meanings.

Hair

Hare

Homophones might be confusing when you hear them being read aloud. Pay attention to the words before and after the homophone to find its meaning.

Understanding
Homographs, Homonyms, and Homophones

	Pronunciation	Spelling	Meaning
Homographs	may be the same or different	same	different
Homonyms	same	same	different
Homophones	same	different	different

Homographs

tear

tear

John

ear

Homonyms

ear

berry

bury

Homophones

Dictionary

A dictionary is a book that explains the words of our language. The words in a dictionary are in alphabetical order.

punc•tu•al **1** (pungk'chu al), **2** *ADJECTIVE* **3** prompt; exactly on time: **4** *He is always punctual to the minute.* **5** -**punc'tu•al•ly** ADVERB.

1 This part of the entry shows you how to pronounce the word.

2 The dictionary entry tells you the word's part of speech. *Punctual* is an adjective.

3 Here is the word's definition.

4 The word is used in an example to help you understand its meaning.

5 See how the word changes when it has a suffix added.

Thesaurus

A thesaurus is a book of synonyms. The words in a thesaurus are in alphabetical order.

cute
adjective
attractive, appealing, amusing, charming, adorable, enchanting

Keep a thesaurus handy when you write. It can help you find just the right word.

Spot is so cute!

SPOT